Software Portability

Olivier Lecarme
Laboratoire d'Informatique
Université de Nice, France

Mireille Pellissier Gart
Intermetrics
Cambridge, Massachusetts

McGraw-Hill Book Company
New York St. Louis San Francisco Auckland Bogotá
Hamburg Johannesburg London Madrid
Mexico Montreal New Delhi Panama
Paris São Paulo Singapore
Sydney Tokyo Toronto

Library of Congress Cataloging-in-Publication Data

Lecarme, Olivier.
  Software portability.

  Bibliography: p.
  Includes index.
  1. Software compatibility. I. Pellissier Gart,
Mireille. II. Title.
QA76.754.L43 1986   005.1   85-23656
ISBN 0-07-036948-8

1234567890 DOC/DOC 8932109876

ISBN 0-07-036948-8

*The editors for this book were Stephen G. Guty and Susan Killikelly,
the designer was Naomi Auerbach, and the production supervisor
was Thomas G. Kowalczyk. It was set in Primer by T. C. Systems.*

Printed and bound by R. R. Donnelley & Sons Company.

Contents

v

Preface

Software portability is an idea whose time has come. More and more often, potential software customers are asking whether a specific software product is portable. More and more often, advertisements and promotional literature use portability as a sales feature.

The fact that software has become more and more expensive in comparison with hardware costs has led to this state of affairs, heralded several years ago when vendors introduced "unbundling," or separate sales of hardware and software. Computer users often perceive this relatively recent development as a major advantage, because their investment in software no longer necessarily ties them to one hardware vendor, and portability is now considered one of the major features of software products.

It should also be noted that the increasing complexity of programs has more and more often required that they be written in higher-level languages. This factor has contributed greatly to (at least partial) program portability.

As frequently discussed as the notion of portability is, however, it carries many different meanings. Portability problems are often underestimated, partly because so many different aspects of computer science may affect portability. Thus, though a unifying synthesis seems especially desirable, it is presently lacking. Two books have been published about the subject: the collection of papers edited by P. J. Brown [Bro77a] and the small monograph by P. J. Wallis [Wal82]. The first book, because of its very nature, lacks unity, and it fails to treat some important aspects of the subject. It is becoming somewhat outdated. While the second book constitutes a good introduction, it is too short and too general to provide all the necessary information.

The purpose of this present book then is to answer the need that we feel for a relatively complete synthesis of software portability. Of course, we are fully aware of the imperfections of our work, and although we hope we have omitted no important facet of the subject, we also hope that our very extensive bibliography will help those readers who are eager for further study.

This book can be used in any of three ways. First, it can be read by computer users who want to self-study the subject. Whether they are application programmers, system programmers, or computer project managers, all interested readers should find something of value in our text. There should be no part too difficult for a reader with a computer science degree or with equivalent experience.

Second, our book is designed to serve as a complementary textbook for a general course in software engineering, such as those found more and more often in undergraduate computer science curricula. Although it considers the vast subject of software engineering from a specific point of view, our text covers a large part of what is generally taught in this area.

And finally, our book is designed to serve as a basis for a specialized course on software portability. Such a course could occur at the graduate level in computer science curricula, probably following a general software engineering course. Or it could be used in a special seminar of one or two weeks. In such a course, lectures could emphasize new case studies, while our book could provide students with the necessary bases and references.

The idea of writing this book first occurred to us in 1980. Work in the software engineering group of the computer science laboratory at the University of Nice led to two doctoral theses [ThP77, Pel80] and two papers [LPT78, LPT82a]. We studied software portability as thoroughly as possible, and we came to regret the lack of a comprehensive textbook in the available literature. Thus we proposed to give a course on this subject during the annual informatics summer school of AFCET, the French computer society. The idea was submitted in July 1980 and was accepted for the 1982 session of the school.

The first version of this text [LPT82b] was written as course support between December 1981 and June 1982. The course was given at the summer school in Namur, Belgium, as a sequence of eight 1½-hour lectures. Comments and criticisms from the audience, together with the experience we gained in giving the lectures, helped us to revise that first text and to enhance it with the addition of two important chapters containing case studies.

Thus the division of the present book into parts and chapters evolved rather slowly, the text itself passing through at least five stages. Broad organizational changes finally brought about a scheme that makes sequential reading of the text as easy as possible.

The most interesting and novel aspects of our work deal mainly with the collection under one cover of ordinarily scattered or inaccessible information and with the system of classification and clarification that we have devised. The size of the bibliography will give the reader an idea of the amount of documentation we examined and of the quantity of more-or-less relevant information we sifted in writing this book.

In its final state, this book is signed by only two authors. We wish to acknowledge especially, however, our debt to our colleague, Marie-Claude Thomas, of the University of Nice. She not only worked on the whole subject until 1981, but she attended all the discussions and working sessions that preceded the summer school at Namur. She wrote the French text of two very sensitive sections, those dealing with data portability (Sec. 2.3) and with software property rights (Sec. 2.4). She is presently working in a completely different research area, and it is because of this, and only at her explicit request, that she does not appear as an author.

This book was first published in French [LeP84], then translated into English. This work was done by the authors themselves, with the invaluable aid of Mitchell Gart, Mireille's husband, who also wrote the first draft of the case study based on the Unix system (Sec. 7.2). Contributions by Mitchell and by Reba Krause to Sec. 2.4 were especially helpful in adapting this part of the text to the American environment.

Finally, we wish to thank the 1982 AFCET summer students, and especially the AFCET summer school director, George Stamon, as well as all our colleagues at the Informatics Laboratory at the University of Nice, at the Research Center of CII-Honeywell Bull in Louveciennes, France, and at Intermetrics in Cambridge, Massachusetts.

Olivier Lecarme

Mireille Pellissier Gart

Software Portability

Software Portability

1

Introduction

Computer hardware is only as useful as its available software. It is very expensive, in time and in other resources, to re-create software for every new machine, and it is often desirable, from the user's point of view, for the software environment to be as similar as possible on different machines. Since the available software usually "hides" most or even all of the hardware from the user—that is, it is the software with which the user interacts—it is useful to try and implement the same familiar software on many different computers.

Thus, it is very frequently desirable, even at times necessary, to change the environment of any given software product to make it work on more than one computer and with more than one operating system. This change in environment we call "software transport" (or sometimes "software port"). A software product is more or less useful according to the relative ease of its "portability."

There are many cases in which software products, to be useful at all, must demonstrate portability. For instance, utility depends upon portability in the cases of software packages sold by a commercial vendor; a matrix inversion subprogram that is part of a library of scientific subprograms; computer games programmed and distributed by a club of hobbyists; a compiler for a new programming language, distributed by the authors of the language as a means of promoting their work; a mailing list distributed in machine-readable form. . . .

The list of examples goes on and on, but one can readily see the variety and complexity of the problems of portability involved. The purpose of this book is to demonstrate how most of these problems can be solved. The rest of this introductory chapter raises three important questions and provides some tentative answers.

1.1 Why should existing software be transported?

We shall often hereafter have occasion to note the differences in point of view between designers—those who build a software product so that it can be transported to other environments—and installers—those who install a software product, built elsewhere, in a new environment. For now, we state the problem from the point of view of the installer; the point of view of the designer will be considered in the next section.

There are several possible answers a typical installer might have for the question asked in the title of this section. It might be said that:

- It takes less time and effort to use a program already built by somebody else than to attempt to rewrite it. This argument assumes that the transport operation itself takes less time than does the creation of a software product, thus freeing the programmer to do other work. Independent of the work saving, time will also be saved. (The distinction between time effectiveness as measured by work and by calendar is important: It is not likely that a programming job demanding one person-year could be done instead by 6 persons in two months; nor is it conceivable that such a job could be done by 52 persons in one week.)

- The designer of a software product is most likely a specialist in the field addressed by the product, while the installer is likely not a specialist but simply a user; or perhaps nobody with enough expertise to build such a product is available locally.

- The particular software product might be an excellent one, a standard in the field. (This assumes that the transport will not, as a side effect, severely damage the qualities of the product that made its transport so desirable in the first place.)

- It is advantageous to have always at hand, even when traveling, the same software environment to which one is accustomed. (This argument was originated by William Waite, who will be quoted many times in this book. It presumes a somewhat special situation, where the installer is also the designer.)

- A change of hardware (or operating system, or both) may be anticipated in the near future, and it would be desirable to continue using the same software products on the new hardware. (Reluctance to change, which sometimes causes stagnation, may have a more positive effect in this case.)

- Transporting an existing software product helps to guarantee conformity with what is done elsewhere. Programs will be compatible with other installations, and validity will be improved.

- In the case where the choice is between building one new program or choosing between several existing transportable programs, the result might be better with the wider choice.

Let us note that, of course, most of the above answers have negative counterparts that give rise to possible arguments for *not* transporting existing software. In all fairness, those counterarguments should be considered:

- If the software product has been designed specifically for portability, its performance may be inferior.

- No software product is immune from errors and weaknesses; to transport it is to perpetuate these shortcomings, perhaps even to increase them.

- Rewriting an existing software product, instead of using it as is, may be a good way to improve it. Often, when one builds and tunes a complex program, he or she learns from the experience; if then the program has to be rebuilt, it will inevitably be better.

These objections are serious, and it is not easy to answer them in a few words. But in the succeeding chapters we will give some fairly strong reasons why portable programming practices generally add to the overall quality of a program.

1.2 Why should we build portable software?

Taking here the point of view of the designer, we can suggest some answers to the question we ask in the title above:

- A software company builds and sells software: if its products are portable, they will appeal to a much wider market. Furthermore, instead of building new products for every possible computer environment, it is in the company's own interest to reduce the effort needed to change from one environment to another. The overall cost of developing a portable program once, and then transporting it several times, is bound to be advantageous compared with rewriting the same program several times.

- The designer as employee might contemplate changing employers and might want to reuse programs in the new environment. (This argument is another presentation of William Waite's argument.)

- Since software is becoming more expensive than hardware, its life cycle must be made longer; that is, it must be designed to survive hardware changes.

- In the case of a newly designed programming language, portability almost ensures broader, faster implementation.

- Further, the portability of the implementation will serve as a strong incentive to maintain compatibility in subsequent implementations.

- Even in the case of an established, well-known programming language, highly portable implementation will influence the shape of the official standard and promote the ideas included in the implementation.

- In an environment that comprises several different computer systems, the same application may be needed on each system, perhaps at the same time.

- A portable software product presents a positive sales argument.

- Anticipation that a software product will be portable is likely to have a beneficial effect on its programming: The style will have to be cleaner, more systematic, more disciplined, and more readable. Hence the reliability, adaptability, maintainability, and overall quality of the program will be improved.

Here again, of course, one can provide several counterarguments, most of them similar to those given in the preceding section:

- A portable software product may be more reliable and adaptable, but at the same time it might be less efficient. (Still, we have to ask: Is it so important to produce an efficient but erroneous program?)

- If one of the main goals of a software company is to develop software for new customers and computer systems, and the software is *too* portable, the company's employees could conceivably be left with nothing to do. (Still, we have to point out that they would then be available for developing more new software.)

- Perhaps, as stated above, the overall cost to a company of developing portable software is less than that of rewriting the same program many times over, yet time or other resource constraints may require that the secondary goal, portability, be sacrificed so that the first version will be ready on time and/or within a fixed budget.

- If the implementation of a programming language is both easily transported and adapted, users may be encouraged to devise their own variations, thus negatively affecting compatibility and hampering the portability of programs written in this language.

1.3   What software is potentially portable?

By "software product" we mean here a set of programs with a common purpose. We will not attempt to provide a more precise definition (partially because that would require us to define precisely what a program is). But, we can give some typical examples of software products that can be built to be portable. These various examples will all appear again in the case studies found in Part 2 of this book.

- A compiler can be portable in its entirety if it generates an object language that is independent of the target computer. This is what we will call a "compiler-interpreter," of which a typical example is Snobol4 (see Sec. 6.3).

- A compiler can also be divided into two main parts, the front end depending on the source language, the back end on the object language. The interface between these two parts, if well designed, can be independent of both languages. In this case, the front end can be built to be portable (see Sec. 6.4).

- A large number of utility software products can be designed to be portable, at least in the major part. This is the case, for example, for text editors (see Sec. 7.5), general-purpose macroprocessors (see Secs. 3.1 and 7.4), various program-conversion tools (see Sec. 3.2), and tools for verifying and filtering a language (see Sec. 3.3). In fact, even file-management systems can be portable, in which case they further the portability of the above-mentioned utilities.

- Application software products that can be portable are still more numerous, and in fact their design constitutes the main reason for the existence of many software companies. We can mention, for example, company payroll, library management, stock or portfolio management, accounting, text processing, and the software packages and computer games that are increasingly popular for personal computers. But neither these applications nor the techniques used in making them portable are usually described in scientific literature, and we have no case studies for them.

• Finally, and somewhat unexpectedly, whole operating systems are now built to be portable. The first systems of this sort were only demonstration models, but those that will be considered in Secs. 7.2 and 7.3 are full-scale systems now in actual use.

All things considered, a software product may be designed to be portable if its purpose does not depend on the environment in which it will be implemented. By contrast, it is impossible to build a software product whose specifications refer to a specific environment and expect that product to be portable. This may be the case, for example, for the back end of a compiler, which generates machine language, or for a link editor or an assembler, the purpose of which is also to generate machine language. Let us note, however, that even in the cases just mentioned, an attempt is often made to design as much of the program as possible to be independent of the target machine; it is also true that we are beginning to develop the expertise to build portable code generators, link editors, and even assemblers.

Still it is not yet within the state of the art to build a portable peripheral handler, a supervisor nucleus (the part of an operating system that processes interrupts), or even a text-processing utility linked to a specific peripheral. There are still some cases where the major part of software development is too closely linked to a specific computer environment to permit portability in programming.

In addition, it must not be forgotten in many cases that it is simply not desirable to transport software products. Transport will be useless, or even of negative value, if (1) the initial qualities of the product do not warrant its broad use; (2) the transport would be too expensive; or (3) the expected performance after the transport would be calamitous.

Thus, we can summarize in one sentence: The transport of a software product can be considered for any product of satisfactory quality, independent of its environment, provided the costs involved warrant the transport.

The Bases of Portability

2

The Major Problems
in Software Portability

There are some major problems that must be recognized in ensuring the portability of software, problems that can occur at any time from conception through initial implementation, actual transport, installation in a new environment, and maintenance. We will study here the problems that we could call "primary," or "initial." This means that these problems are present at the outset, even before one meets the problems that arise from a given implementation or from inadequate solution to basic discrepancies. As an example, the difference in representation of real numbers on various computer systems presents a primary problem in software portability. The unsatisfactory performance of a program because of a failed attempt to resolve the difference is a secondary problem.

In the first section of this chapter we will show the difficulties encountered in various software environments. As we mentioned above, the characteristics of real arithmetic are quite important and are well-delimited. This type of problem and the range of possible solutions form the subject matter of the second section; we will not consider numeric software again in the text. In the third section we will study the specific problem of data portability, as opposed to program portability. Finally, in the fourth section we will discuss a very particular aspect of portability, one not directly related to computers but of increasing importance as software becomes more portable. It involves the question of property rights and the extent of legal protection available for software producers.

2.1 The portable software environment

2.1.1 Introduction

Some basic terms that will be used in the rest of the book should be precisely defined at the outset in order to avoid any confusion. Here we will define the general terms; the more technical ones will be defined later.

A given program is used in a certain environment that consists mainly of two parts: the material environment (the computer and its devices) and the software environment (the operating system with its various programming languages). The "portability" of a program depends upon the ease with which it can be transferred and made useful, without modification of its properties, in a new environment. The "adaptability" of a program is defined by the ease with which its properties can be modified. Adaptation is made without changing the program environment, and remains an adaptation only so long as the new properties are closely related to the old ones. On the other hand, if a program's properties are partially dependent on its environment, as in the case of a compiler, then the program is portable only to the extent it is adaptable.

A program is portable if the effort required for its transport is much less than the effort required for its initial implementation and if it retains its initial qualities after the transport. The portability of a program can be evaluated by measuring the transport effort. For example, if I is the work involved in initial implementation, and T is the work involved in transport, then the program's portability can be evaluated as $(I - T)/I$. Hence any program can be mathematically determined to be 100 percent portable (that is, there is no transport effort involved), 80 percent portable, 50 percent portable, and so on.

In the same way, we can evaluate a program's adaptability. Note that for some authors, adaptability includes portability, since they consider adaptability to be the overriding characteristic. We prefer to distinguish these two terms, although the distinction between them might be unclear in cases where transport implies adaptation.

Note also that some authors distinguish "portability," where no modification is necessary, from "transportability," where a certain effort in adaptation is required. This distinction seems artificial since 100 percent portability is almost never achieved, and we will use the terms synonymously.

A given transport involves several elements that we will try to clearly distinguish. First there is the software that is to be ported; this can be a program or a set of related programs or subprograms. Beyond the software itself, it includes the complete documentation that must go with it: detailed specifications, user's and implementor's manuals, internal descriptions, etc.

There is also the environment within which the software is to be considered. We will call the environment in which the software works before its transport the "source environment," and the one in which it works afterwards, the "target environment." It often happens that the transport involves the use of specific tools. The environment in which these tools are used will be called the "porting environment"; this is usually the same as the source or the target environment.

Finally there are the people who accomplish the port. Griswold [Gri77c] provides a simple but usually sufficient model; it distinguishes the designer and the installer. The former writes the software and makes it run in the source environment; the latter ports it and makes it run on the target environment. Designers can accomplish their job in such a way that the installer's job is reduced (in which case the software is highly portable). On the contrary, designers can write a program having some qualities that make it worth porting to new environments, but they leave the program in a state such that performing the installation becomes a major job. In that case the designer and the installer both work on the transport environment, working either independently or as a team and sharing the title of implementor.

The remainder of this section is divided into five parts. In the first four, we will speak of the main components of an environment: the computer, the operating system, the devices (files, input-output, and communication), and the programming languages. For each case, we briefly describe the problems involved and then discuss possible solutions and their consequences. Most solutions will be described and evaluated in more detail in later sections of this chapter and in Chap. 3. Finally, the last part of this section is a deceptively simple but often irritating aspect of software portability—the act of physically transporting programs and data.

2.1.2 The computer

Problems in portability

Internal representation of information.* Since all computers now use binary representation, one of the governing characteristics of a system is the length of a word, even if the notion of "word" itself is not perfectly defined in all cases. The variety of lengths is large—from 8 to 64 bits—and affects the method of representing values in integers and other numbers, the method of addressing data, the number of characters permissible in a word, etc. The two methods of representing negative integers give different results: In 2's complement representation, the representable domain is not symmetric, and binary shifts allow fast multiplication or division by 2. In 1's complement representation, the addressable domain is symmetric, but there are two distinct representations of zero, and shifts give correct results only for positive numbers. On some computers, often those with a large word size, some binary configurations have a special meaning (defined or undefined, for example). There is a subtler problem related to the representation of data: Integer operations are almost always used to manipulate characters and pointers (or addresses). However, this mix of operations on different machine-level types is rarely uniform, and therefore rarely portable, because their size may not be the same and because the parts of a word used to represent the operations are often not the same or do not have the same meaning.

Use of registers. Using the register as our basis, we could separate computers into five different categories:

- Those having no registers, all operations being done in memory. This category is now almost nonexistent.

- Those having one register or accumulator for common operations, usually with an extension for multiplication or division, and some index registers.

- Those having a set of general-purpose registers. Ordinary operations take one of their operands from a register and the other from memory. In most cases,

---

* The representation of floating numbers and associated operations will be discussed in Sec. 2.2; it will not be discussed here.

only some of the registers are used for addressing. Most computers fall into this category.

- Those having several sets of specific registers, with most operations dealing with one or two operands, which are in registers.

- Those having few actual registers, but an operand stack where operations find their operands and put their results.

The main differences among these five categories are seen in the management of intermediate results. Only the stack mechanism allows an intermediate language to be independent of the computer.

Organization of memory.   The smallest addressable element in computer memory can be a byte or a word (though some specific instructions can access a part of a word). If the addressable unit is a byte, words and larger objects can easily and transparently serve as targets of addresses; the converse is not true.

We can distinguish three main categories of memory organization. In "linear memory," addressable components are consecutive, numbered with a single integer, and equally accessible (even if addressing protections limit the part of memory that is accessible). In "segmented linear memory," each segment is linear but is independent of the others, and an address typically consists of segment plus offset. Addressing can be said to be two-dimensional. In "hierarchical memory," there are several levels of memory, each having a different speed and independent addressing, with explicit transfer between levels.

The different mechanisms of pagination or of topographical modification make this distinction more complicated; it is even possible to simulate one type through use of another type.

Addressing computation to access structured-data components.   Three mechanisms may be used to access structured-data components, although only two are of practical importance:

- Deferred computation, then modification of the access instruction. This access mode had so many drawbacks that it has completely disappeared.

- Deferred computation, then indirect addressing. This addressing mode is mainly used to implement the idea of pointers.

- Computation done by the computer itself, with a pair of registers—a base register and an index register. This is the most frequently used addressing method in large computers; even so, it does not generally do all the work necessary since on most computers the distance between two components of the structured data must be explicitly computed. On a few other machines, the addressing computation can be automated for the most frequent sizes (1, 2, and 4 bytes), but no general mechanism is provided. The combination of indirect and indexed addressing is not always available and does not in any event present any really useful options.

Storage of useful data at procedure calls. The most important thing to save is, of course, the return address, but there may also be other kinds of information to save. There are four main mechanisms to accomplish this:

- Storage of the data in memory at the beginning of the code. This method is rare, since it does not fit with recursive or reentrant procedures and treats a program as a data area.

- Storage of the information in a particular register, usually chosen from among the general-purpose registers.

- Storage of the information by specialized instruction.

- Storage of the data on top of the execution stack.

Except in this last case, access to the parameters of the procedure is not provided in the instruction set; several methods of providing access are possible and depend on the programmer's preference.

Possible solutions and their consequences. The differences in computer architecture and instruction sets mentioned above make it difficult to establish a general model for the different mechanisms. However, this is what in effect has to be done in order to design a general intermediate language, as we will see in Sec. 5.1. Some aspects of the problem are more frequently faced than others—for instance, working with a set of general-purpose registers or saving return addresses in a register. Differences in word length and in the internal representation of the common data types also impose barriers to providing portable programs.

The designer of an intermediate language can even make some restrictive suppositions without being aware of them, such as the assumption that adding 1 to the address of an integer-array component gives the address of the following component. This is true only on a word machine, not on one based on bytes. Another example is the assumption that once a character has been loaded into a register, that register represents the ordinal number of the character: This is true only if the load operation puts the character on the right side of the register and clears the left side.

Therefore the model that is actually portable must be heavily parameterized and must make a systematic distinction between each data type and the associated operations that are available. When a choice must be made between different solutions, the one least difficult to simulate by the others must be chosen. For example, it is much less difficult to simulate a stack machine on a register machine than vice versa. Thus the model should be a stack computer.

If the model does not have to be universal, but must cover only a family of similar machines, its definition is obviously much simpler. The suitability of the model is crucial, because a badly adapted model can lead to unacceptable performance. Only the transport environment, if separate from the source and target environments, is not a part of this problem.

2.1.3 The operating system

Problems in portability

The command language. The command language is often the most troublesome element of an operating system. The lexical and syntactic aspects of the language are usually incomprehensible, and the semantics, even the existence, of some commands often cannot be justified. The language itself is very often so complex that it cannot be analyzed. Moreover, there are huge differences between the capabilities of specific systems—as any reader who has had the chance to compare at least three operating systems will attest.

Resource management. Resource management is one of the major functions of an operating system, which is constantly called on to balance timesharing between processes, main memory sharing or simulation of a virtual memory, space sharing on direct-access devices, sharing of devices themselves (of tape drives in particular), and allocation of nonsharable resources such as the specialized devices. Problems that may arise in the design of portable software are caused not only by the existence of these various resources but by the limitations that a system can impose on the resources. Some systems impose absolute constraints and ask that all resources be requested before execution of a program; others impose dynamic constraints and constraints applying to the maximum number of resources that can be used at one time.

Of course, the existence of a given resource on a given system and the different naming conventions used to access the resource also pose problems for portable software.

Various services. Several services may exist on different systems; here the major problem vis-à-vis software portability is that their presence on an operating system can never be assumed. We cite, for example, the overlying facilities for a program, the control points used periodically (or at critical junctures in a program) to save a very long job and/or to restore it in case of failure, the initialization of memory when a program is loaded, the specification of parameters and access to them, and the possibility of direct program-to-program calls without explicit commands.

Error handling.* When an error occurs during the execution of a program, it may be handled in three different ways: by terminating the program (either the current step or the complete job), by calling a specific module to handle it, or by completely ignoring it. In certain cases, termination may be required, and in other cases ignoring the error may be the preferred course of action. Whichever method of error treatment exists, the nature of the information provided and the actions allowed also vary. Let us finally mention that in many cases errors in the operating system itself, unknown to that time, are discovered during the transport of a large software system, sometimes endangering the transport.

---

* We are not including in this discussion the methods of error treatment that occur within the run-time systems implementing high-level programming languages; for such discussion, see Sec. 2.1.5.

Possible solutions and their consequences.   The problems that an operating system may pose to a person wanting to port a program are so great that they are practically unsolvable by a general model. Usually one can adopt a set of various solutions, depending on the nature of the problem. The question of the incompatibility of command languages is usually completely ignored. The designer does not even try to suggest a solution to the problem, since there is little comparability between systems, and the installer is invariably forced to build the bridge.

The software to be ported could be encapsulated in a specific subsystem that serves as the interface with the target system. Requests to the operating system are thus isolated, but the subsystem may prove unportable in many ways. Moreover, its definition is not easy since it must be careful to specify all the services that are needed by the program in the way that these services are most likely to be implemented on each receiving system.

Whatever method used, the best solution consists in avoiding the resources provided by the source system, or at least in not depending on them. This can be very expensive; it may involve several complicated and inefficient methods, duplication of work, even loss of performance capability to the extent that the software itself becomes unusable. (Imagine, for example, the result of a programmed pagination system implemented on a system already providing another kind of pagination.)

Let us note in passing that the system on which the most demands are placed is the operating system of the transporting machine, since the transport operation may involve much larger, more complicated programs than the ported program itself.

2.1.4   Devices and files

Problems in portability.   In the following discussion, we consider devices and files as means of local input-output and as places to store large amounts of information over time. In Sec. 2.1.6 we will consider the problems that may arise during physical transfer from one site to another.

Ordinary devices.   Punch cards are becoming less and less popular, yet when the 80-column card and the Hollerith punch code were the standard of the industry, they fostered widespread portability of data.

Printers, while presenting greater ease of use, also present more problems, in portability, with line lengths varying from 72 to 160 characters, or even more. (Ironically, the less expensive printers allow more format flexibility.) Specification of line or page feeds, the existence and configuration of programmed tape, the number of lines on a page, and the possibility of superimpression—each of these variables represents a source of difficulty, as do the discrepancies between the printed character set and the character sets accepted by other devices.

Magnetic tapes present serious problems only in transmission between different installations (see Sec. 2.1.6). Disks, diskettes, and related devices have their own unique and disparate characteristics. The major problem here is the maximum length of blocks allowed.

Interactive terminals.   To suppose that a program can carry on an interactive dialog with a terminal is often the surest way to make it unportable. One of the first difficulties is that too often a terminal cannot be considered as separate input and output files connected to the same device (perhaps even with the same name) and must be programmed at the lowest level of a given terminal. Then the question of whether the terminal transmission unit handles one line or one character at a time arises. End-of-line conventions are different from one character set to another, from one system to another, and, of course, from one terminal to another. Tabulation notation is also often bothersome, since its meaning depends on the context, making it impossible to guarantee what shape the printed text will have. The other control characters, if used, can be even more unportable, even if standardized character sets theoretically define their meaning. Erasing, deleting, backspacing, various escape sequences—all present problems. Even simple spacing may raise some difficulties, in particular when a space occurs at the end of a line or when there is an empty line. The major problem in all these circumstances comes perhaps from the nontransparency of the operating system, which almost always transforms the characters transmitted. Finally, the advanced system of screen handling on some terminals is so different from that of others that this capability must be sacrificed if the program is to be portable.

Files.   Files are certainly the most indispensable service offered by an operating system; they afford a level of abstraction above raw I/O devices. Unfortunately, even the very notion of a file is system-dependent. The term "file" does not even always have the same meaning—it can be a primitive way of linking a program's internal description to a physical address, or it can be a sophisticated tool associated with hierarchical directories and access and usage restrictions. Aside from purely sequential files, which are universal, nothing in the domain of the "file" has the same meaning everywhere. It is impossible to find a satisfying model for describing a direct-access file. Even sequential files can raise some problems— particularly if their support is a magnetic tape and if one wants to store several files on the same tape or to have one file span several tapes. Finally, the so-called standard files, which imply standard input and standard output, are very often treated so individually that they cannot be exchanged with other files.

Possible solutions and their consequences.   The source, transport, and target environments must be considered for all computer input-output. A way to solve at least a part of the disparity problems we mention above usually consists of designing an intermediate level of software to form a standard interface for input-output. Such an interface must be as simple, and hence as primitive, as possible, but it does not always have to be efficient, since the cost of input-output is generally many times greater than the cost of machine instructions. It is usually sufficient if the treatment done in the interface is not *excessively* long and inefficient.

This kind of standardized interface, since it is primitive, will not allow high-level operations on the files themselves; thus these operations should be avoided, as should almost any procedure related to the operating system. In fact, all high-level operations should be avoided, even if the programming language provides them, since they cannot be given universal meaning.

The major consequence is that most portable software has to be severely limited in its use of input-output, which consequently limits what such software can do. Because of these restrictions, efficiency becomes a secondary problem.

2.1.5 Programming languages

Problems in portability. In Chap. 4 we will establish that high-level programming languages are the basic tools for writers of portable software, and we will see in detail in Sec. 4.2 the problems they raise. In this section, we will mention only a few of those problems.

Dialects. The main problem related to high-level programming languages stems from the existence of dialects. Either because the official language definition is not fully usable, or because it is incomplete or ambiguous, it is almost impossible to find two different implementations of a language that are rigorously compatible, even if they run on the same computer and the same operating system. Moreover, implementors often do not even try to attain this compatibility, adding instead extensions and improvements to various implementations.

Low-level resources. Correspondence between what is written in a programming language and what actually happens in the computer can be explicit or implicit, depending on the language. Explicit assumptions by a programmer about the implementation of a specific language feature make it difficult to achieve the machine independence that is needed to make a program portable. Implicit assumptions occur when a programmer who is used to a certain language and a certain computer makes implicit hypotheses on how a given construct is implemented. A hypothesis that may be true for most implementations may be false in a new setting—and everything collapses.

Error treatment. The interpretation of error differs from one language to another and from one implementation to another. Compilers that allow some compile-time and run-time errors to pass undetected are particularly dangerous in this regard. They will accept a program that would be rejected by a stricter compiler. This problem occurs so frequently that it is almost a constant in all transport operations of sufficient size.

Possible solutions and their consequences. Various solutions have been adopted to solve the problems cited above. One of the most reliable consists in the use of only a common subset of a programming language, one that is expected to be implemented in the same way on all target machines. There exist some automatic verifiers to facilitate this approach, as we will see in Sec. 3.3.

Another solution also makes use of an automatic tool—this time to translate from one dialect to another. This approach will be studied in Sec. 3.2.

It is possible that the common subset is so small as to be unusable, or that the search for truly implementation-independent solutions will lead to something so inefficient as to weaken the entire program. Thus the last solution, one often forgotten, is simply to use another programming language. The newer languages promise so much in the domain of portability that they should discourage the continued use of obsolete programming languages.

2.1.6 The distribution of portable software*

One of the least considered and most underestimated phases of a transport is the purely physical aspect of the operation and the technical problems that arise between designer and installer. Three main classes of problems may occur, and although they seem trivial, they can jeopardize an otherwise successful transport if they are not correctly handled.

Character sets. A 500-page book [Mac80] has recently been published on the use of character sets, an apparently limited subject. Although a hundred pages could have been saved by avoiding a systematic description of each set each time it is referred to, the book does prove that character sets may be a vaster subject than once thought—as we ourselves will show.

Problems in portability. A character set can be used to describe several different elements: It can be used for binary representation (5-, 6-, 7-, and 8-bit sets), for representation on a particular medium (card, punch tape, or magnetic tape), for graphic appearance ("|," "¦," "!," for example), or to carry procedural instruction (control characters such as "newline" and "delete," or the minus sign). The definition of a character set does not usually include all these aspects, nor does it even entirely describe all the elements it includes. For example, the EBCDIC code does not define the graphic representation of all possible characters, and the 7-bit ISO code leaves positions available for representation of national variants (diacritic characters of some languages). None of the codes define the representation on a punch tape, and another code is necessary to establish that correspondence.

The different character sets are defined by various private organizations (IBM) and by national (ANSI, IEEE, Afnor) and international (ISO, CCITT) organizations. They are defined according to various and often contradictory goals; some are concerned with numerical or alphabetical order, others with the simplification of decoding numbers or of changing letter cases or of device-decoding circuits, or of changing from one code to another. Some points cannot even be addressed—for instance, the respective places of upper- and lowercase letters and the totality of characters that must be provided in the first place. Thus there is nothing surprising in the great disparity between character sets, although the different interpretations given to the same, supposedly standardized character set can be surprising. It is not rare to find, on the same computer, some incompatibilities between devices having the same function—for example, between two printers or two terminals. We can propose, as an exercise for the interested reader, a study of the different external appearances of the string "\{/!}^%#[]" transmitted from an EBCDIC internal code to different interactive terminals pretending to use the ASCII code. One can readily see that designing a portable program in which these characters play an important role would not be wise, and it is not uncommon for the installer to spend a lot of time trying to reproduce a text with the same external appearance on two implementations. The problem

---

* The following discussion is taken largely from an article by Waite [Wai75].

can be compounded if the internal functioning of the program depends on a certain order in the character set, for the order may change when the program is ported.

Possible solutions and their consequences.   These problems in the use of character sets can be avoided if the designer takes several precautions:

- A truly standardized set should be chosen. Currently it can only be the 7-bit ISO code, better known by its American variant, ASCII.*

- A truly common subset should be used. The subset should have no control characters and no national variants.

- Substitute characters must be considered for letters not available in the common subset—for example, "(." or "(/" instead of [.

- It should be assumed that upper- and lowercase letters are equivalent.

- The problem should not be underestimated. Consider every possible source of trouble.

Transport media

Listings.   Hard copy, or a listing on paper, is only usable for a program of few pages in length, but it is the only distribution medium that does not raise any problems in automatic conversion. The important condition is its readability, which must be assured in order to avoid transcription errors. The algorithms published by the Association for Computing Machinery (ACM) have been distributed in this way for a long time.

Cards.   The use of punch cards presents several drawbacks (besides the fact that they are no longer universally employed). Among their disadvantages are their weight (and hence the expense of packing and mailing), their sensitivity to moisture, the necessity of numbering them to avoid mixing, their limitation to the use of printable characters (since binary cards have no relation between two systems), and their nonnegligible cost. Their major advantage is that character data on cards is very likely to be readable between systems. For weight and space reasons, cards should only be used for programs of under 2000 lines.

Paper tape.   The use of paper tape has practically disappeared (except perhaps in England). However, paper tape has the same advantages as do cards, without most of their disadvantages. Paper tapes are light, strong, and inexpensive; there is no possibility of mixing the sequences, and the explicit ends-of-line allow much saving of space. They should be used to transport programs that are under 5000 lines in length.

Magnetic tape.   For reasons of capacity, magnetic tape is by far the most commonly used medium of transport. An ordinary 2400-foot and 1600-character-per-inch tape can theoretically contain 46 million characters; but and because of the

---

* ISO is currently studying an 8-bit code.

intervals between blocks, it can in fact hold about 30 million, with 2000 character blocks. This allows almost anything to be transported on one or two tapes.

Unfortunately, though, magnetic tape is also the medium that raises by far the most problems. The first difficulty comes from the high cost of a tape reader, which is disproportionately expensive compared with the cost of most microcomputers. Thus microsystems rarely have tape readers. Even on systems with tape drives, there are still several problems: There are two kinds of tapes, one having seven, one having nine tracks, with no compatibility. There are many different densities in magnetic tapes, and, because of the parity bit, many different ways to represent the same character. There is the possibility of information damage during the transport; there are minimum and maximum block-size limits and different ways of grouping logical blocks into physical blocks. The use and formatting of labels vary, even though all these aspects are supposedly standardized. The use of blocks and labels, depending on the file manager of an operating system, can cause so many difficulties that it is sometimes impossible to read a tape produced on another installation; in this event it is necessary to write the conversion tools in assembly language.

Floppy disks or diskettes.   Diskettes are the favorite medium for microcomputers and often the only way for micros to have access to new software. The advantages of diskettes include their low cost and their relative security. Their drawbacks stem from their reduced capacity and their differing densities and organization. In their current state, floppy disks (and cassettes and cartridge tapes) are an excellent way of distributing software between the same machines and same operating systems but not a practical or convenient way of transporting software.

Direct transmission.   The increasing availability of computer networks often allows direct transmission of files between computers, without intermediate external support. By definition, a network should present no compatibility problems, since all of those were presumably solved when the network was created. Thus direct transmission can be used for average-size files, and it is certainly the best method . . . when the net is available and works correctly.

Software maintenance.   A service company should deliver its software, not simply abandon it on its customer's doorstep. The same is true for portable software, even if the designer's commercial motivations are reduced. Three important points should be considered in the distribution of portable software; they are discussed below.

Documentation.   Complete and usable documentation is often voluminous and difficult to produce. It should include four kinds of manuals for four different kinds of readers:

- The user's manual, which should include a standard section valid for the target environment and a section to be adapted by the installer according to his or her experience. The fundamental component of the user's manual should be complete examples of the program in use.

- The installer's manual, which must be a step-by-step guide. It has to take into account that the installer will usually know both the target and transport environments well, but may not know the transported programs and/or the source environment at all.

- The working manual, directed to the person who wants to understand the principles and the practical details of the program. The working manual should allow the installer to locate and correct errors.

- The adapter's manual, which is often confused with the installer's manual and/or the working manual, though it is distinct from both. The adapter's manual should allow a person, not necessarily the installer, to adapt the program to new specifications. Hence it must outline the critical design points, give the meaning of all parameters, and suggest likely modifications or extensions.

The best programmers are not always the best documenters, and well-written programs are not automatically self-documented. The best and safest organization is to deliver programs in machine-readable form, with documentation on paper.

Testing. A battery of tests provides an indispensable tool for the installer, especially if the tests are complete enough to be used as validation tools. They must be numerous and varied and must cover all parts of the program. A good way to ensure that is to have them produced automatically whenever possible (see Sec. 3.5). If they are designed to give a bulk of results, it is important that the implementation kit provide, along with the listing of these results, a tool to verify their conformity and flag eventual differences. In some circumstances, the designer cannot provide an exhaustive battery of tests, in which case the description of the installer's responsibility must be carefully written. Finally, an often forgotten aspect of the tests is that they must be portable to be useful. In any case, examples of use of the program cannot replace the tests themselves.

Updates. A program is never finished; there is always debugging, improvements, and modifications to consider, all of which implies more or less frequent updating, partial or major. The designer can proceed in two different ways: He or she can provide the installer with a version of the latest update, which is to be imposed on the previous versions (that is, a patch), or, alternatively, the designer can provide a complete new version of the program with each update, announcing the new version to all installers and giving it to those who ask for it. Patches can be used if nothing fundamental is changed in the program, if only a few corrections of errors detected after distribution are involved. Patches imply that the designer has established, from the first release, a unique identification of program source lines; they also usually imply that the implementation kit contains a small, specialized updating program. But if the source program is not available, patching cannot be used as a method of updating, and entire modules have to be replaced each time. Thus, the second method, where the installer is given a complete new version and an implementation kit similar to the first, may be easier. The same implementation method can be used, providing it is not too expensive. The general distribution of complete successive versions also has the advantage that the designer need not record what has already been given to each installer.

2.2   The portability of numeric software

The major problem in designing and transporting numeric software is the defini-tion of arithmetic in programming languages. Numeric types are very machine-dependent, both in the range of values that can be represented on a given com-puter and in the representation of numbers. Moreover, the semantics of arithmetic operations is not always well defined and can prompt different inter-pretations, especially when the limits of representation are reached.

On top of this, there are other problems: Numeric software involves a large number of algorithms for the resolution of linear equation systems, for handling matrices, etc. These algorithms must be described in a machine-independent way, so as to be useful in different contexts and on different machines. Thus, numeric software needs library-management facilities, and therefore file sys-tems, to regroup useful algorithms and allow the user to choose whatever is needed. Here the programming again depends on the operating system software and file systems, and some of the same problems we discussed in the previous section result.

The choice of a programming language is especially critical. The language used to write the algorithms must provide the ability to manipulate large parameter-ized arrays, to be called in different contexts, and in particular, to be called by programs that may be written in another language.

In the following paragraphs, we are first going to examine some of the problems encountered in designing portable numeric software and then discuss some of the ways they are solved in different programming languages: Fortran, since it is by far the most widely used (though not the most appropriate) in this area; Ada because of its effort to provide solutions; PL/1; Algol 68; and others. Finally, we will give some examples of portable numeric software, such as the library de-signed by the Numerical Algorithm Group (NAG) in England.

2.2.1   Numeric types and their problems

Integers.   Integers present two kinds of problems, one stemming from the lim-its of the representable interval and the other from the approximate computation for operations, such as division, that do not have integer results. Depending on the machine, such computation can result in truncation or rounding. Different behavior may be prompted by interval limitations. An overflow, in an extreme case, can lead to a reset of the memory location. More often, an error message is given, with or without stopping the execution of the program.

Rational numbers.   Rational numbers are not present in all programming lan-guages, especially not in Fortran. However, they are found in PL/1 and Ada (fixed-point numbers). They are represented as a mantissa and an exponent, which implies a limitation of the interval of rational numbers that can be repre-sented, either because of the number of digits allowed for the mantissa or be-cause of the domain of the exponent.

Real numbers.   Real numbers can only be approximately represented, more or less accurately. Therefore every operation on a real number yields an approximate result, which, repeated several times, can introduce major error. The result thus depends on the representation of the real number and on the precision with which it is obtained. Moreover, it depends on the method used, by a machine or a software library, to implement floating-point arithmetic.

The base of representation.   The number base used to represent numbers can also have an influence on the interval of numbers that can be represented and on the precision of computations. In fact, high-level programming languages reason in terms of numbers in base 10, although these numbers are most often represented in base 2, 8, or even 16.

The precision of arithmetic computations.   As we have seen above, numbers are often represented by approximations, either because a given number does not have an exact representation or because the results of arithmetic computations do not belong to the right type. The more such operations are repeated, the less precise the results obtained.

2.2.2   Solutions offered by some languages

The only ways of implementing machine-independent arithmetic are either to enforce strong restrictions on numeric types (intervals), which may not be the right solution since even in the general case it would prevent the use of all machine capabilities, or to define an arithmetic flexible enough to accept any kind of numeric object. Programming languages usually offer a mixture of these two solutions.

Fortran.   Fortran does not propose any actual solution, but it is useful to mention it here, since it is the most widely used programming language in the scientific domain. Most of its drawbacks come from its lack of standardization (see Sec. 4.2) and its lack of precise definition. Aird, Battiste, and Gregory [ABG77] studied it from this point of view.

Lack of standardization.   The lack of standardization in Fortran has led to the development of many different constructs, each of them accepted by only a single compiler. In Fortran one finds different kinds of loop statements, different input-output constructs, different data types (for example, INTEGER*2 in IBM Fortran), and different predefined functions. In this latter construct particularly, the differences are numerous; in some instances the same function has different names, in other cases the function is available on one computer and not on others.

It is always possible to avoid the inconvenience of extensions by limiting a program to a more-or-less standard subset of Fortran. However, it is much more difficult to overcome the other deficiencies that make the portability of Fortran programs rather difficult. Some of the problems would disappear if the compiler had the ability to choose the method of representation of numbers (single or double precision), rather than leaving the choice to the programmer.

Lack of precise definition.   The constants that determine the use of integers, real numbers, or double-precision numbers depend on the host computer and the compiler and are inaccessible to the programmer. Hence, it is conceivable that a program would give different results on different machines. Further, the representation of a real constant can be different from one machine to another. This implies that a given program might not be accepted by all compilers. Then too, compilers react differently to errors: For example, encountering an integer overflow, one compiler might signal an error, while another might automatically give the result in double precision. And finally, results of arithmetic operations, such as integer division, are not precisely defined in Fortran.

Ada.   In Ada numeric types have been defined with special care, reflecting a real evolution of the state of the art in this domain.

Indeed, some groups such as the International Federation for Information Processing (IFIP) working group WG 2.5, the American National Standards Institute (ANSI) committee X3J3, and Brown and Feldman [BrF80] have been studying the problem of parameterization of numeric environment for several years. Well-defined parameters, together with an arithmetic model and axioms, should allow a certain independence between numbers and their representation on different computers.

Ada is inspired from the model defined by Brown [Bro81] having certain restrictions—in particular Ada supposes that all computers use binary numbers. According to Brown, a system of model numbers is defined with four integer parameters and with three real parameters derived from the integers. A model number, different from zero, is represented by $x = b^e f$ where f is a signed rational number such as $1/b \le |f| < 1$, composed of p digits in base b, and e is an integer such as $emin < e < emax$.

Ideally, these parameters should be the same as the parameters describing floating-point numbers in the host system. In reality, these parameters must be adapted in such a fashion that they verify some of the axioms defining operations on the model numbers, which in fact form a subset of the numbers that can be represented on a particular computer.

Parameters Proposed by Brown and Feldman

Base of computations	b
Precision	p
Minimal exponent	$emin$
Maximal exponent	$emax$

Derived Parameters

Maximal relative domain	b^{1-p}
Smallest positive number	b^{emin-1}
Largest positive number	$b^{emax}(1 - b^p)$

For a given computer, it is always possible to choose parameters in such a way that the arithmetic system is optimal. All the results of computations are then explainable in terms of axioms. The most difficult task is, of course, to choose these parameters.

Numeric types in Ada are copied from this model, although they are much less flexible. The predefined type FLOAT has a precision determined by the host system. However, the user can declare a new type for which he or she can fix the minimal precision needed. This is the only parameter the user has the liberty to choose, the others being fixed by the implementation. However, their values are accessible by the following attributes:

F'DIGITS	D, precision given in the type declaration
F'MANTISSA	Number of significant digits, defined as the first integer greater than $D*\log(10)/\log(2)$
F'EMAX	Maximal value of the exponent, defined as $4*$F'MANTISSA
F'SMALL	Smallest positive number, defined as $2^{-\text{F'MAX}-1}$
F'LARGE	Largest positive number, defined as $2^{\text{F'MAX}}*(1.0 - 2.0^{1-\text{F'MANTISSA}})$

All this allows the user to write a program in terms of model numbers, without worrying about their actual representation; this makes for much more portable programming. As opposed to Fortran, in Ada the compiler chooses the representation according to user specification.

As we have seen, these numbers are only a subset of what can be represented on any given machine. A user who wishes to take advantage of the machine and who is not preoccupied with portability can still access the limit parameters, which are machine-dependent.

Therefore, Ada allows a programmer, albeit with many precautions, to write machine-independent scientific programs. The Ada-Europe subgroup studying the portability of Ada programs gives a list of these precautions in Nissen et al. [NWW82]; the limitations are constraining, and even frustrating, for the programmer who is working on a powerful machine, but they favor portability. For example, the precautions include recommendations not to use integers that cannot be represented in 16 bits; not to declare floating-point types with a precision greater than five digits (if the application absolutely needs them, a new type can be declared, limiting the portability problems to this type, but not involving the whole application); and, of course, not to depend on implementation attributes.

Other languages.   Besides the two languages we cite above, which represent two extremes, other languages such as PL/1 and Algol 68 address some of the problems of portability, but their solutions are not precise enough to be very helpful.

For example, in Algol 68, a programmer can choose between several precisons (or for integers, between several intervals) by defining the types of variables as real, long real, long long real, etc. However, aside from the fact that a particular implementation can choose to define only one precision, the meaning of the precision itself depends on the implementation. Thus Algol 68 should not be used to write functions the result of which relies on the precision with which the computations are performed.

In PL/1, the definition of real numbers is a little more precise, but still, each implementation can choose its own definitions. Reals can be declared in base 2 or 10, with a certain number of digits, but the interval of the exponent cannot be specified. However, PL/1 does provide some operators and mathematical functions that are useful for numeric software. Some of these predefined functions take as a parameter the precision needed for computations, but in fact the operations are still performed with the usual precision, and only the result is modified to satisfy to the requested precision.

Other languages are even poorer from the point of view of numeric operations; Pascal has only one real type and very few predefined functions, and Basic has a single arithmetic type.

In summary, an adequate language for numeric software, even nonportable software, should allow several formats of reals, depending on the significant digits of the mantissa or on the maximal exponent, to ensure that such operations as subtraction, division, modulo, square root, comparison of reals, and conversion from one format to another are executed with the desired precision. We have seen that most current languages do not have these possibilities.

Let us mention that the Institute of Electrical and Electronics Engineers (IEEE), within its work of standardizing microprocessors, is designing a model for the representation of reals and real arithmetic [Fe182], seeking to influence the development of future languages.

2.2.3 Examples of numeric software

Numeric software deals with a certain number of general algorithms that are the same for various applications (such as the resolution of an equation system, statistics, approximations, etc.), whether used by chemists, geologists, physicians, or mathematicians. Therefore, it seems important to standardize these algorithms and make them available in centralized libraries. There is the additional advantage that algorithms in such general use can be certified by specialists to be of good quality. Although the writing of portable numeric software is difficult, there are today many examples of mathematical libraries.

Library One. Library One [GeT68] was developed at Bell Laboratories in order to gather into one library the subprograms solving the major problems of applied mathematics. To be admitted into the library, the subprogram has to be "the best," selected after a series of tests in different environments. Then the subprogram is modified so that it can be called by simple interface from programs written in different languages. Documentation is also considered very important.

The portability of these subprograms is ensured because they are written in a subset of Fortran ANSI, which is common to several Fortran dialects on different machines. The compiler used for these tests accepts only this subset. The first algorithms were written in Algol W, which did not prove to be available on enough machines, then in Algol 60. But Fortran has the advantages of being much more widespread than Algol 60, and more efficiently implemented.

A second example will show in greater detail the kinds of problems the construction of such a library raises.

The NAG library. One of the projects of the Numerical Algorithm Group (NAG) at Oxford [RiH77, FBC79] is to build a portable library of numerical subprograms that can be used on at least the nine different configurations the group can access. These subprograms were first written in Fortran 66 and Algol 60, then from 1973 on, in Algol 68 and later in Fortran 77. More recently, some of them have been written in Pascal to satisfy the needs of microcomputers. A portable file system to manage the library has also been written.

Algorithms.   To be included in the NAG library, an algorithm must satisfy the following criteria:

- It must be of enough interest to be used in several domains and must provide the best solution for the problem considered. Also, the algorithm must not depend on a particular machine.
- It must be parameterized enough to be adaptable in different contexts.
- It must pass validation tests.
- It must be documented according certain rules.

The file-management system.   To manage the library efficiently, a file system must satisfy the following criteria:

- It must be portable over a large range of machines.
- It must be usable on different information media.
- It must be reasonably compact.
- It must be flexible and easily modifiable.
- It must be reasonably efficient whatever its environment, computer or media.

The portability of the system has been ensured because it is written in a small subset of Fortran, one common to all the available implementations, and programmed in a modular fashion. (Fortran is also the principal writing language of the algorithms.)

To solve the problems of incompatibility between different support media, files are built as a series of card images, and the system accepts an arbitrary number of files. A control block is associated with each file, allowing easy modification of the library structure (which may be needed for reasons of efficiency or to pass from one support medium to another).

A comparison of the languages used.   One of the most important points in assuring portability of the NAG library, besides the specifically numeric aspects mentioned above, is the subprogram calling sequence, since it is the only linguistic aspect visible to the user. This problem is not specific to numeric software, but it is particularly critical in this domain.

Calling sequences must be as simple as possible, though they should allow the user to specify more information in special cases. From this point of view, Fortran is the least flexible of the languages used to write the NAG library, in particular when array parameters (about 77 percent of the subprograms need them) or default parameters are involved.

Let's take the example of a calling sequence to a subprogram to solve a linear equation system. The function F called computes $X = (A^{**} - 1)B$, where A is an $N*N$ matrix and X and B are $N*M$ matrices.

In Algol 68, the calling sequence would be simply F(A, B, X). The dimensions of each array can be accessed inside the function by calls to "lower bound" or "upper bound."

In Algol 60, dimensions must be explicitly given, for example, F(A, B, M, N, X).

But in Fortran, the call becomes CALL F(A, IA, B, IB, N, M, X, IX, W) because the dominant dimension must be specified for each array—IA, IB, and IX—and the working area W cannot be declared but must be passed as a parameter.

Fortran is even less flexible when some parameters have default values. In the previous example, if X was equal to B, the call in Algol 68 would be F(A, B, nil); in Fortran the parameters would have to be repeated: CALL F(A, IA, B, IB, N, M, B, IB, W).

More specific to numeric software, the problems of precision are also important and cannot be easily solved in Fortran; the strategy adopted in the NAG library is to have two versions of each subprogram, one in single precision and the other in double precision. Even passing from one version to another is not always easy, because of the incompatibility of the constructs: Some, but not all, objects can be declared in both precisions, and a program may sometimes have to be modified. Algol 60 and Algol 68 are hardly any more satisfying from this point of view.

One major reason to use several languages inside one library is that most languages do not allow calls to subprograms written in another language; or even when they do, parameter passing and the representation of objects can be so problematic that calls from one language to another are usually avoided.

The NAG library was built gradually, according to user needs, and has been available for some time; this partly explains its reliance on Fortran, a reliance that is continuing with the development of Fortran 8X and of supercomputers such as the Cray I.

Besides, to completely rewrite the library in other languages, even given the advantages of some of the more modern languages, would be much too tedious and expensive—unless it could be done automatically (see Sec. 3.2).

2.3   The portability of data

2.3.1   Possible problems

It would not be right to overlook the problems of data portability, even though very little has been written on the subject. The chapter on this subject in *Software Portability* [InK77] is primarily oriented toward the specific problem of data portability between Cobol programs. The recent book by Wallis [Wa182] dismisses the problem in 1½ pages of generalities. Does this mean that all is resolved in this domain? That no problems of data portability occur when a program is ported? Hardly. In the simple case of a small Fortran or Pascal program that works on a data file, using the same program on another machine is likely to necessitate the complete transformation of the file. Furthermore, format conversions are needed if a Fortran program is to use data written by a Cobol program. Most programmers are likely, sooner or later, to be faced with the job of converting data to render it usable, and this job can sometimes be very complicated.

In fact, files are not very portable; the solutions that are currently proposed offer some additional portability, but fail to address the full scope of the problem. There is one obvious reason for this: Data, which is dependent on its physical medium, is intrinsically unportable. To be usable, data must, of course, have a logical representation, and this can aid in portability.

2.3.2 Categorizing problems in data portability

A definition of success in transporting data is that the data, in its physical representation, be susceptible to the same interpretation before and after transport [InK77]. The transport may be to another storage medium, another operating system, or another programming language.

Change of storage medium. The problem is to render a file that is used on medium X usable on medium Y. For example, if textual data is created for machine X, and if machine X and machine Y have different character sets, it is likely that, without format conversion, the data will be unusable on Y. A change of machine, or of peripheral device, may be involved. A part of the problem— machine representation of data, memory, and addressing—was already covered in Secs. 2.1.2 and 2.1.4 and will not be treated again here.

The use of machine-dependent characteristics must be avoided as much as possible if data is to be reused on another machine, and this goal often is in conflict with program efficiency.

Data transportation almost always involves the use of a physical medium to hold the data, and thus the data is dependent on some transport medium. The physical characteristics of different peripheral devices were discussed in Sec. 2.1.4; because of their standardized format, punch cards and paper tape have historically been the most portable media. Magnetic tapes often pose serious problems because of different densities and encoding strategies, different number of tracks, the presence or absence of labels, and so on (see Sec. 2.1.6). As for disks and diskettes, their standardization is still far from complete; they are in fact very dependent on the machine to which they are connected, and different computer companies often support their own formats. Machine size, as well, can pose a problem, for instance, when trying to transfer diskette data between a minicomputer and a micro, or even between micros (5-in versus 3½-in sizes, etc.).

Change of operating system. On a given storage medium which is the same, even identical, a change of operating system (OS) is not without influence on the data. The OS manages memory and peripherals; in particular, the physical organization of data files is decided by the system. It is difficult for the system to distinguish a physical malfunction of a peripheral device from a file of a different format (e.g., one that uses different sector control information on disks).

In the case of files, their physical organization is determined by the OS, and the only files that do not pose major problems are those organized for sequential access. For example, an indexed sequential file created by a Cobol program on system S1 is likely to be difficult to use, even with another Cobol program, on system S2. In fact, there are many different ways to represent indexed sequential files. The index table may be fixed or it may be a binary tree that is updated with each modification or . . . .

Change of programming language. Data portability also poses problems when data written in language L1 is to be reused by another program written in language L2. For example, a Cobol program may create data that will then be processed by a Fortran program. In almost all cases, the data format must be modified. (A special case of this kind of problem occurs when L1 and L2 are two versions of the same language—for example, two versions of Pascal that feature static and dynamic file allocation.)

Programming languages offer diverse ways to structure data, and the representation in memory of these structures may vary from one implementation to another; two-dimensional arrays in Fortran are organized by columns, but in most other languages they are organized by rows. Data organization in Pascal is practically unportable; nonformatted Fortran files are unusable. Data organization in Ada is similar to that in Pascal, but representation specifications should allow format conversions. Cobol and PL/1 both allow relatively easy access to the representation of data.

2.3.3 Possible solutions

There are no miracle methods of transporting data without subjecting the data to modification. Often the transfer of a file or of a group of data requires that the data be logically and physically restructured. The program using the data necessitates large or small changes, depending on the nature of the programming language (use of logical structure, dependence on physical representation, etc.). If the data is sequentially organized (as in a sequential file), the codifications may be minor; this is also the case if mainly character data is used. But more complex organization poses greater problems: Either the data must be entirely reorganized or an intermediate sequential file must be used. (Indexed sequential Cobol files are often treated this way when being copied between storage media.)

Different university research groups have proposed methods to automatically translate files from one form to another: Two such projects took place at the University of Michigan [BiF76] and Cambridge University [Atk77].

Over the course of four years, the Michigan group developed a generalized translation method based on physical reformatting and logical restructuring of data. A data translator consists of three mini-interpreters: a reader, a transformer, and a producer. The reader reads source data, the transformer changes the data into the logical structure of the target, and the producer physically constructs the output file. The complex logical restructuring done by the transformer requires that it have direct access to all file elements.

The Cambridge project proposes a low-level data description language (IDL), which is a machine-independent representation of data structures. In short, IDL offers a compact, symbolic, machine-independent way to describe data structures, along with a set of procedures that translate IDL structures in both directions between symbolic and binary representations. IDL has recently found a practical application in the implementation of Ada compilers, where it is used to describe intermediate structures that are passed between compiler phases and to automatically generate the routines that manage these structures.

2.3.4   The portability of databases

Data portability diminishes as data structures become more complex. Text strings and sequential files scarcely pose any problems. But structures such as lists and trees—nonsequential files—are poorly portable, and portability becomes even more problematic in the area of databases. A database system is physically organized in a certain environment. Its dependence on its environment makes it intrinsically unportable, at least without great logical and physical restructuring. The problems encountered and the solutions proposed in this area are the same as those for other complex data structures (see Sec. 2.3.3).

But a database is used with a manipulation language that does not depend on the physical organization of the data. According to Demuynck, Moulin, and Vinson [DMV79], it should be possible to transport a program written to use one database for use with another database. To achieve this goal, it is necessary to (1) transform the data description by hand; (2) transform the data managed by one system into data managed by the second, probably by transforming the first base into simple files and then reloading these files into the second system; and (3) transform the program using the first data-manipulation language into the second data-manipulation language.

The authors propose an ideal description of data structures and data manipulation, translated into a program and an internal description of the data. They make use of the basic idea of the ANSI-Sparc report, which proposes a three-level architecture for modeling database systems: internal schema, external schema, and conceptual schema.

The external level corresponds to the perception of data by the user; the internal level corresponds to the adaptation of the external level to the technological constraints of the material; the conceptual level, which is logically between the two others, translates the data semantics by taking into account the relationships between data objects. This departmentalization permits a separation of the logical description of data structures from the physical implementation and from the user formulation. We find here the same idea that pertains in other portable software. As a consequence, a change of environment does not call into question the entire logical data organization. A certain level of description—the conceptual level—will thus be preserved.

This work, which is still as a whole in the domain of research, has become essential for some computer system teams, and a few experimental prototypes are starting to surface in an industrial context. For example, considering the classical Management Information Systems (MIS) approach of combining all information into one large, monolithic database to be a failure, a new method for Automatic Information Systems (AIS) proposes the separation of data into several distinct databases. To each database are attached certain processing capabilities, and the internal organization can be adapted to reflect either a relatively centralized or a relatively distributed approach. The system is referred to as being "logically evolvable"—the location of a database and its processing may be modified.

Let's summarize the work involved in passing from one data model to another, including the associated database-management system. Every approach proposes a division into several phases, using an intermediate model. Let's refer to the intermediate model as IM, to the phase that allows passage from the source model to IM as PH1, and to the phase that passes from IM to the target model as PH2. PH1 and PH2 will be different depending on the distribution or centralization of the context; for example, in a centralized context, PH2 represents the physical implementation by a DBMS; IM is almost always a conceptual model guaranteeing data independence, whether a relational or an entity-relation approach is used. IM may also allow enriched access functions—for example, selection or projection.

Most of the work that has been done on database model transformation has focused on transformations between the relational and heirarchical modes; nevertheless, it is possible that a systematic method will soon exist for the transport of data that is organized in databases (see Sec. 2.3.5). If such solutions are found they will certainly be welcome, since the problems of restructuring data when changing machines or systems occur frequently.

In conclusion, we will mention one small example of the potential magnitude of such database transports. A French company recently had to change its database to improve efficiency and at the same time to incorporate some modifications. The customer database contained 11.5 million accounts, a total of 7 billion characters. The transformation was performed by the approach we cited above: division into logical entities, creation of a file containing the data of each logical entity, restructuring, and finally re-creation of a new database with modified organization.

2.3.5 Perspectives and standardization

In the previous section we discussed a pair of recent research projects, showing their similarities especially in the separation between the conceptual and the implementation aspects of data management. One can hope that in the near future it will be possible to build portable applications by collecting large amounts of data into an appropriate structure, without thinking about future maintenance and transport. Here, of course, the subject of standardization becomes important.

An article about the problems of standardization and departmentalization in conceptual data models [Tab82] shows the effect of standardization, as applied to two formal methods of data conceptualization, and offers a critical comparison.* The two methods studied are individual [ISO81] and relational. The conclusion of the study was that standardization allows structural restraints to be expressed implicitly (and has the added benefit of reducing redundancy of information in this regard); but it also showed that standardization multiplies the relational schemas in a relational formalism, even as it multiplies relational types in the individual formalism. In any event, large methodologies such as MEGA

---

* Remember that conceptual modeling of data involves the specification of meaning and structures.

(Meurise-Gamma) pass data that is processed through a standardization phase, even if this phase imposes certain constraints.

Standardization may be imposed at another level in data transportation, such as the standardization in the model for interconnection of open systems proposed by the International Organization for Standardization (ISO) [Afn82, Iso80]. Before describing the objective of this model, we must first briefly review the vocabulary used in teleprocessing.

A "system" is a set of one or many computers and the associated software, peripherals, terminals, data-transmission equipment, etc., that constitute an autonomous unit capable of processing or transferring information (ISO document DIS7489). A system is referred to as "open" if it may be connected to other systems (as opposed to a "closed" system). Open systems may be connected via networks, such as the telephone system or a packet-switching network.

The ISO open-system connection model is only concerned with the parts of systems that are involved in interconnections, not with the internal functioning of a given system. For this, each system is divided into seven logical layers, and information exchange takes place between layers at the same level, via the lower levels, eventually relying on whatever physical connection is used for data transmission between the systems. These layers progress from the lowest level, the physical level (which allows data exchange over a physical data-transmission medium), up to the application level, which is the level at which a user or an application functions.

Currently, the four lowest levels—physical, line, network, and transport—have been standardized. The European Computer Manufacturers Association (ECMA) transport protocols and the X25 network layer are examples currently in use. Standards for the session and representation layers are now generally accepted (for example, file-transfer protocols). The application layer, on the other hand, seems to be progressing toward a group of standards, one for each class of related applications.

The adaptation of this model to different methods of data transmission, such as local networks, is the subject of work by several groups in industry and academia. An important group in France is the RHIN pilot project of the *Agence de l'Informatique.*

Different networks are compared in Berera [Ber82], and the conclusion is that in spite of the diversity of such networks as Transpac, X25, Decnet, and Ethernet, they are, in fact, complementary, and it is possible to construct heterogeneous networks. For example, when it comes to communications with IBM, Digital users can make use of file-transfer procedures to communicate with central IBM sites; many programs have been written for PDP-11 and VAX to allow communication with other systems such as IBM, Univac, and Control Data.

An analysis of the situation with local networks [Pia82] has stated that the situation resembles the choice of a computer in the early 1960s. There are international standardization groups (ISO, CCITT, IFIP); American (ANSI, IEEE, NBS, DIX, NVA); and European (CEPT and ECMA). A proposal for the standardization of local networks, based on the ECMA/CD protocol with X25 public interface, had received the support of about 20 computer manufacturers by the end of 1982. In the near future, software gateways between local and area-wide networks are likely to become standard programs, evolving into open-network standards, and these programs should become available on many different machines.

The problems of data transport will perhaps become less burdensome as languages, operating systems, machines, networks, and their interconnections are submitted to more and more precise standardization.

2.4 Software property rights and protection

2.4.1 An overview of the problems

It is hard to avoid mentioning problems of protection when studying software portability; this section will deal with why portable software must be protected and with the different methods of protection.

Since the earliest computers, there have been techniques to save programs—for example, by making backup copies of an important program or by stopping a program at checkpoints from which it can later be restarted in case of machine failure. But larger programs pose larger problems in security. Recently the problem has been compounded by fraudulent attacks on the integrity of software systems. The rising number of such attacks raises the problem of legal protection of software, which was already written about 10 years ago [Par76]. According to an investigation published in *01 Informatique*, the French weekly computer newspaper, the number of such attacks, per computer, has multiplied by 5 over the last 10 years, and the total loss to companies in Europe will be a half billion dollars by 1988. It has even become a commonly accepted practice among owners of micros to trade, or to copy and sell, programs that are copyrighted.

It becomes even more important to protect software that is designed to be portable. The production of such software is more expensive in time and money. Its qualities of documentation, readability, and maintainability make it more susceptible to being copied than a relatively obscure program that is written to run on only one machine. And we mention in passing that certain methods of protection can have a positive side effect on software, making it more portable in the long run.

"Software protection" is a term of many different connotations; we use it to speak of physical, technical, logical, and legal protection, as well as of data security and confidentiality. In all cases the objectives are the same: First, to avoid accidental physical losses (that is, the actual loss, destruction, or degradation of a program), and second, to avoid the attacks to which software is subject (for example, theft, malicious destruction, and unauthorized copying).

We cannot hope to present here solutions to all the problems of software protection, but we hope to at least acquaint the author or user of portable software with the existence of a number of protective methods that are at least partially effective. It is sometimes only necessary to observe a few, sensible rules in order to avoid the partial or total loss of software.

Methods of guaranteeing the security and confidentiality of software may be split into two main categories—technical and legal—and these means can be discussed independently of the definition of actual ownership of any given program. Since the organization of data into large databases is accelerating, we will mention some of the problems of protection that are specific to this category of software.

Finally, without going into all the economic aspects, we want to mention that for different reasons portability is not always desirable. For example, porting programs from machine to machine represents a large part of the business of certain software companies [Nib77a]. It is sometimes in the interest of such a company for a program not to be portable or to be portable only for its original authors. Machine-language programming can be used deliberately to make a program less portable.

2.4.2 The legal protection of software in France and Europe

Introduction. It has been said that one cannot talk of a "set of software laws" [Ben82a]. In the legal system of many countries, there are no basic computer laws. Traditionally, laws that govern a new technology are taken from the existing body of law. Nevertheless, the vital need for computer laws, and especially laws to protect software, has been noted, and a body of law is starting to emerge.

It is not surprising that most of these laws emanate from the American system. In France, the Computers, Files, and Liberties Law of 1978 contains a special chapter on penalties, and in addition a 1981 decree instituted several penalties for computer crime. In fact, computer law comes mostly from two sources [Ben81a]. The first is the above Computers, Files, and Liberties Law, which takes the point of view that a computer scientist doesn't need any special authorization to use normal legal protections. The second source is Article 1134 of the French Civil Code, which, in the current context, states how a contract may be established between a software supplier and a client.

Nevertheless, enforcement of the law against infractions remains problematic [Ben82b]. There are diverse causes, but the main one is perhaps the anarchy of terminology—particularly of the new technical terms that are usually in English—which inhibits the establishment of precise texts to interpret the law. And there are problems with the legal vocabulary. One example is that it is difficult to define exactly what it is that makes a "program" or a piece of "software technology" valuable property. A second example is that it is not easy, using the text of laws against theft, to classify taking a program as "theft." In the French legal system, theft is a crime against property, but when does software qualify as "property"? It is relatively easy to establish this classification if the software is on a storage medium that is physically stolen, but it is much more difficult if the software is copied or taken from a network.

The definition of theft is evolving; "theft" is no longer strictly the taking of another's property; recently a programmer received a short jail term for making a personal copy of a program he himself had written while employed by a software company. (This case was tried in the court at Montbéliard in 1978.)

Since legal protection is still far from perfect, it is wise for the owner of a program to try to protect it by applying for a patent, a copyright, or a trademark; by classifying it as a trade secret; or by making an explicit agreement with the user.

These different legal protections were not, of course, expressly conceived for the protection of software, and each must be carefully evaluated for its usefulness on a case-by-case basis. Classically, in seeking protection for a software product three stages may be distinguished: the conception, the functional design, and the coded implementation. One could add to this the program's maintenance and follow-up. Decisions must be made as to which stages of production are to be protected, and at what price. In the case of portable software, the product's conception and functional design would seem to need the most protection, but for each case the different needs must be studied in detail.

Patents.   A patent gives to the party who invents or discovers a new product, combination, or process a monopoly on its use for a certain number of years. The lack of industrial standards for software has inhibited it from being patentable [LeS80]. In France, laws drafted in 1968 and 1978 specifically exclude software from patent protection.

Nevertheless, a ray of hope recently came from the Paris Court of Appeals in the Schlumberger case. Briefly, the facts are these: In 1977 Schlumberger applied for a patent for a process for diagraphic data processing. The application was rejected in 1980 by the National Institute for Industrial Property (INPI), but the rejection was overturned by the Paris Court of Appeals in 1981. The invention was a process that reconstructed underground physical formations, from instrument readings, which could determine the existence and size of oil deposits. The fact that the information was mostly processed by a computer motivated the decision of INPI.

It therefore appears that programs like compilers, or other large systems, can benefit from patents in certain cases—for example, if the program uses novel data structures, algorithms, or architecture. Here it would be the program's conception that was patented, and a particular implementation would not be protected. In addition, it would be necessary to show that the conception represented a really new industrial process based on a new invention or method, and this is very rare in software.

It would be going too far to say that French law was called into question by the Schlumberger case, because an industrial invention was undeniably involved. In other countries there has been no specific rejection of the possibility of patenting software, in accordance with the 1973 Munich Convention on European patents. One of the few European countries to allow this protection is Belgium. The Belgian doctrine generally allows a program to be patentable in its role as a process that makes a computer work, in spite of certain objections citing the abstract character of software. But patentability is limited to scientific and commercial applications; industrial applications are excluded [Luc81].

Judging by the Munich Convention of 1973 and other recent European conventions, there is little hope for international cooperation on the subject of software patentability [Bra80].

Copyrights.   A copyright gives rights of exclusive use; it is given to whoever requests it for an original creation in literature, science, or the arts. Currently this seems to be the type of software protection receiving the most attention in

France. Software may be considered a "work of language," thus permitting this protection. In practice, things are not so simple because a "copyright gives to a creator a monopoly on the reproduction of the work, and not on the use of its contents" [Luc81]. And even the protection against reproduction has an exclusion in a French law of 1957 that allows private use by the person who makes the copy.

Since a software author typically wants to protect a program's contents and also wants to protect the program from being copied for individual use, copyright protection is problematic. In an article about software copyright protection in Europe [LeS80], both the possibility and the effectiveness of copyrights are covered.

Copyright possibilities. The possibility of using copyrights exists, and the difficulties related to the nature and character of software seem to be resolved. For example, it is the creation of the product, not the application for copyright, that initiates this protection, at least in France, Italy, the Netherlands, and Luxembourg. In addition, written expression can be protected, even if its destination is a machine.

Judicial protection sometimes extends beyond written expression, and similarities can be detected between computer programs and other forms of expression that may fall under copyright protection (like a literary work that is produced in several stages—that is, the choice of theme, the outlining of chapters, and the actual writing).

The effectiveness of a copyright. The effectiveness of this form of protection lies with the designation of the holder of the copyright and with the identification of the contents to be protected. Does the unauthorized introduction of a program into a computer constitute copy or use of the program? The definitions are questionable, and the sanctions are inappropriate.

In summary, the problem is to know whether it is in one's interest to protect the specific use of a program rather than to protect the program's ideas, which are abstract by nature.

Copyrights and software portability. Copyrights are more or less justified according to the type of software they are intended to protect, because what is protected is essentially the source or binary code, not the ideas that are reflected in the code. Nevertheless, for portable software, Mooers [Moo75] states that this form of protection is not only appropriate, but that it will have indirect, beneficial effects on the quality of the product. First, the copyrighting will accelerate language standardization and compiler validation. It will also promote the accelerated development of really portable packages (since the source code will not be altered).

The current situation. The only country where copyright laws have recently been revised is the United States. Since 1964, the Copyright Office has accepted registrations of sufficiently original programs. The revised law of 1978 proclaims that any program transcription on any medium constitutes a reproduction [Bra80]. Reproduction of a copyrighted program is therefore prohibited, although the ideas represented in the program are not protected from reuse.

The National Commission on New Technological Uses of Copyrighted Works concluded that a program would be fraudulently acquired if it were reproduced at some stage of its existence—for example, from a magnetic disk—to make a copy that was directly usable [Van79].

In continental Europe, a similar revision of the copyright laws is needed, even though in some countries, like Belgium, the protection is directly applicable [Got81]. In France, some recent decisions effectively allow the application of copyright laws to computer-based creations. In one case involving a company and its chief accountant, some personalized programs written by the latter while on the job were returned to him because of his rights as an author [Ben82a].

Nevertheless, many reservations about copyright protection may be expressed: It lasts too long, it is too personal, and (despite Mooers' opinion [Moo75]) it seems to offer poor protection for software, especially portable software, since it protects the form and not the substance of a program. To be protected, a portable program would have to be copyrighted upon each new implementation.

Trademarks.   The author of a program also has the right to protect a program by giving it a trademark. Currently, the documentation, the user manual, and all the input and output of the program can be covered by a trademark. An unauthorized user of such a program may be sued for the equivalent of counterfeiting or bootlegging; furthermore, if the unlawful user tries to hide the trademark, an act that destroys a part of the program, he or she can be sued for practices of unfair competition.

In fact, a trademark protects the container and not its contents. Trademark laws in France do not forbid copying a program, at least in part. And it is not always easy to associate a trademark with a given program, if only because of the nature of some programs. Nevertheless, when used in combination with other means, the association of a trademark with a program can protect it against certain abuses. An example of this kind of protection strategy, used by IBM, is given in Sec. 2.4.4.

Contracts.   This method of protection is based on the establishment of a contract between two parties, typically, between a software producer and a client. The contract explicitly states how the software is to be used. It is necessary, for example, to stipulate that the program remains entirely the property of a software producer; the client has no right to modify, sell, or give away the program. If the contract is broken, the act is classified as unfair competition under the French Civil Code.

This "obligation to secrecy" naturally requires both legal and technical precautions; in particular, the company that receives the program must keep it in a secure place and must inform its employees of the contract. Currently, contracts seem to be one of the most practical and widespread protections in use, even though the protection is far from guaranteed, especially if the program crosses a national border. The fact that a certain client has distributed a program is always hard to prove, but one remedy open to the supplier is to refuse to maintain the program. A contract offers written proof of the ownership of a program, as long as the program has never been published in any form.

2.4.3 The legal protection of software in the United States

Like those of the different countries of Europe, the U.S. system for legally protecting software consists of a patchwork of laws that were mainly written to
protect either industrial technology or literature. These laws have recently been
extended to protect software.

The three main types of legal protection that are available are trade secrets,
copyrights, and patents. "Each of these options provides a different scope of
potential protection, makes certain demands on the software developer, and is
liable to specific shortcomings" [Gra84]. Patents and copyright laws are not very
different in the United States from the corresponding laws in Europe, which were
previously discussed in detail.

Trade-secret laws.   Trade-secret laws have been the most popular and effective method of protecting software. A "trade secret" is generally any intellectual
product or idea that has a business purpose and that is a secret. The last condition
excludes any knowledge that is already public—e.g., if the material has been
published—and serves to protect the ideas that are developed by a company for
competitive purposes.

The major limitation of trade secrets is that they can be "lost"; once an idea has
become known outside the company by legal means, it is considered to be irre-
trievable and hence usable by anyone.

The concept of a trade secret is certainly not unique to the United States;
witness, for example, the fact that in France someone who steals software may be
guilty of violating unfair competition laws. Within the United States, trade-secret
laws are a part of state code and vary, by and large, from state to state. Traditionally, a trade secret is a formula, pattern, device, or idea that is valuable to a
business. In software, it might be a new algorithm or organization, or simply a
unique combination of known functions.

A requirement for legal protection is that the matter is truly secret. Typically a
company establishes nondisclosure contracts with its employees and business
associates and has restrictive license agreements with customers to keep the
program a legal "secret," when it is disseminated.

Like a patent, and unlike a copyright, a trade secret covers the basic ideas
behind a program, rather than a specific implementation of the program. Thus
this kind of legal protection is particularly appropriate for portable software, since
(theoretically) it suffices to protect the concepts behind the program once, probably via a license agreement made with each customer and not subject to change
with different implementations of the portable program. There is no need to
devise a new means of protection or to apply for a new copyright with each new
implementation.

There are differences, and sometimes conflicts, in the protection afforded by
trade-secret laws, patents, and copyrights. For example, although both patents
and trade-secret laws apply to the basic ideas behind a program, they are very
different; applying for a patent is a public process that will obviously endanger
the very secrecy of the idea.

As analyzed by Graham [Gra84], protecting a program involves a choice of strategy, based on the available alternatives and the target market, as to what is appropriate for the specific program.

The problem of hackers.   A form of breaching software security that has recently received wide publicity is the break-in, usually via telephone lines, to computer systems by people whose main aim is often to bypass a computer system's security, not for financial gain, but only because of the intellectual challenge involved. These so-called hackers are often teenagers who treat the breaching of a computer's security system as a game and who consider the gaining of unauthorized access as "winning" the game.

The positive aspect of this phenomenon is that it often leads to the improvement of security, with less loss involved than if the person who beat the security had been a real criminal. There are several negative aspects, such as the general disrespect for the law that is shown by hackers and the fact that in a few cases valuable information has been destroyed—such as in the recent case where medical records at a New York City hospital were damaged in the break-in. The relation between such actions and computer crime committed for profit is subtle, often involving no more than motive and degree of loss.

There have recently been many newspaper stories about this phenomenon, and there is growing alarm over the fact that such actions are often legal, or are illegal only if the action can be shown to be trespassing. This is another case where a law is used for a very different purpose than that for which it was written, with dubious applicability.

There is certainly a need to reexamine existing legal code and its application to computer crime and software protection, and it is ironic that recently more attention has been focused on the need to protect software from teenagers with modems, than on the need to protect against software piracy and other unfair business practices.

2.4.4   Summary and perspective

The efficacy of any method of software protection is, of course, based on proof that an illegal diffusion of the software has occurred [Luc81], and such proof can be difficult or impossible to obtain. The penalties involved have already been discussed and will be mentioned again below.

Very few countries, to our knowledge, have laws that specifically protect software. Belgium has its own patent and copyright systems, which seem satisfactory [Got77, Got81]. The United States has partially revised its legislative codes, but the relatively small success of the system (for example, the small number of copyrights actually issued) continues to inspire the search for more efficient solutions. In France, even more than elsewhere, the legislation in this area is inadequate.

The hope for the future seems to rest with international, not national, laws. To the extent that a program is portable, it must be protected internationally, unless its diffusion is to be arbitrarily restricted to one country. What international protection is likely to be adopted? Braubach [Bra80] contains a good summary of the situation. It would seem that there is consensus, among many international institutions, in favor of a new system of protection. Two proposals, that of Gabler (IBM) and the framework law of the International Organization for Industrial Property (OMPI), are contrasted in Braubach's article. Both propose new solutions, that of OMPI being closely based on copyrights and patents. The author of a program would be protected against both unauthorized use and unauthorized copying [Luc81]. But until these international standards are in place, it is necessary to rely on the laws of each country.

We now will discuss two examples of legal protection: the protection that governs the diffusion of the Unix system and the diffusion of IBM software.

The Unix example. The phrase "Unix is a trademark of Bell Laboratories" (or ". . . of AT&T) is contained in every article mentioning Unix. AT&T offers three categories of Unix licenses, each designed for a different kind of user: The licenses are extended to (1) commercial use; (2) administrative use in educational institutions; (3) and academic use. The licensee is precluded by contract from distributing Unix. The programs that are furnished are different, depending on the kind of license; an educational license includes the source code. Until recently, AT&T offered no maintenance. As part of the Unix license, a customer must specify the serial number of one computer, and of one backup computer, on which Unix will be run.

In academia and industry there are many "bootleg" copies of Unix—for example, the famous Lyons *Commentary on Unix* (6th ed.), which consists of two volumes, the first containing the Unix sources and the second explaining them in detail. In France, pillaging a program constitutes theft under the penal code, but proving that a program was acquired illegally remains problematic.

The IBM example. For its programs that are licensed products, IBM uses a mixed-protection strategy that might be considered to offer maximum security. IBM mainframe programs and documentation are copyrighted, both in printed and machine-readable form. Such programs and documentation are only furnished to users after they have signed an "IBM Program Products License Agreement." In addition to furnishing the serial number of the machine on which the program will be used, the user must agree "not to provide or otherwise make available any licensed program and/or optional material . . . to any person other than customer . . . without prior written consent of IBM." With the exception of patents, every available software protection method is used.

This said, fraud and unauthorized use still occur, even in the largest companies. There are many examples; many well-known programs were developed for a company by a group, some of whom subsequently left to set up shop elsewhere and sell the program. This is why legal protection is currently insufficient and why it is in the interest of the owner of a program to take every possible means of protection. At the same time, physical protection of the program against accidental loss should not be neglected. The next section will deal with this kind of technical protection.

2.4.5 The technical protection of software

The necessity of such protection.   There are a certain number of technical precautions that the possessor of a program should take: Some are of greater concern for the program's distributor, others primarily concern the user, and some are of common importance. These precautions may protect the program from unauthorized access (if such controls are required) or may be designed simply to avoid accidental losses. In contrast with the previously discussed legal protections, which are justified only if the program's diffusion must be controlled, technical protections are generally inexpensive and can help to avoid many problems.

Access control.   There are two kinds of access to protected software: physical access to a computer and access to software resources. The control of physical access to software includes prohibition of illegal possession—actual theft of a program for later use, reproduction of the material, or simply reading protected information [DeB80]. It may be prudent to take a few simple precautions, such as putting listings into personal mailboxes or controlling the machines used to make copies (photocopies, diskettes, microfilm, and so on). Wastebaskets have sometimes been the source of listings and documents that have been sold afterwards, as is. Access to computer facilities over telephone lines can cut both ways in this sense: If poorly managed, modems allow unauthorized access; well managed, they can be an effective means to control access to programs or data.

When software resources must be protected, different kinds of access can be put in place for different people. Both confidentiality and security become important. For example, a company may want to allow a few employees the right to modify a program or change the contents of a database, may want to allow some people the right to use the information, and finally, may want to preclude entirely access for some people. The general techniques to control access in these ways include identification of user and authentication of access.

Identification of users.   There is a wide range of choices for user identification—from the simple use of name or code number, to digital voice or fingerprint analysis, up to the scanning of an optical or magnetic identity card or badge. In a network architecture, the location of the user can itself be used to confirm the user's identity and control access.

Authentication of access.   If the system of user identification is sufficiently sophisticated (for example, if fingerprints are analyzed), authentication becomes superfluous. A password system is the most commonly used method, but its effectiveness depends upon its confidentiality, and perhaps, upon periodic password changes. Other, more research-oriented methods exist. For example, in one system each user creates his or her own function, which is recalculated at the start of each session and is controlled by the system.

In addition, when software security or confidentiality is necessary, it is possible to specify what access and what software resources will be allowed to each user. Often a code is assigned to each file and program, stating which users may be allowed access. Different techniques are used to specify selective access depending on the system: For example, in database-management systems there is often a system of locks that provide fine-grain control over access to confidential data.

Other methods of protection.   Other methods of protection are often necessary, including backups and control of software distribution. Even if the access to resources is carefully protected, there is never total guarantee of safety. Control of physical access might be difficult—for example, in the case of a university computer center—or the small size of a computer installation might not justify the cost and the onerous style associated with strict controls.

In most cases, software backups constitute one of the most effective methods of physical protection. By "backups" we mean the set of procedures used to recover the maximum possible amount of information after the failure of a computer, a peripheral device, or a program. Since backups have been effectively in use for years, we will simply mention a few methods:

1. Files can be copied onto another physical medium, with storage of the medium in a fireproof place, if possible at a certain distance from the computer center. Magnetic tapes are often the most practical way for computer centers to store large amounts of information; diskettes are very popular for backing up relatively small files, especially on personal computers.

2. In case of machine failure, checkpoint/restart procedures, correctly used [Bou79], will roll a program back to a state from which it can be restarted. A common technique involves the use of journal files that record interactive sessions over a period of time, permitting the reconstruction of a session.

3. When needed to preserve the continuity of processing (and when physically possible), all the software may be shifted to another machine—for example, in the case of very large, uninterruptible, real-time applications. When a teleprocessing system uses a public network, data security can be reinforced thanks to the communication function of the system, which permits a terminal to connect to an emergency computer center simply by dialing another telephone number [Gui80].

Finally, control of software distribution must not be overlooked, especially if the software is portable. A few methods to assure control are listed here:

1. Massive documentation that is very difficult to reproduce may be a separate, necessary adjunct to a program. For example, the RT-11 system is included in the price of an LSI-11, but the documentation is sold separately.

2. A maintenance contract may be used to protect the program's distributor; if the buyer misuses the program, the distributor can refuse to continue maintenance.

3. A program may be installed in such a way that it works with only one hardware configuration; this gives some protection to the distributor, since the program would be very difficult to move to another machine that is not configured in exactly the same way.

The protection of database-management systems. It may be necessary to make a greater investment in security and confidentiality for the programs that manage databases than for other programs. The major reasons are the size of databases; the nature of the managed information, which may attract fraud; the organization of so much important information in one place; and the risk of diffusion of information over a network. All the methods of protection already mentioned are equally applicable to databases, so in the following section we will describe in detail only those protections that are specific to databases. For more detailed information, we refer the reader to Miranda [Mir80].

To ensure physical protection, there are special techniques that depend on database organization. In the case of a relational organization, one technique consists of maintaining two copies with sufficient information to do a rollback in case of failure; there are similar journal techniques for the transactions that occur in relational databases.

The methods of access control discussed above may be used to protect databases, as may data-flow control, interference control, or cryptography. Interference control consists of preventing the deduction of protected information from already known information: In effect, starting from a relational system such as Ingres, one can indirectly deduct private information from nonprivate information. As for cryptography, this consists of encoding information in such a way that it can only be decoded if a key or a password is supplied. Numerous cryptographic systems exist, up to the "public key" systems, which have not yet been broken. Cryptography is presently one of the most secure methods of protection available.

If a database system is designed from the outset to emphasize data security and confidentiality, the effort to achieve these goals is considerably reduced [DeB80].

In concluding this chapter, it may be stated that very diverse methods of software protection exist. Their effectiveness and appropriateness for a given program vary widely, and a method should not be chosen without careful study of the type and level of protection desired and of the cost one is willing to pay. The cost of protection may be measured in money, calendar time, and person time, as well as in the possible loss of efficiency if too complex a method of protection is chosen. For example, some legal protections are disproportionately expensive compared with the value of the program to be protected.

This brief study is not, by any means, a complete one; the study of software protection still contains many open questions, which are documented in Remer [Rem82] and which will be the subject of the upcoming AFCET study on computer fraud.

Chapter

3

Software Tools
of Transport

In the present chapter, we will study the software tools that serve as aids to portability; these tools are automated and relatively self-contained—that is, they are generally not integrated into larger software systems, although they may be used in the construction of such systems.

Macroprocessors, which are covered first, have been in existence for many years and are used in many situations; still, they are rather little known. In fact, their usage seems to be decreasing, maybe because of their poor adaptability to current programming habits. However, we shall discuss their use rather frequently in the following chapters.

The other tools we consider in this chapter are much more specialized. They are used to ease the transport of programs written in a programming language, without need to modify the original program and without need to install new software tools (in contrast with the methods that will be considered in Chap. 5). It is somewhat difficult to define a single context in which these tools are used. Rather, we can simply enumerate the various tools we will consider:

- Higher-level translators: A program given in some language, HLL1, is to be translated into another language, HLL2, of a similar level and used in a new environment, in which a compiler for HLL2 will be needed to execute the program.

- Verifiers and filters: These two tools are very similar in concept and are often confused. They serve to check the conformity of the programming language with a specific model, i.e., with a particular official definition or standard.

- Generators: Given the formal definition of some aspect of a programming language, these tools generate (or simply help in the production of) the part of the compiler that processes this aspect.

- Other tools, though simpler, are less frequently used. They include, for example, tools for changing the version of a language, which generally avoids the work of an actual translation; decompiling tools, which do the opposite of compilers, translating from a low-level language to a higher-level one; and finally, tools that verify a posteriori the result of a transportation, by checking that the product obtained on the target computer is equivalent to the source product.

3.1 Macroprocessors

In the available literature one finds the term "macroprocessor" applied to several different things that have little in common and can hardly be collected under one global definition, however general it might be. Brown [Bro69] defines a macroprocessor as "a piece of software designed to allow the user to add new facilities of his own design to an existing piece of software." This definition encompasses a lot of tools, and needs to be refined. Cole [Col81] adds to the definition a distinctive property of macroprocessors: Namely, they work by text replacement. This more precise formulation leads us to exclude the Macro-Spitbol [DMC77] "macroprocessor," which is actually a translator. In contrast, some text editors may be considered macroprocessors by Cole's definition. Text replacement may mean the simple substitution of one fixed character string for another, as well as the replacement of one sequence with another one generated by various kinds of parameters, embedded macro calls, etc.

In the next section, we give some definitions of frequently encountered terms. In the succeeding sections, we distinguish several classes of macroprocessors that group together different tools. Specific examples will illustrate this classification. We distinguish macroassemblers from string-handling macroprocessors. Those macroprocessors that modify the syntax of a language will be considered more specifically in the section on extensible languages (Sec. 4.3).

3.1.1 Definitions

The definition of a macroprocessor varies widely between authors. For us, a "macroprocessor" is a program that reads a source text and scans it for occurrences of macro calls. Unrecognized text fragments are copied unchanged into the object text. When a macro call is encountered, the macroprocessor executes the corresponding macro definition. With the exception of its special behavior in the case of unrecognized text, a macroprocessor is similar to an interpreter, since it directly executes the highly specialized program represented by the macro calls, a program written in the language defined by the macro definitions.

The following definitions, which may differ between authors and between applications, are the same as Cole's [Col81] and will be the ones operative here.

A "macro definition" is made up of a macro header, followed by a macro body (definitions below). It is generally distinguished by a special character, often followed by a keyword, and it terminates with another special character, possibly followed by another keyword. A typical macro definition would be

```
$MACRODEF
header
macro body
$MACROEND
```

The "macro header" is a character string, which may contain some special characters for defining the parameters. This header is a sort of a skeleton, to which a character string will be compared during the macro expansion phase. The differences between macroprocessors result from the complexity of parameter substitution allowed, which can range from no parameter at all (simple substitution) to any number of recursive macro calls. An example of a macro header is

```
SUM $1,$2,$3
```

where the $n's represent formal parameters or variables.

The "macro body" represents the character string that will be substituted for the header during the macro expansion phase. As with the header, the macro body may be very simple, as in the case of a simple character substitution, or maybe much more complex, as in the case of special processing depending upon parameter values. The macro body may also contain calls to other macros, or even new macro definitions. For example, the macro body corresponding to the preceding macro heading would be

```
FETCH $1
ADD    $2
STORE $3
```

During the expansion phase, the call

```
SUM P,Q,R
```

will be replaced with

```
FETCH P
ADD    Q
STORE R
```

If the computer has an accumulator, an improvement to this macro could be

```
$MACRODEF
SUM    $1,$2,$3
IF $1 = ACC SKIP
FETCH $1
ADD    $2
IF $3 = ACC SKIP
STORE $3
$MACROEND
```

in which a conditional substitution is used.

A "macro call" is a string to be compared to the macro header, and replaced when a match is found.

The "expansion phase" deals with the replacement of the input string by the macro body. It may involve the expansion of embedded calls, conditional evaluation, etc.

Finally, an "embedded macro call" is a macro call internal to the body of another macro.

The syntax of macro calls varies widely between macroprocessors. The call may have a rigid format, giving a meaning to ends-of-line (in the case of macroassemblers, for example); it may be delimited by initial and final special characters; or it may have completely free format.

3.1.2   Macroassemblers

Most assemblers allow the insertion of a code sequence at a given place in a program. This insertion, in contrast with what would be done in the case of a subprogram, is done at compile time. This saves program execution time at the expense of code space.

The use of macros can also ease the writing of assembly-language programs, since they allow the user to define a unique set of macros suited for a specific problem. Although the present use of higher-level languages for writing programs in almost any area makes the use of a macroassembler much less vital than it was 20 years ago, this capability may still be useful in making program modifications easier, since each macro may be separately debugged, in standardizing an interface, or as an intermediate language (see Sec. 5.2).

3.1.3   An example: The IBM 360 macroassembler

A macro definition for this macroassembler has the following format:

```
MACRO
name and parameters
macro body
MEND
```

Keywords MACRO and MEND serve as delimiters. Embedded definitions are forbidden, and all macros used in a program (and not cataloged in library) must appear at the program's beginning.

The macro header is simplified, since the macro name must appear in the name field of an instruction line. In contrast, parameters may be quite complicated.

The macro body will replace the macro call after evaluation of the parameters. Embedded macro calls are allowed. The expansion of an embedded macro call is not done when the embedding macro is defined, but each time it is expanded. This avoids code redundancy, but at the expense of macro processing time.

Parameters must be recognized in two different contexts: in the macro header and in the macro body, where they can occur several times, and correspond to partial fields of the instructions. Formal parameters are prefixed by the "&" sign in the macro definition. After macro expansion, nothing distinguishes them from other operands.

Parameters are listed after the name of the macro, as in:

```
LANDT &REG,&ITEM,&COND,&TO
```

A parameter may also appear in the label field of the macro header, as in the following complete example:

```
        MACRO
&HERE LANDT &REG,&ITEM,&COND,&TO
&HERE L    *   &REG,&ITEM
        LTR    &REG,&REG
        B&COND &TO
        MEND
```

A corresponding macro call would be

```
ICI LANDT 3,LA,Z,VA
```

which would be replaced by

```
+ICI L 3,LA
+     LTR 3,3
+     BZ  VA
```

The "+" sign signals in the program listing that macro expansion has occurred.

Parameters can be given names and default values at macro call. In the macro header, they must then be marked with an "=" sign after the formal parameter:

```
        MACRO
        MOVE   &FROM=,&TO=,&LNTH=80
        MVC    &TO.(&LNTH),&FROM
        MEND
```

A call to this macro would be

```
MOVE FROM=HERE,TO=THERE,LNTH=100
```

which would produce

```
+ MVC THERE(100),HERE
```

Alternatively, the call

```
MOVE LNTH=100,FROM=HERE,TO=THERE
```

would produce the same result, since the order of parameters is irrelevant in that situation. If &LNTH were omitted, it would be replaced by its default value, 80.

In the preceding macro definition, the period denotes the concatenation of a parameter to the rest of the line. It is made necessary by the lack of an end delimiter for parameters.

The macro body may be more complex than in the preceding examples if one uses conditional substitution. A language internal to the macroassembler is needed for providing directives: It gives internal labels, which will disappear after expansion (they are prefixed with a period), as well as instructions branching to these labels. AGO is an unconditional branch, while AIF checks a relation between its parameters before branching. The following macro definition illustrates this:

```
        MACRO
        ADD    &A,&B,&RESULT
        AIF    ('&A'EQ'').NOLOAD
        L      1,&A
```

```
.NOLOAD A        1,&B
        AIF      ('&RESULT'EQ'').DONE
        ST       1,&RESULT
.DONE   MEND
```

The call

```
        ADD      X,Y,Z
```

produces the following code:

```
+       L        1,X
+       A        1,Y
+       ST       1,Z
```

while the call

```
        ADD      X,Y
```

generates

```
+       L        1,X
+       A        1,Y
```

The internal language of the macroassembler is actually more complete, since it also has iterations and typed variables, which may be local to a macro or global to all macro definitions. For a detailed description, see Strubble [Str69].

The power of the IBM 360 macroassembler stems from its internal language and from the parameterization of the macros.

3.1.4   General-purpose string-processing macroprocessors

In contrast with macroassemblers, which are linked to a particular assembly language, and consequently to a particular computer and operating system, general-purpose macroprocessors are fully independent programs. Moreover, the range of their application is larger since they are not linked to a particular language.

We can mention in this category macroprocessors such as TRAC (*text reckoning and compiling*) [MoD65], GPM (*general-purpose macrogenerator*) [Str65], and ML/1 [Bro67]. There are no recent models. The first two were developed at the same time, but independently. They have many characteristics in common, but their implementations differ entirely.

TRAC was designed to be used in a timesharing context. Its internal mechanism works by recursively scanning input character strings, evaluating functions as information is obtained. Every character string may be handled as an executable procedure, a name, or a string. TRAC contains a very limited number of primitive functions, which are part of the system and which cannot be extended, but the user has the capability of defining his or her own functions.

GPM was designed specifically for system applications and also works on an input character string. Its interest here is mainly historic, since it is now rarely used.

3.1.5 ML/1

ML/1, which we are going to describe in more detail, is also based on string processing, although, in contrast with TRAC and GPM, it works on atoms rather than on individual characters. An "atom" may be a single character (other than a letter or a digit) or any character string delimited by special characters.

The simplest way to do text replacement in ML/1 is to define a macro, using the keywords MCDEF (which specifies that what follows is a macro definition) and AS. For example,

```
MCDEF P AS Q
```

allows the replacement of every occurrence of P by Q in any given text; P and Q may be arbitrarily complex. If the first atom, P, is made of several words, the keyword WITHS must be used; as for the second atom, it needs only to be embedded within angle brackets:

```
MCDEF green WITHS apples AS <red fruit>
```

If the definition part of the macro is made of more than one sequence of atoms, it means that a parameter occurs between each sequence. In the macro body, these parameters are referred to as %A1, %A2, etc. For example,

```
MCDEF concatenate to WITHS list.
   AS<YPTR := YPTR+1;
      %A2.[YPTR] := %A1.;>
```

In this definition, the absence of a keyword between "concatenate" and "to" denotes the presence of a parameter. The period after "list" denotes both the end of "list" and the presence of a second parameter.

A call to this macro could be

```
concatenate x + 1 to list Y.
```

which would generate

```
YPTR := YPTR+1;
Y[YPTR] := x + 1;
```

The sophistication of text processing may be augmented via the use of other keywords. Thus OPT, OR, and ALL allow acceptance of several atom alternatives. For example,

```
OPT + OR - OR * OR / ALL
```

can match every arithmetic expression. Similarly, MCGO, IF, and UNLESS give the capability of conditional replacement when used with one of the conditions BC (belongs to class), EN (equals numerically), GE (greater than or equal), GR (greater than), or =. When used alone, MCGO is equivalent to an unconditional branch. Macro labels have a special syntax: %Li.

An example of a macro definition is

```
MCDEF  SET = OPT + OR - ALL;
AS      < L   3,%A2.
MCGO   L1 IF %D2. = +
        S   3,%A3.
MCGO   L2
%L1.    A   3,%A3.
%L2.    ST 3,%A1.>
```

The notation "%D2." refers to the second word of the macro name. A call to this macro might be

```
SET P = Q + R;
```

which would generate

```
L   3,Q
A   3,R
ST  3,P
```

ML/1 provides three counters, local to every macro call (more can be declared if necessary), as well as global variables, which can be used for passing information from one macro to the other. Before beginning a working session with ML/1, the user defines his or her own delimiters; atom delimiters, parameter markers, etc.

ML/1 was designed to be relatively independent of any computer, and its implementation system, based on the low-level intermediate language LOWL, provides for its portability to new computers. Combined with its processing power, this makes it a very interesting tool.

3.1.6 Stage2

As a part of the Mobile Programming System (MPS), described in Sec. 7.4, Waite defined the macroprocessor Stage2 [Wai70b], used for implementing abstract machines on actual ones. Each instruction of the abstract machine is replaced by the corresponding instruction sequence of the actual machine, by way of macro definitions. Thus every software product built on the abstract machine is immediately transported as soon as Stage2 is implemented on the actual machine.

The main design goal of Stage2, consequently, is to be sufficiently powerful for use in various applications, and at the same time to be easily implemented on any given computer, since it is only a tool for more important operations and not a goal in itself.

From the user's point of view, Stage2 has several concepts in common with ML/1. A macro header is any character string containing formal parameters and terminated by a special character. As in ML/1, the user defines the delimiters.

Compared with other macroprocessors, some original ideas are found in Stage2, especially in its use of parameters in the macro body and in the method it uses for matching macro headers in order to make this phase efficient.

Like other macroprocessors, the macro call in Stage2 is matched to the header by matching every fixed substring of the header, then identifying parameters between substrings. This may lead to ambiguities; for example, the string

```
A + B + C
```

compared to the header

```
@ + @;
```

(where "@" marks the place of a parameter and ";" is the end of the header), may be interpreted differently, depending on whether the first parameter is A or A + B.

In order to solve these ambiguities, Stage2 first tries to match parameters with the shortest possible substrings, then longer and longer substrings, balanced by parentheses if necessary. In the preceding case, the first parameter is consequently A, and the second is B + C. Similarly, if the string

```
A + B * C
```

is matched with headers

```
@ + @ * @;
```

and

```
A + B * @;
```

the second header is chosen, since it matches the parameters with the smallest number of characters.

Headers are collected in a dictionary that is organized as a tree. During the expansion phase, macro calls are recognized by searching this tree. If the input line does not correspond to any header, it is copied without modification. Otherwise, substitution is done on a line-by-line basis in the macro body. Actual parameters are first evaluated, then substituted. The line thus built is scanned again for possible macro calls, in which case the expansion phase is recursively entered. As a consequence, the line built is not copied into output (in the absence of special indications) until no more macro calls are encountered during scanning.

Parameters are evaluated according to their position in the input string, but also according to the conversion type specified in the macro definition. Thus nine conversion types are available, from a simple "as is" copy of the parameter to more sophisticated conversions.

Stage2 has a command language too, which provides for conditional or iterative substitutions. One can thus build pseudoprograms with macros, unfortunately rather unreadable, as the following example [Wai73] demonstrates:

```
+$'$.                    Header, immediate operand with apostrophe
'20*2'96$                Character conversion
'10IM BASE+'94$          Build a compound operator
$                        Macro end
—$ $.                    Header, general operand
IF '25 GT 1 SKIP 3$      Symbol or integer?
'28*2'96$                Character conversion
'10 BASE+'94$            Compound operator
'FO$                     Macro exit
'20'370123456789$        Integer, check the front character
IF'30 = SKIP 1$
```

```
Z'22'20'26$           Convert the entire symbol
'10'20$
$                     Macro end
```

Finally, the most important characteristic of Stage2 is surely its system of implementation, which will be described in Sec. 7.4 and which is actually an implementation tool for other software products. Its main defect, however, is its inefficiency, especially critical when Stage2 appears in the final product it was meant to implement.

3.1.7 Syntactic macroprocessors

All macroprocessors considered to this point have an independent syntax and can be used as preprocessors (see Sec. 4.4) for other languages. Syntactic macroprocessors are a part of a compiler, and may be used to add constructs to the language compiled. Other uses will be considered when we study extensible languages (Sec. 4.3).

The macroprocessor is used during the compilation process, and consequently it uses the compiler itself—for example, to check the validity of parameters or to evaluate parameters, which can become rather complex expressions. It can hardly be considered as an optional part of the compiler, unless the compiler is especially well structured. Most often, it is an integral part of the compiler, and we shall not consider this matter further here.

3.2 Higher-level language translators

3.2.1 Goals and principles

Suppose a program written in a higher-level source language HLL1 is to be translated automatically into an equivalent program, written in an object language HLL2 of a similar level. This transformation is useful if HLL2 is available on the target machine while HLL1 is not, or even if HLL1 is available but one does not want to use it. In the first situation, one is probably changing the entire computer environment of a group of users who want to be able to save the investment already made on programs written in HLL1. In the second situation, one is probably trying to encourage a group of users to change to a new programming language—perhaps even the source and target computers are the same.

Another possibility is that the translator is intended for use only for a temporary period; the long-term objective is to use HLL1, but only an implementation of HLL2 is currently available. This situation, consequently, is the opposite of the preceding ones, since the long-term goal is to get rid of HLL2, while in the other cases one wants to forsake HLL1. It is already assumed that there are not many reasons for both languages HLL1 and HLL2 to be of the same level. One may distinguish three different cases:

1. HLL1 is more primitive than HLL2. This is the normal case, when one wants to use old programs, numerous and well debugged, in a new context. One can then find translators from Fortran to Algol 68, from Fortran to Pascal, etc.

2. HLL2 is more primitive than HLL1. This is normally the case when HLL1 is preferred to HLL2 but is not yet usable in the new environment. Here one can use a translator from Ada to Pascal or PL/1. This can also be used for a small-installation program previously written for a big installation in a powerful language and now impossible to implement in the new environment. (Admittedly, this is not a very realistic example.) To build the translator then would avoid building a cross-compiler, supposedly a more complicated task. Finally, there are cases where HLL2 might simply be considered a normal (portable) means for implementing HLL1, as in the case of translators from Pascal to C, or from Icon to Fortran.

3. The respective situations of HLL1 and HLL2 are irrelevant. Generally, this simply means that HLL1 is available on the source environment, HLL2 on the target environment, and the translator is built as a general transportation tool. Or it may result from the simple desire to use both languages indiscriminately, and in this case it is likely that a translator symmetric with the first is also needed. This case occurs when an installation wants its users to forsake their customary but obsolete programming language and to have a gentle transition to a new and more up-to-date language, hoping that the law of natural selection will then come into play in favor of the new language. Similar operations have already been attempted, but apparently in vain: The inertia of users, reluctant to change their habits, most often prevails over other considerations. The evolution of animal species by natural selection took several million years, and Fortran celebrated its twenty-fifth birthday only recently . . . .

3.2.2 Techniques

The problems facing implementors are rather different, depending upon the respective levels of HLL1 and HLL2, and we shall consider them separately.

If the target language HLL2 is more primitive than the source language HLL1, one encounters almost the same problems and the same solutions found in ordinary compilation. This is particularly true if the difference in levels between the two languages is great. The second language is considered and handled as a pseudomachine language, in which the higher-level concepts of the source language are to be expressed.

In translating from Algol 68 to Fortran, for example, Fortran is treated as a machine language, and consequently, as is the case in most true compilers, Fortran's capabilities are not all used. Features of Fortran that are ignored include not only input-output operations and equivalences, but even the repetitive DO statement, since it does not correspond to any control structure of Algol 68. Procedure recursion, dynamic memory allocation, and complex object structures, all are simulated in Fortran as they would be in machine language, and Algol 68 input-output is translated into calls to subprograms in the run-time support, probably written in machine language.

In such a situation, one generally uses, as we said, only a small subset of the target language. This could lead to rather disastrous performances by the object program finally generated, since the parts of the target language HLL2 that are best suited to the generation of efficient code are generally the first to be omitted.

The compiler used for translating programs written in HLL2 must use the most sophisticated optimization techniques if there is to be a chance of producing acceptable object-code performance. This situation is somewhat similar to what is encountered, in the case of an augmented language, with the code generated after preprocessing the source program (see Mersson and Pyster [MeP79] and Sec. 4.4).

If the difference in levels between HLL1 and HLL2 is small, but HLL2 is still more primitive than HLL1, the situation is, paradoxically, more difficult than in the preceding case, since an important drop in performance is no more acceptable when the source and target languages are closely related. One may be led, in that case, to restrict HLL1 to a subset, easily translated into HLL2, and maybe forced upon users by way of a filter (see Sec. 3.3). Therefore, one can limit oneself to an elementary conversion from HLL1 to HLL2, every notion having a counterpart in the target language. In that case, the translator is much closer to a preprocessor than to a compiler, since it can probably pass on many statements unchanged.

If HLL2 is of a higher level than HLL1, the problem is much more difficult, contrary to what might be imagined. The expression of low-level constructs in a higher-level language may be awkward. Take the case of the branch statement, which may be present in HLL1 but completely lacking in HLL2. A thorough analysis of the program's control flow is necessitated in order to establish what high-level control structures are expressed by each branch statement in the source program. In many cases, one is simply confronted with an unstructured section of a program, and the only solution is to duplicate some code.

Other difficulties may occur if HLL1 provides a weaker type checking than does HLL2. For example, how could a translator change into Pascal a Fortran subprogram that considers its parameters to be of various types, depending upon circumstances? Of course, such a Fortran subprogram would not conform to standard, but that's irrelevant here. In the same manner, common blocks and equivalences of Fortran have no exact counterpart in any other higher-level language. They raise almost unsolvable problems if the same storage location is used in several incompatible ways. Again in the case of Fortran, input-output operations are impossible to translate into any other higher-level language.

Because of these difficulties, a translator from a relatively primitive higher-level language (typically Fortran) into a more advanced higher-level language cannot be a total translator. Severe restrictions must generally be placed upon what is allowed in HLL1, and in some cases the translation of several constructs must be completely abandoned. Thus one may speak more of "translation aids" than of fully automated tools. The user must entirely revise the result of the translation, and at times the work has to be completed by hand. The most favorable use of such a translator is when one wants to process a coherent subprogram library, especially for numerical problems.

3.2.3 Examples

The work of Prudom and Hennel [PrH77] consisted of translating Fortran into Algol 68, the goal being to convert the very bulky library of numerical subprograms produced by the Numerical Algorithm Group (NAG). The purpose was to make this library available to Algol 68 programmers, taking into account the fact that most Algol 68 compilers did not provide for calling subprograms written in Fortran. The nature of the subroutines to be converted made the work easier than is customary, since they did not often use any structured objects, except arrays, and they used no input-output.

The method chosen was to translate word for word, without any attempts to rebuild structured statements of Algol 68 from Fortran statements. In a sense, this amounted to casting Algol 68 back to the same level as Fortran. The only restrictions needed in Fortran, as we anticipated in Sec. 3.2.2, were related to the COMMON and EQUIVALENCE statements and to input-output. The Fortran constructs that needed special study were the arithmetic IF statement, the DO statement, and the tricks used in ordinary programs to obviate the lack of the character data type in Fortran. But the major problem dealt with the transmission mode of subprogram parameters, since it could be established only by a global study of all subprogram calls, especially when subprograms were passed as parameters.

Here again, as anticipated, the automatic translation produced a result that had to be revised by hand. Thus it was a means for saving much time when translating a subprogram library, but not a means for updating and maintaining a single version of a library written in several source languages. On the other hand, the authors studied the comparative performances of subprograms, before and after translation. After the differences resulting from input-output were deducted, they found globally similar performances (with wide local variations, however).

The translator from Fortran to Pascal, built by Freak [Fre79, Fre81], has a similar goal (to allow the use in Pascal of subprograms initially written in Fortran), but is much more ambitious. Instead of making only a simple word-for-word translation, this translator tries to build Pascal programs of good quality, making use of the language's control structures. Using the principles of structured programming, Freak's translator generates programs without any branch statement, and in difficult cases it uses the well-known techniques of code duplication and boolean flags.

From a Fortran program made of a sequence of subprograms all of the same level, Freak's translator generates a Pascal program where procedures are embedded as deeply as possible. Of course, this necessitates a reordering, depending upon the way in which subprograms call each other, and use of global variables. Common blocks and equivalences are simulated with Pascal variant records; here again declarations are embedded as deeply as possible in their procedures.

Because of its ambitious goal, it comes as no surprise that this translator has the size and complexity of a compiler. Because of the reordering actions, its processing time is not negligible. The author claims that resulting programs are much easier to understand and to modify than their original counterparts, thus warranting the work of the translator and the slight downgrading of performance.

The translator described in Filipski, Moore, and Newton [FMN80] has very different goals, which would normally cause it to be considered among the various combinations of transport methods that will be seen in Chap. 6. It is a translator from Ada to Extended Algol 60, intended as an intermediate step in the building of an Ada translator for the Burroughs 6700 computer. On this computer, Extended Algol 60 is the base language; there is no assembly language, hence the choice of the object language of the translator. This translator is written in Pascal, and it is intended that it will be reprogrammed in Ada in order to compile itself. The full operation is designed as a way for transporting a very large set of software products from the Burroughs 6700 to an as-yet-unknown computer. An Ada compiler will be developed in several successive steps and will be transported using the Ada to Extended Algol 60 translator.

The set of tools described in Albrecht et al. [AGG80] has yet another goal. Its purpose is to provide for the translation of programs from Ada to Pascal, and vice versa, in order to ease the transition from one language to the other, to transport them to installations where only one is implemented, and even to aid the implementation of the translator itself, since it is written in Pascal and it would be desirable to have it in Ada too.

The method chosen is original and complex. The authors defined subsets of Pascal and of Ada (PascalA and AdaP, respectively), such that there is between them an elementary correspondence that makes the translation from one to the other (and vice versa) easy. Then they defined two extensions of these subsets, PascalAE and AdaPE, respectively, which are still subsets of the initial languages, such that the extensions can be expressed in terms of the unextended subsets. Finally, a unique tree representation was designed for all these subsets; it is used by most components of the translation system.

This translation system has eight components; their purpose loosely is expressed by their source and object languages:

1. Pascal (source) → PascalAE (tree)   Elimination of the constructs not provided
2. PascalAE (tree) → PascalA (tree)   Transformation of the constructs
3. PascalA (tree) → standard tree   Elimination of the constructs not provided
4. Standard tree → Pascal (source)   Decompilation
5. Ada (source) → Ada (tree)   Acceptance of all constructs
6. AdaPE (tree) → AdaP (tree)   Transformation of the constructs
7. AdaP (tree) → standard tree   Elimination of the constructs not provided
8. standard tree → Ada (source)   Decompilation

You can see that, with various combinations of these components, you can fashion translators from one subset of a language to another. From the subset AdaP, by using components 5, 7, and 4, you can produce the subset PascalA (since it is compatible with AdaP). From a source text in PascalAE, by using components 1, 2, 3, and 8, you obtain a text in AdaP. No component is of insuperable complexity, and the success of the method comes from the judicious (and critical) choice of the various subsets, as well as from the fact that no attempt is made to produce constructs of the extended subset of the target language, to say nothing of the full target language. Thus the situation is similar to what occurs when the object language is of a lower level than the source language.

3.3   Verifiers and filters

3.3.1   Goals and principles

Two different and incompatible terminologies are sometimes used here. For some authors, verifiers and filters are two categories of tools with the same purpose: to verify whether programs written in a programming language conform to the rules and restrictions established in a definition of this language (maybe a standard definition, but not always). Filters make only those verifications that can be done during a purely static analysis of the program, as does a compiler. Verifiers perform a dynamic analysis, which makes it necessary to study all the possible paths in the program.

Other authors consider this distinction to be rather specious and above all useless, since it is based on the verification techniques used more than on the specific features verified. Thus they use the word "filter" for all tools that force programs to conform to some language subset, and they reserve the word "verifier" for a dynamic program-debugging tool, especially one that uses assertions explicitly interspersed in the program. We prefer the second set of definitions, and we shall be content to use the word "filter" in its broader sense, being aware, however, that the verifications made by some filters go much farther than do others.

One may ask why this family of tools, distinct and different from compilers, even exists. The best reason is that compilers and filters are not built by the same people. Compiler writers are interested above all in processing correct programs in the correct way, and they take much less care in forcing users to systematically follow some definition of the language they compile. Whether lazy or careless, they sometimes forget to verify that all restrictions are satisfied, and consequently they provide users with unique, undocumented extensions of the language. But if the source language is not properly defined, a systematic checking of the validity of every construct might cost a lot of compile time.

Filter writers, on the contrary, are interested in program correctness and portability. Their method of choice is to take a subset (maybe extended) of the source language, such that its implementation on every known computer (or at least, every intended computer) is compatible. A subset is thus defined, even if the compiler is not limited to the subset. Hence a new tool, the filter, is needed to ensure that a program is compilable by all intended implementations, and above all that the meaning of the program will be unchanged.

The verifications to be made may be divided into three classes. "Syntactic verifications" are concerned only with checking the conformity of the source text to the language syntax, and they use customary parsing techniques. "Semantic verifications" deal with all that cannot be described by syntax, and are divided into two subclasses: "static semantics" deals with the set of problems related to variables—types, life span, and visibility; "dynamic semantics" deals with all that depends on the order of evaluation of program components and that cannot be discovered by verifications of the two preceding classes.

3.3.2 Techniques

Of course, there are close relationships between the techniques used in filters and those used in ordinary compilers. The differences stem from the fact that filters stop before generating any object code, even an intermediate one, but they make a more thorough verification than do most compilers. A typical filter is very similar to the first part of a syntax-directed compiler, with advanced checking facilities, error detection, and error correction. A tree-structured representation of the source text is generated for use by the dynamic semantic-verification phase.

The static semantic-verification phase works using the symbol table, which represents the declarations that occur in the source program. Of course, this phase checks the correct use of names, but that is a part of any compiler. It can also detect some side effects normally forbidden by language definitions—for example, the modification of the record reference in a **with** statement in Pascal or the modification of the upper bound of a repetitive statement in Fortran or PL/1. It can note that the usage of a function, known to have a side effect, in some arithmetic expression may change the meaning of this expression if the compiler reorders the operands during optimizations. It can detect, in Fortran or Pascal, the forbidden use of the value of the control variable after a repetitive statement. It can detect forbidden branches into loops or other structured statements.

In summary, this phase can detect all that can be seen in a single sequential pass on the source text, knowing that some decisions can be postponed to the end of the pass. In fact, it is possible—for example, in order to detect what variables may be modified by a procedure call—that computation of the transitive closure of some dependency matrix may be needed, the initial contents of this matrix being known only after a complete pass over the program. Peculiarities of the source language, where the use of names does not always follow their definition (only Fortran, Pascal or Ada try to enforce some rules in this area), may make a second pass necessary, before the verification pass, in order to build and fill the symbol table. All in all, the techniques used, succinctly described in Griffiths [Gri77a], are often more complicated and costly than those encountered in ordinary compilers.

But the real difficulties occur in semantic verifications, and this explains why most filters stop just before that point. In fact, in this case, it is necessary to refine the work done during static semantic verifications, by following all possible paths in the program. This work is done on the directed graph that represents these paths, by using techniques ordinarily encountered in the optimization phase of compilers. Thus one can follow the order in which assignments occur and in which variables are defined and undefined. (A variable becomes undefined, for example, if it is the control variable of a repetitive statement that ends normally.) If at least one path leads to the use of an undefined variable, and if it is impossible to prove that this path will not be followed, then the filter flags a possible error.

The dynamic part of the filter is normally useful for eliminating a large part of potential causes of error that the syntactic part flags after a primitive analysis. It is also possible, in the dynamic part, to study the possible value ranges of variables, according to the paths followed. One can check the a priori validity of array references or of assignments to subrange variables in languages like Pascal and Ada.

Thus it is possible to prove, without executing the program, that one reference or assignment is always valid, that one is always invalid, and that another needs run-time verification. The more the dynamic analysis made by the filter is refined, the more precise and certain its diagnostics become. This is a necessary condition for the filter to be usable; a major defect of the early filters was abundance of imprecise messages produced. Without aid, the user had to find in the middle of a large number of useless messages, the precise message corresponding to an actual problem; a finer analysis would not have produced the useless messages.

3.3.3 Examples

PFORT [Ryd74] is a well-known filter for Fortran. It is a purely static filter, intended to check the conformity of source programs to an extended subset of standard Fortran. This subset was chosen for its portability; i.e., its implementations on the various target environments is guaranteed compatible. In that sense, and probably this is its main weakness, the language with which PFORT checks conformity is not itself a language that conforms to any widely accepted standard, but only the result of the choices and trade-offs made by its author. For example, PFORT accepts some extensions to standard Fortran simply because they are accepted by the target Fortran implementations.

Such an approach would be warranted if these extensions were the result of an observed consensus of all implementors, but this is far from being the case. Thus it was observed, some years later [PyD78], that PFORT considers as valid some programs that are not handled in the same way by all Fortran compilers, including different compilers on the same computer with the same operating system. For example, PFORT considers as valid the use of the value of the control variable of a DO statement after it is exhausted; unfortunately, such a control variable does not have the same value with the G and H compilers of the IBM 360/370.

Moreover, since it is purely static, PFORT cannot, of course, check that all variables used are actually initialized or that all parameters of a DO statement are positive, if that value is specified by variables. On the other hand, this filter performs a critical verification of the use of common blocks across subprograms and of the use of parameters that may depend upon the particular implementation of standard parameter passing (i.e., the transmission of reference or of value and of result).

In the case of programs intended to be portable, the language accepted by PFORT has become yet another de facto standard. Basically, this constitutes a benefit; another important benefit is the bulk of static information about a program that is provided as a side effect by the filter. By contrast, one can regret that this standard comes in addition to the existing ones, is not even a subset of them, and is incomplete. The feeling of security that PFORT gives its users is all the more dangerous since it is ill-founded, as demonstrated by the preceding examples.

PBasic [Hop80] is a filter that checks the conformity of Basic programs to the standard for minimal Basic. It is built using PFORT as a model, and in fact is written in the Fortran subset accepted by PFORT. Because of the extreme simplicity of the language to be checked, PBasic is a more complete filter than PFORT, but unfortunately it is still only static, and thus of limited utility.

Dave [OsF76a, OsF76b] is a much more ambitious filter, since it makes a dynamic analysis of Fortran programs. It is not a complete filter at all, since it is interested exclusively in two types of anomalies in the usage of variables. The anomalies stem from an infringement of one of the two following rules:

1. A reference must be preceded by an assignment, without any undefinition between them (see discussion of undefinition in Sec. 3.3.2).

2. An assignment must be followed by a reference before any subsequent assignment or undefinition.

A violation of the first rule is clearly an error, but a violation of the second has only a disquieting effect. Since several paths generally exist from one point to another, Dave signals a type 1 error if there is at least one path wherein the variable would have no value and a type 2 error if none of the paths uses the value of the variable.

Programs are supposed to be correct, so Dave is normally used only after PFORT, and then only if the latter has not flagged any errors. However, Dave is able to accept the description of additional statements or constructs not included in the Fortran standard. Dave's analysis of programs follows an algorithm described in Osterweil and Fosdick [OsF76a]. The program itself is written in Fortran.

The available quantitative data about Dave is rather troubling; this program of 25,000 statements needs about 500K bytes and 10 minutes on a CDC 6400 in order to analyze a program of 2000 statements. The subprograms in the analyzed program have a maximal size of 200 statements. The results generated by the system consist of dozens of pages full of results and messages, in which the user must painfully search for something of real interest.

The fundamental limit of Dave is that it can properly handle only simple variables. Arrays yield problems that cannot be solved without running the program; Dave considers a whole array to have a value as soon as only one of its components has a value. In fact, it appears that the most important information that Dave establishes is that Fortran is very ill-suited to the writing of reliable programs, an already well-known fact.

The filter called Lint, built for the C language in the frame of the Unix operating system [JoR78], exists as a supplement to an overly permissive compiler, as is generally the case with filters for Fortran. It was built after the implementation of C on an Interdata computer, since this later work was done in a way not fully compatible with the original implementation for the PDP-11. C users, who employ the language for system programming (supposedly "dirtier" than any other programming), insist that the compiler not make too many checks. Thus the filter was designed so as to avoid any modification to existing compilers, and to force an interpretation of ambiguous features of the language that is identical on both target implementations. This means that a program accepted by the filter may run with indifference on both implementations. Thus this filter is a typical portability tool: It flags in a program all points that are actually illegal, as well as any that may give rise to problems at transport time. However, like PFORT, and for practical reasons, it makes only a static analysis, and is therefore incomplete. It may give its users an unwarranted feeling of security.

3.4 Generators

3.4.1 Some observations

As we shall see in the next chapter, compiler-writing systems will generate, from an appropriate description of a given language, a more-or-less complete compiler for the language. In this chapter, we are not interested in proper compiler-writing systems, but rather in the specific tools that provide for automating the production of some compiler phases. In this case, the compilers are necessarily generated in several phases, in contrast with those produced by some compiler generators—see, for example, Lecarme and Bochmann [LeB74] or Milton et al. [MKR79]—which generate one-phase compilers.

In this section, we will consider the work of a compiler, using specific points of reference:

- Lexical analysis or scanning
- Syntactical analysis or parsing
- Semantic analysis
- Code optimization
- Code generation

All these phases may be considered as independent processes, which may occur separately or may be combined. For example, scanning may be done at the same time as parsing, processing a token at a time, instead of a whole phase. Similarly, code optimization may be merely a part of code generation.

Program generators, more or less specialized depending on the task, are used for each phase. A generator is itself a program, accepting as input a description of the task to be done and generating the program that will do the job (Fig. 3.1). One can thus imagine generators for each particular task of a compiler. Each task communicates with others by using common tables. In most cases, a specialized generator is used to produce a given phase of a compiler.

As we shall see, this method is closely related to auxiliary languages (see Sec. 5.2), especially in the case of the optimization and code-generation phases. If the

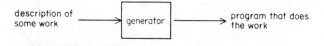

Figure 3.1 Diagram of a generator at work.

semantic-analysis phase generates an intermediate language, optimization can be done on this language itself, or it can be done during or after code generation.

The first two phases—scanning and parsing—are well documented, and usable, compact, efficient generators have existed for many years. By contrast, the last three phases are still being researched, and satisfactory results are only now being achieved.

We shall now consider in turn the five phases, presenting examples to demonstrate the use of generators.

3.4.2   Lexical analysis

In the lexical-analysis, or scanning, phase, character sequences of the source text are grouped into larger units, the "lexical tokens" or "lexemes," which are the terminal symbols of the language for the syntax-analysis phase. Secondary tasks of the scanner deal with clerical processing of the source text—the physical reading, the handling of lines and comments, the production of a listing of the source program, the searching of a source text library, macro expansion, etc. However, only the grouping of character sequences is accomplished by automatic generation.

The lexical aspect of a programming language can ordinarily be described by a regular expression grammar, the most restrictive subset of phrase-structure grammars, which excludes recursion. Automated scanner generators are programs that accept as input a regular grammar, expressed in some adequate notation, and that produce as result the deterministic finite-state automaton that recognizes this grammar. More specifically, the generator generally produces tables, which direct an already programmed automaton.

For every rule of grammar, the user may associate an action that specifies what must be done by the scanner when it recognizes the corresponding lexeme. In particular, the action specifies what information must be transmitted to the parser. The following example describes the syntax of a real number, but omits the corresponding actions:

```
integer        = digit+
sign           = '+' | '-' |
signed-integer = sign integer
number         = signed-integer '.' integer
real           = number |
                 (number | signed-integer) 'e' signed-integer
```

The process that builds the automaton, given the description, is outlined in Johnson et al. [JPA68] and Aho and Ullman [AhU77]. A relatively well-known scanner generator is the Lex system [Les75].

The method just sketched may have disadvantages. On one hand, several programming languages have a lexical structure too complex to be accepted by a deterministic finite-state automaton. This is especially the case in Fortran, where the statement

```
DO 10 I = 1.25
```

contains three lexical tokens ("DO10I"; "="; "1,25"), and the statement

```
DO 10 I = 1,25
```

contains seven tokens ("DO"; "10"; "I"; "="; "1"; ","; and "25"). A similar situation occurs in PL/I, where keywords are no more reserved than in Fortran, but even a very recent language like Ada sets up some delicate problems. (Consider, for example, the quote, which occurs by pairs in some cases and alone in others.)

On the other hand, and above all, the main work in the processing of an identifier or a number is not to recognize it, but indeed to build a characteristic value to represent it. In the case of an identifier, this work is rather trivial, but in the case of real numbers it is very difficult if no loss of precision is acceptable (so that the statement PRINT 2.0 actually prints 2.0, and not 1.99999998). But this work has to be done again, in an almost identical way, in every compiler. Thus there are some scanner generators that are more useful, even while they are more rudimentary [LeB74, Gie79]. The main classes of lexical tokens are built in: identifiers, numbers, keywords, operators, comments, etc. The work of the user is only to specify the classes needed, the value of the information to be transmitted to the parser, and the representation options that must be chosen. It is even possible, if the scanner generator and the parser generator are integrated in the same compiler-writing system, for the interface between both analyzers to be handled in a completely automatic way. This idea is the opposite of what is found in the generators of the Unix system [JoL78].

Those scanner generators that work according to this principle do not produce a general finite-state automaton. They only fill in several tables (for example, the keyword table or the operator table) for a built-in scanner in which the common parts are included. A good parameterization of this scanner allows it to be adapted to any ordinary situation, and generally an additional escape is provided in order to allow the user to program directly some special uncommon functions (e.g., special characters in strings and pragmats in comments).

3.4.3 Syntactic analysis

In the syntax-analysis, or parsing, phase, the syntactic validity of the source program is checked, i.e., its conformance to the grammar of the language. Above all, it must establish the way in which the rules of the grammar are activated to generate the source text. This is the most thoroughly studied part of the whole compilation process, and thus it is the best known. Countless studies in this area, spanning more than 20 years, have resulted in the definition of many practical, efficient methods, and there are no serious theoretical problems still pending. In fact, it is almost impossible to describe clearly all that is known about the subject in a few words, and we will limit ourselves here to describing parser generators from the user's point of view. For more information, the interested reader is referred to the numerous textbooks dealing with syntax analysis—especially see Abramson [Abr73], Aho and Ullman [AhU72, AhU77], Bauer and Eickel [BaE74], Cunin et al. [CGV80], Ershov and Koster [ErK77], Gries [Gri71], and Lewis et al.

[LRS76]. Note, however, that the survey textbooks—e.g., Aho and Ullman [AhU72, AhU77], Cunin et al. [CGV80], Gries [Gri71], and Lewis et al. [LRS76]—give a great deal of room to parsing, perhaps too much, and give relatively limited treatment to parser generators. They seem to imply that production compilers still cannot be built with these tools, which is far from being the case.

A parser generator is a program that takes as input a context-free grammar, describing the syntax of a language and conforming to some restrictions, and generates as output a syntax analyzer for the language. The differences between generators come from the input format of the grammar, the restrictions to which it must conform, and the performance (in time and space) of the resulting parser. Moreover, if the grammar does not conform to the required restrictions, some generators attempt to modify it, some make suggestions to the user, and still others give up with an error message.

There are probably as many different input formats as there are different generators. They range from a grammar already coded with integers, input in a fixed format, up to a powerful and complex metalanguage. In most cases, the formalisms used are derived from Backus Normal Form, generally with simplifications and improvements, or from Van Wijngaarden form. The same grammar rule is illustrated below with both notations:

```
<while statement> ::= 'while' <expression> 'do' <statement>
whilestatement    : whilesymbol,expression,dosymbol,statement.
```

The relatively uncommon generators that produce top-down parsers also accept notations for empty right parts, repetitions, etc. Some generators also accept factorizations and other metasyntactic guiles.

The restrictions to which the grammar must conform depend above all upon the parsing method used by the generated analyzer. Except in the case of the most primitive methods, it is extremely difficult for the user to decide a priori whether these restrictions are satisfied, and the preparation of a grammar for a generator is unfortunately very similar to the work of a sloppy programmer, who tries to run a program in order to see whether it is correct, having no guarantee of certainty. It is still easy to check the absence of conflicts in precedence and of identical right parts. With weak precedence, the rule for compatibility in the right part is much more difficult to check, even intuitively. In the case of mixed-strategy, bounded-context, and a fortiori LR methods, the problem becomes impossible. Of course, with some practice, the user can manage to know what kind of constructs raise problems for the generator. In fact, however, these restrictions are not important, because most programming languages are designed explicitly to raise no serious syntactic problem.

If the restrictions are not satisfied, the generator is unable to produce a correct parser. In several cases, however, it can transform the grammar to make it conform to the required model. Of course, this is impossible if the grammar is ill-conditioned, having blind-alley rules, unreachable rules, left and right recursions both on the same nonterminal, etc. In several cases, depending on the chosen method, it may be enough to introduce additional nonterminals, which replace others in some rule positions. It may be possible, too, to divide rules into parts, or to replace some nonterminals with their various derivations, and so on. All these transformations must be described to the user—on one hand, they might modify the sequence of events in the subsequent compilation; on the other, if they are not enough, the generator describes the problem to the user in terms of the transformed grammar.

Even in the latter case, all generators do not behave in the same way. For some, if the restrictions required by the chosen method are not satisfied, the generator says so, and stops. For others the generator uses built-in heuristics for choosing what to do in case of ambiguity. If the choice conforms to what the user intended, the generated parser is satisfactory, and it is not necessary to restart the work from a modified grammar. In still other cases, the generated parser will call a user-supplied procedure when encountering an ambiguous situation. For example, this procedure may search the declaration table and thus help the parser in separating a function call from an array reference if the notations are the same.

In most cases, the generator fills in several tables, which will direct the working of the predefined parser. In the simple precedence method, for example, the table is the precedence matrix, along with an internal representation of the grammar itself. In the LR(k) method—or better, in its practical simplifications, the SLR and LALR methods—it is the transition table of a stack automaton, along with a branching table. The variants of the general LR(k) method differ according to the techniques used for reducing the size of these tables, and for representing compactly the still-bulky tables that remain.

In less frequent cases, the generated parser is somewhat different. In the weak-precedence method, for example, the final parser is in fact the interpreter of a very simple language, and the generator produces an internal representation of this interpretable language. There are also some generators that produce a recursive descent compiler; i.e., they generate an actual program instead of the tables that will direct the working of a predefined parser. From the user's point of view, the differences between these various methods have mainly to do with the way in which the generated parser may be modified. To modify or to complete a bulky table is generally impossible, especially if it is already compacted, while it is much easier to retouch a recursive descent parser, even if it was automatically generated.

A last characteristic that distinguishes between parser generators is the way in which they place themselves in the general frame of a compiler-writing system. Several examples will show the variety of possible cases.

The generator Yacc, described, for example, in Aho and Ullman [AhU77] and Johnson and Leak [JoL78], is a completely independent system, whose only context is the Unix operating system and the C programming language. It can be used in relation with the scanner generator Lex, already mentioned in the preceding section, but it can also act independently, and no additional module exists for helping to build other compiler parts.

The generator XPL [MKH70] is the center of a compiler-writing system, the other components of which are much smaller. It generates tables, which must be included in a compiler skeleton. This skeleton comprises a predefined parser, an already complete scanner (without a previous generator), and several predefined utility procedures for bookkeeping of the source text or of the declaration table.

The user must complete this program by writing, in the XPL language, the code-generation part of the compiler.

In the Montreal system [LeB74], the parser generator is only a component (although the biggest) in the sequence of generators that produce the various parts of the compiler. The user provides, in a single so-called integrated description, all the aspects of the language to be compiled. These various aspects are dispatched to several independent modules, which generate the scanner, the parser, the error processor, and the semantic-attribute processor.

In the MUG2 system [Gie79], the integration is much deeper, and the user may almost ignore the parser generator. The user describes in turn the methods of lexical analysis, by way of regular expressions; syntactic analysis and syntax tree generation, by way of a context-free grammar that specifies transformations from a string to a tree; semantic analysis, by way of an attribute-definition language; optimization of the intermediate language, by way of an attributed transformational grammar; and code generation, by way of instruction patterns.

As we progressed in the enumeration of these four systems—Yacc, XPL, the Montreal system, and MUG2—the reader may have noticed that we also progressed in the range of matters encompassed by the system and in the scope of the compilers the system is intended to generate. At the same time, the relative importance of the parser generator decreases, even if the generator itself is still a bulky and complex program whose cost is far from negligible.

3.4.4 Semantic analysis

During the semantic-analysis phase, the compiler checks that some constraints on language components are satisfied and establishes relations between them. The correctness of the program is checked for such cases as variable declarations (if required by the language), type compatibility in expressions and assignments, correct number of parameters and subprograms, and so on.

The semantic analyzer can also help the parser, in case of ambiguities. For example, in Algol 68, a statement reduced to a single identifier may denote a procedure call, as well as a branch to a label. Also, the meaning of the sign "+" placed between two variables changes according to whether the variables are integer or real.

A semantic analyzer generator must use the description of actions that are difficult to formalize, at least in a context general enough to be used in various languages, in order that it can automatically generate those actions.

Two formalizations of semantic actions are in current use: "attribute grammars" and "affix grammars." Attribute grammars are especially well suited to the production of analyzers by hand. They are still the object of many studies, and their use by automatic analyzer generators is not yet really satisfactory. The generated analyzers are usually extremely slow and expensive in storage space because they necessitate the presence of the whole syntax tree in memory at one time.

Attribute grammars. An attribute grammar [Knu68] is a context-free grammar in which some attributes are associated with every terminal or nonterminal. Attributes have validity scopes, which allows different attributes for the same symbol if it occurs several times in different contexts. Attributes contain information acquired from the context. They are separated into "inherited attributes," which are computed with information from upper levels, and "synthesized attributes," which use information from lower levels.

For example, a representation of the syntax tree of the Pascal expression "$i := j+4$" is seen in Fig. 3.2a. A first phase of the semantic analyzer "decorates" the syntax tree with attributes, as shown in Fig. 3.2b. Then the attributes are propagated along the tree, top-down for inherited attributes and bottom-up for synthesized attributes, thus yielding the tree seen in Fig. 3.2c.

Thus the attributes provide for expression of constraints by checking their values on each use of a particular rule, or for expression of evaluation rules by evaluating some attributes as a function of others.

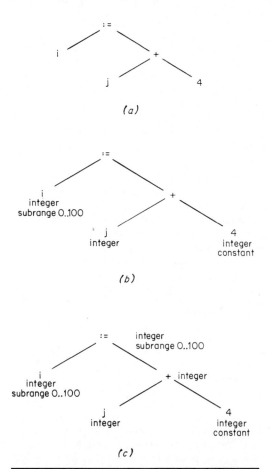

Figure 3.2 Semantic attributes: (a) syntax tree; (b) decorated tree; (c) decorated tree after propagation of attributes.

An example of a semantic analyzer generator that uses attribute grammars is the MUG2 system [Gie79]. It is a compiler-generation system developed at the Technical University of Munich, Germany, which attempts to give the users automatic production tools for all phases needed in the implementation of a new language. Means of description for the various phases are rather high-level. For the description of the syntax analyzer, MUG2 uses a language called Adele, which is, in fact, a metalanguage for attribute grammars. From this description, it is possible to describe the semantic analysis of the language, at compile time as well as at run time.

An attribute grammar written in Adele is structured in subgrammars, each working on a special subtask and representing a specific pass in the generated compiler. For a given language, a first subgrammar could cover syntax analysis, a second could process declarations, a third could handle constants, etc. The generated compiler is thus entirely built around the semantics of the language.

Affix grammars.   An affix grammar can also be used for formalization of programming language semantics. The formal description of an affix grammar appears in Koster [Kos71a]. Here we describe affix grammars only intuitively. In fact, affixes may be considered as local variables and parameters, added to a context-free grammar. A second level is thus introduced in the grammar, in the form of identifiers associated with every nonterminal. This is not really enough for expressing the full semantics of the language, so additional predicates and actions are needed. All these additions transform the context-free grammar into an affix grammar.

The CDL compiler-compiler [Kos71b, Kos77] uses a system of macros, which provides for the generation of actions and predicates. It is a classical system (see Sec. 3.1), in the sense that it is actually a sequence of rules for replacing a piece of text, matching some pattern with another one corresponding to it (the macro body).

In fact, CDL is more a compiler-description language (similar to Adele in MUG2) than a compiler-compiler in the true sense. The implementor of a new language who wants to use CDL must rewrite the macro bodies in order to adapt them to the new language, especially the macros that describe actions. For example, the following macro describes an assignment:

```
"macro"  "action" assign =
   load     acc,v('1')
   store    acc,v('2').
```

where "1" and "2" represent macro parameters.

3.4.5   Code optimization

In this compiler phase, the intermediate code generated during lexical, syntactic, and semantic analysis is improved—not actually optimized—made more compact and more efficient. This is necessary because object code is usually produced in short sequences in a systematic way. Considered separately, each sequence is compact and efficient, and maybe even optimal, but when concatenated, the sequences may introduce redundancies or even unreachable code. More generally, they can often be improved by the use of registers or by careful use of the life span of variables, hence making it possible to share some memory locations.

During the seventies, the studies in this area dealt more often with improvements in optimization algorithms than with the design and realization of automatic code-optimizer generators. There is not presently any satisfactory formalization, either of the instruction sequences of a given language or of the optimizations needed, although such a formalization would allow automatic generation of code optimizers.

However, if no actual generator exists, there are examples of portable optimizers; we divide them into two main categories:

- Those that process the intermediate language and are a part of the object-independent part of the compiler. Their optimizations, however, may be oriented toward some classes of computers; at least, they may be better adapted to some actual instruction sets than to others.

- Those that are based on the description of a particular object computer's instruction sequence, with associated semantics, and on the associated description of optimizations that may be applied to the instruction sequences.

Intermediate-code optimization.   A more detailed optimization is useful after completion of code generation. If code generation is simple and fast, it generates instruction sequences in a systematic way, barely using the context where they occur or the surrounding instructions. Consequently, it is useful to subsequently rearrange these sequences, removing useless instructions (a store immediately followed by a load of the same variable, a sequence of branches, etc.), or to replace them with more appropriate instructions that will probably be more efficient on the target computer.

The first optimization made in the intermediate language is to reduce some instructions (operations on constants, for example), replacing an instruction sequence by a single, supposedly more efficient instruction of the intermediate language. A multiplication by 2 may be replaced by a binary shift, or the addition of a constant followed by a store may be replaced with a special increment instruction, and so on.

For example, a sequence optimizer was built at the Free University of Amsterdam [TSS82]. The intermediate code that is the basis of the optimizer is the assembly language of a stack computer, called EM-1. The optimizer works using a table that contains instruction sequences, along with equivalent improved sequences. Thus

```
LOC A; NEG ⇒ LOC −A
```

means that a load followed by a negation may be replaced by a load of the negative value.

Object-code optimization.   In this case, the optimizer processes the object code. However, it is portable since it uses a formalization of the description of machine instructions, along with their semantics. It analyzes the object code, replacing some instructions with others that are more efficient but have the same meaning. These are often called "peephole optimizations."

Such an optimizer has been built at the University of Arizona [DaF80]. The description of instructions is made using a context-free grammar. Their semantics is described by moves of register or memory contents. For example,

```
R[3] ← R[3] + 1
```

represents the increment of register 3 by 1.

```
M[C] ← 0
```

represents the store of zero in memory address C.

```
PC ← (NZ = 0 ⇒ 140 else PC)
```

represents a branch to location 140 if register NZ is zero.

The optimizer works by matching patterns of instruction sequences. It considers every instruction pair, with all its consequences, and makes reductions if applicable. It is integrated in a simplified code generator and is written in Snobol4. Descriptions of machine instructions are translated into Snobol4 patterns.

This last example is a first step toward formalizations that will allow the automatic generation of optimizers. Such an approach is being studied at the Technical University of Munich [Gie82]. The optimizer generator accepts as input a formalized semantic description of the target-computer instruction set, and builds the context descriptions needed by the optimizer.

3.4.6 Code generation

Code generators work on the intermediate language code, generated by the preceding analysis phases. They constitute the last phase of the compiler, according to the model we used, since they generate executable code for the target computer. This phase is difficult because a code generator should try, as much as possible, to produce optimal code. Many algorithms have been suggested—for general cases (algorithms for optimal code generation for arithmetic expressions [AhJ76]) as well as for special situations (code generation for arithmetic expressions on two-address machines [SeU70]). However, as with semantic analysis and code optimization, the lack of mechanisms for general formalizations for computers and code generators makes the development of really automatic code-generator generators presently impossible.

There are two main approaches to the simplification of code-generator production [Cat80]:

- To develop specific languages, i.e., the procedural language approach [FeG68]
- To formalize machine descriptions, i.e., the descriptive language approach

All the examples we are going to describe pertain to the second category, which corresponds to the present orientation of research in this area.

The method used is based on transformations of intermediate code patterns into equivalent machine-language sequences. For each instruction in the intermediate language, the corresponding sequence depends on several factors: localization of operands (memory or registers), occupation of registers, complexity of the instruction set, etc. To build a code generator for a new machine, machine-dependent descriptions cannot be used just as they are, and most of the generator must be rewritten. A code-generator generator gives the additional capability of automatically generating correspondence tables.

Table-driven code generation.   Code generation may be automated, similar to lexical and syntactic analysis, by using methods based on transformation tables and programs for automatic generation of these tables. Such an approach is used at the University of California at Berkeley [Gra80]. The code-generator generator consists of a table builder and a code generator that uses the generated tables. In order to obtain a code generator for a computer, one must give a description of the machine to the code-generator generator.

Code generation is supposed to be completely independent of the analysis phases. Thus the generator assumes that all that can be done at compile time is already done. Instead, it undertakes machine-resource management (although in separate phases): memory allocation for program and compiler-generated variables, register allocation (in parallel with code generation), and so on. After allocating these resources, the main task of the generator is to select the instruction sequences to be generated, depending on the order of evaluation of the intermediate program form used as input. (This form is assumed to be a tree.)

The main difficulty is to find a deterministic algorithm for choosing the best sequence without fail, using the context if possible. The algorithm chooses a solution only after traversing the whole subtree, using the following criteria:

- Generation of this instruction cannot be avoided; i.e., the subtree cannot be treated in a wider context.

- In its particular context, the generated sequence is the best.

- The tree is traversed "regularly" (in prefix order), which allows a subtree to be represented using a linear code sequence, each operator preceding its operands.

The various possible solutions are represented in a table automatically produced from the machine description. For a given intermediate language pattern, at least one corresponding machine-language sequence must exist, without any context restriction, but other sequences may correspond to special cases. The generator itself proceeds by pattern matching and replacement.

Generation from a machine description.   The code-generator generator of PQCC, the compiler-writing system of Carnegie-Mellon University, uses about the same approach; i.e., it generates tables from a description of the target computer. This description contains, in particular, a description of the various memory categories, the instruction formats, and the actual address computations, as well as a full description of the target-machine instruction set. For each instruction, all the actions are described. Along with this description, the table builder uses a set of axioms, which describe some characteristics; for example,

```
E = -(-E) |
E + 0 = E }    Machine-independent axioms
-E = (-E) + 1  Machine-dependent characteristic (complement of 2)
```

The generation of translation tables is made in two phases: First interesting subtrees are selected, then instruction sequences are generated [Cat80]. These tables are built by a preprocessor and sorted to speed the search for a particular pattern. The tables contain subtree patterns that represent the intermediate form of programs, as well as the corresponding code sequences that will be generated each time the pattern is encountered.

The code-generator generator produces patterns in the form of Fig. 3.3. The notation "$1:register" means that operand 1 must be in a machine register, while "$2:memory" means that operand 2 must be in memory. In Fig. 3.3c, it is seen that limited context should allow generation of better code.

Instruction selection is made by traversing the tree in prefix order. Selection of the best pattern is made on every node, but code generation is deferred so that the largest possible pattern will be chosen. Thus, the subtree of Fig. 3.4a, matched to the model of Fig. 3.4b, will trigger generation of

```
TDNN $1,$2
JRST $3
```

on a DEC PDP-10, instead of first generating the code for "and," followed by the test for zero value, and then the code for "if."

3.4.7 Interpreters

The generators mentioned up to this point generate parts of actual compilers, either analyzers or code generators. We do not know of any systems that automatically generate interpreters. However, MUG2, the compiler-writing system of the Technical University of Munich anticipates this problem. It is intended that an interpreter be generated by an "attribute evaluator" from a definition of the interpreter written in Adele (described in Sec. 3.4.4). This will occur after semantic analysis of the program.

3.5 Other tools

3.5.1 Changing language versions

Tools that convert a program from one version of a language to another version of the same language are related to higher-level language translators, as well as to filters. These tools resemble translators, since the problem is to translate from a higher-level language to another, except that in this case the two languages are very similar. They resemble filters, since they must consider only those features of the language that differ from one version to the other, and they can ignore all other constructs. They even have some relation with preprocessors, since they copy without modification all the text that is not of interest.

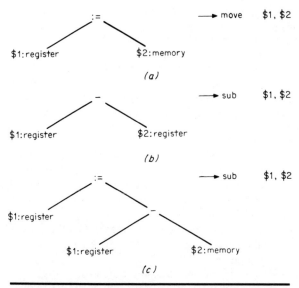

Figure 3.3 Patterns for the code-generator generator: (*a*) simple assignment, (*b*) register subtraction, and (*c*) subtraction and assignment.

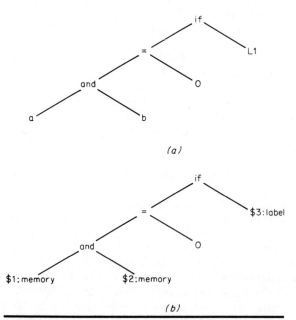

Figure 3.4 Pattern selection in code generation: (*a*) code subtree and (*b*) matched pattern.

In the case of two successive and official versions of the same language, the change is difficult; furthermore, the usefulness of an automatic tool may be limited since a very inefficient program may be generated. Normally, one wants to change versions only because the second one is incompatible with the first. Incompatible constructs generally cannot be expressed using the rest of the language, thus forcing the use of complicated tricks or a costly simulation. If the representation is easy and efficient, then the new language version is useless (except for the trivial case where additional control structures can be expressed using conditional branches).

Such a situation occurs, for example, with the original and revised versions of Pascal: The suppression of the class concept and the replacement of constant parameter passing with value parameter passing are relatively easy to process by hand, but not automatically. This would be the same for the new definition of input-output in Ada or for the two incompatible standards for Cobol, for which changes in the keyword set would be a severe obstacle.

Tools for version change, consequently, are much more useful in the case of parallel variants of a poorly standardized (or nonstandardized) language, as demonstrated by the following two examples.

A typical example of a widely used, nonstandardized language is Lisp. The conversion program of H. Samet [Sam81b] is used for passing from Lisp version 1.6 (Stanford University) to the Interlisp version (Xerox PARC). Neither is a subset of the other; both are supersets of the Lisp 1.5 version, the only one to be described in a somewhat official way [MCA62]. The work of Samet's program cannot be easily described. Mostly it searches the source text for specific cases to process, processes them in an ad hoc way, and adds a set of function definitions that redefines for each object program all the predefined functions of Interlisp not exactly equivalent to those of Lisp 1.6. An important point is that the construction of this program is made very easy by a remarkable property of Lisp—programs and data are represented in the same way.

Another example of a version-change tool is Lint, the filter for the C language already mentioned in Sec. 3.3.3. This is a typical case of an imprecisely defined language, as demonstrated in the only official textbook [KeR78]: The introduction and the reference manuals, published in the same volume, contain incompatibilities. Note that Lint warns of all version differences, but makes no actual conversion.

There are also some tools that use a slightly different idea: Instead of converting from one version of a language to another, the goal is to choose, from a general model of the source text, one of the possible variants of the language. The input text, therefore, is not written in some particular version of the language, but rather in a form that encompasses all anticipated variants. The system of Ford and Sayers [FoS76] does this for Fortran. One must note that the work automatically done by the conversion tool is in the end very simple. The user must explicitly anticipate in the source text all the possibilities pertaining to each variant, and must specify in which case each possibility is to be used. The work of the conversion tool is to extract from this source text the useful parts, after substituting some constants characteristic of the chosen variant. A general-purpose macroprocessor could easily do the same job.

3.5.2 Decompilers

Decompilation is the antithesis of compilation, which is the translation of a program from a higher-level language into a low-level language. The process of generating assembly language from machine language is sometimes called "desassembly"; we do not consider it here, since it is a tool for program debugging.

A decompiler must rebuild, as completely as possible, a source text which was lost or is unavailable, using the object text generated by a compiler. One generally assumes that the nature of the initial source language of the compiler is known. This process may facilitate corrections or modifications to the program, since they will be much more easily and safely made in a higher-level language version than when patches must be made to a binary text.

Decompilation, followed by a proper compilation, has also been proposed as a method for translating from one machine language to another, using a higher-level language as the intermediate language. Since decompilation can ordinarily be done only to produce the initial source language, this idea makes sense only if the higher-level language version of the program to be transported has been lost. It can not be seriously entertained in the case of a program originally written in assembly language.

Finally, one of the most frequent applications of decompilation, although not the most advisable, is in software piracy. Software vendors try to protect themselves by delivering their products only in binary form, but a good decompiler can get around this protection. Of course, this is feasible only if the nature of the source language used by the software builder is known, but that information is seldom difficult to come by.

A decompiler is used much less frequently as a debugging aid; but decompilation can be used to rebuild the source text of the program from its condition in storage after some irrecoverable error. This allows the programmer to compare it with its original condition. In fact, this is meaningful only in case of a desassembly. In case of an actual decompilation, it would probably be impossible to rebuild a meaningful source text from a severely damaged object text.

The general problem of decompilation is in fact unsolvable [HoM80], since it is impossible to identify with certainty a program from its data, and the types of data objects do not normally occur in storage. If a program modifies itself, this makes the situation worse, and it is almost impossible to distinguish, among the constants that appear explicitly within the instructions, those that represent program addresses and those that are ordinary constants.

Some computer architectures alleviate the situation, especially those that physically separate program instructions from the data they process. There are even those architectures where data types are explicit.

However, knowledge of the source language is the best aid for a decompiler, and more precisely, knowledge of the exact compiler that generated the text to be processed. When this compiler is rather primitive, but even in cases where it is more refined, object programs conform to a specific model, and regular instruction sequences may very often be recognized and related to some source-language constructs. This is especially true of procedure calls and some control structures.

In a more general situation, the techniques in use are partly heuristic and are closely related to those of dynamic filters (see Sec. 3.3.3) or higher-level language translators. For example, Horspool and Marovac [HoM80] describe an algorithm that allows maximal separation of instructions from data, thus isolating the largest possible part of the program that must be interpreted as instructions. This example, the techniques in use, and the tools actually built are very seldom described in the literature, perhaps because of the problems of piracy mentioned before.

3.5.3 Verification and testing after transport

A program, after being transported to a new environment, should do more than just compile and execute. Not only must the meaning of the program remain unaltered after transport, but the qualities of the program, which made its transport desirable, must be preserved, or at least kept as close as possible to the original.

Often this point is entirely neglected. The implementor of the software in the new experiment may feel that as soon as the program runs it is correct; it is even relatively rare for the author to provide a complete battery of tests, though the program may have been extensively tested in its original environment.

Actual tools would be extremely useful in this situation, in order to verify the qualities and validity of the software product after it has been transported. Walker and Harrison [WaH82], for example, propose an integrated set of software tools to do this work:

- A static program analyzer, for use before and after transportation. This tool is very similar to a filter, and the installer of the software product can compare the results generated both before and after transportation, in order to evaluate the success of the transportation.

- A test-case generator, which exercises all possible individual paths in the programs at least once (but not all possible combinations of paths, of course, since this would likely result in attempts to generate really exhaustive test cases).

- A dynamic program analyzer, which examines a program's behavior during execution with test cases generated by the tool cited above.

- A software metric tool, which collects the statistical data needed and presents it in a usable way. A comparison between measurements made before and after transport gives an objective measure of performance changes.

This set of tools is proposed for business software products written in Cobol—i.e., for very specific cases. Such a set would be much more difficult to use in other situations, and the only software products for which a posteriori verification tools are usually available are compilers. In this case, the set of programs to be transported, after the compiler itself, constitutes an extremely valuable test case, even if it is neither systematic nor exhaustive.

Chapter

4

Linguistic Means of Transport

The various software tools covered in the preceding chapter are generally used as aids in transporting existing software products in a more-or-less automatic way. In the present chapter, we will study some means more general than the tools we looked at in Chap. 3, which are normally used to construct a portable software product. In a way, the means we shall study here are of a higher level than the software tools. In fact, those tools can be components of the means, or can be used in their construction.

4.1 Introduction

The discussion here, and throughout the rest of this book, is based upon a very elementary notion: A software product is programmed using one or more programming languages.

According to P. J. Brown [Bro77b], four basic means for implementing portable software may be distinguished:

1. Use of a ubiquitous tool, i.e., a higher-level language likely to be available on the anticipated target machines. Only three languages *currently* qualify in this regard: Fortran, Cobol, and Pascal. When dealing with small computers only, one may rely on Basic; on big computers only, one may expect to use Snobol4 or Lisp, though the C language is now widespread enough to be considered in some cases. PL/1 and Algol 68 are not to be considered.

2. Use of a method sufficiently flexible to be implementable with various tools— for example, with any macroprocessor (most often a macroassembler). In this case, it is assumed that such a tool is available everywhere, even if with very different capabilities.

3. Use of a specialized tool, which can adapt itself to a large variety of target machines; multitarget tools include general-purpose macroprocessors such as ML/1 and Stage2 (see Secs. 3.1.5 and 3.1.6), compiler-writing systems (see Sec. 4.4), and multitarget compilers and assemblers. Any of these specialized tools will run on a host computer, distinct from the target computer, and

constitute so-called cross-tools. (We would prefer to call them, depending on the case, "transassemblers" or "transcompilers.") Otherwise the transportation tool must be implemented on the target machine, in which case it must itself be portable.

4. Use of the method that P. J. Brown calls "telescopic generation": A sequence of software is built, each level being more or less specialized, so that the highest level is the software product to be implemented. Each level is built and implemented using the lower level (or even all the lower levels), and the lowest level is itself portable (by means of item 1, 2, or 3 above) or simple enough to be very easily programmed by hand.

The term "bootstrap" is often applied in referring to items 3 and 4 above (and in completely different contexts as well). We think its usage is too vague and its meaning too ambiguous, and we shall see in Chap. 6 that the methods and combinations of methods that can be put in action are far too varied to be described by a single term, the meaning of which nobody really agrees on.

Coming back to the four basic means for implementing portable software distinguished by P. J. Brown, one can remark that the difference between means 3 and 4 has mainly to do with the division of work between the host and target computers: With the use of a specialized tool, the bulk of the work is done on the host machine, while the use of telescopic generation is generally based on the assumption that only the target machine is available. One may also remark that both these means are normally extensions of the first two means cited, at a more-or-less high level: The specialized tool (means 3) must be itself implemented, of course, and it is hardly probable that it can work on only one computer, which could subsequently be used for generating any software product needed for all target machines. Thus this tool must itself be portable, using one of the other three means. As to the use of telescopic generation, we have already noted that the transportation of the lowest level of the hierarchy necessitates use of one of the other means. Finally, let us note that, except when a macroassembler is used (means 2) this case necessitates a macroprocessor, which itself must be implemented, and consequently means 2 is frequently based on means 1.

All in all, it appears that the most important matter in producing portable software is the use of a higher-level programming language, which itself must be either already available on the target computer(s), or easily portable. Acknowledging this, we must now consider the language from a specific point of reference: How is it available?

1. The language is widely available. This leads us to consider the main programming languages from the point of view of the help they provide to portability (Sec. 4.2.1), and especially the very important and often unappreciated matter of their standardization (Sec. 4.2.2).

2. The language is built by extending a core language. This is the already old idea of "extensible languages," a somewhat fuzzy and catch-all idea that seems to be presently out of fashion (Sec. 4.3).

3. The language is defined by adding some constructs, considered to be essential,

to an existing and widely available language. Since the term "extension" has been reserved for a long time, we call this process "augmentation." The transformation of the augmented language into the base language is done by a preprocessor (Sec. 4.4).

4. The language is built from scratch, using tools which automate a more-or-less important part of its implementation. These tools are the compiler-writing systems (Sec. 4.5), which are themselves software products and consequently may be portable too.

5. The language implementation is itself portable, which comes down to the general problem we are considering. Since this constitutes the most important application of the problem, we will devote a whole chapter (Chap. 5) to it.

4.2   Programming in a higher-level language

Even if everybody agrees to classify PL/1, Simula 67, and Euclid among higher-level programming languages, and to exclude any machine language, it is still debatable just which language should be included between these extremes; the position of RPG, Basic, or PL/360 will not be the same in all cases. We are satisfied with the definition given by Jean Sammet [Sam69, Sam81a], which has stood for more than a dozen years and is, in fact, the only proposal we know of in this regard.

According to this definition, a higher-level programming language has the following characteristics:

1. In order to use the language effectively, a programmer does not need to know the language of the target machine (independent of any considerations of efficiency).

2. The language is by nature independent of any specific computer; consequently it should be easy to take a program written in that language and have it work on many different machines. (This property, required by Sammet [Sam81a], raises the whole problem of software portability and suggests the most fundamental solution.)

3. The translation of executable elements from the source language to machine language will ordinarily produce several machine instructions for a single source-language instruction (independent of microprogramming possibilities).

4. The notation provided by the language is natural to the class of problems to be considered and is not present in a fixed tabulated form. (This rule specifically excludes report generators and decision tables.)

4.2.1   How higher-level programming languages help portability

The first two characteristics applied by Sammet to the definition of a higher-level language are generally summarized in the term "machine independence." Naturally, a program written in a machine-independent language should be machine-independent itself, and consequently it should run on several different machines, which is the true principle of portability. In fact, the situation is not so clear; "machine independence" is a much-too-fuzzy term. Thus we shall study in this section the various forms of independence that can be distinguished. We will consider in turn a product's independence from the hardware, from the computer, from the operating system, and from the programming language.

Independence from the hardware. A software product is "hardware-independent" if its working does not depend on technical properties of the materials and components that constitute the computer on which this product runs. We distinguish hardware independence from computer independence, in the sense that the technical properties of its materials and components are the building blocks of the computer as seen by the program. Thus hardware independence mainly deals with the peripheral devices of a computer system, since they are the only parts for which technical characteristics presently produce differences in properties and capabilities: All present-day computers are automata that use electronics and binary representation of information, and it would be necessary to see a hydropneumatic computer using ternary logic to discover the subtle hardware dependencies in most existing software products. It is clear that a program does not depend on whether a computer is wire-wrapped or has MOS or ECL circuits, as long as the instruction set is the same.

By contrast, the diversity of peripheral devices is often baffling, if not absurd. Twenty years ago, the only input devices were punch cards and paper tape, and legible output was inevitably in uppercase lettering run on a printer. Magnetic tape was the only means for saving and transmitting massive information. Since then, various forms of punch cards have appeared, as have a new representation on magnetic tape, optical mark and character readers, and curve plotters; overall we now have an extraordinarily diverse range of powerful and incompatible devices in two different areas: terminals and direct-access magnetic supports.

It is now clear that programmers' lives would be impossible if they could not ignore, at least partly, the technical characteristics of the devices they use. The variety of these devices is so large that higher-level languages are unequal to the challenge. This is sometimes considered a severe defect of the languages, since some people would like to program the use of a table plotter or of a CRT terminal by means of higher-level constructs. But the effect of this supposed defect on portability can be extremely positive: Programs can use the various peripheral categories as means for realizing rather simple abstract concepts—for example, those of a sequential file or of a direct-access file—or they can call library subprograms which provide access to the peculiar properties of peripherals. In the first case, these properties remain unused, but hardware independence is achieved automatically, and, in fact, is compelled. In the second case, the parts that depend on hardware are clearly localized in calls to library subprograms, and as a consequence subsequent adaptation (by hand or automatically) to other capabilities is made easier.

Despite the demands of many users, it would be catastrophic to introduce into higher-level programming languages such hardware concepts as the floppy disk, the CRT terminal, the vocal answering unit, and so on. Only the abstraction that covers them is of importance, at least from the point of view of portability.

Independence from the computer.   A software product is "computer-independent" if its working does not depend on peculiar functional characteristics of the computer—for example, the bit length of a character or a storage unit, properties of integer or real arithmetic, and peculiarities of the character set. To assume that the computer is built on the Von Neumann model is not to exhibit real dependence on the computer, since all past and present programming languages more or less rely on this model, as noted by John Backus [Bac78, Bac81].

Computer independence obviously excludes any programming in machine or assembly language. Not so long ago, this condition was seen as an obstacle, and program portability seemed a useless goal, since it would inevitably lead to large inefficiency. But advances in the design and implementation of programming languages, and above all the evolution in our thinking caused by the amazing increase of software costs as compared with hardware costs, have caused this argument to lose most of its value. The remaining assembly-language supporters include those with a real or perceived need to save a few microseconds or a few bytes and some neophytes who approach computer science by way of microcomputers.

The main characteristic of higher-level languages, in this respect, is then that they are not linked to any specific machine language. This does not mean, however, that computer independence comes without problems, and the following difficulties may be mentioned:

- Validity range of integer arithmetic
- Precision of real arithmetic
- Contents and ordering of the character set
- Presence or absence of a negative zero, which can make comparisons false
- Result of integer divisions with negative operands
- Detection and handling of arithmetic overflow
- Various limitations impossible to overcome (e.g., the size of a program or of a structured object handled as a whole)

Most of these difficulties deal with integer or real arithmetic operations, and higher-level languages are not all equally helpful in solving them, as we shall see in Sec. 4.2.3. Moreover, this is an area where the great care given to a particular implementation of a language may cause severe difficulties that do not result from the language itself. It is not infrequent, for example, that the reference manual of an implementation describes as a feature of this implementation, to be accepted without question, the risk of producing aberrant results (a feature generally called "unpredictability") in circumstances where the implementor did not judge it necessary to achieve predictability.

In a general way, however, and except in the case of numeric software already discussed in Sec. 2.2, one can state that computer independence is one of the most successful aspects of higher-level programming languages, and one of the most dependable properties of software products built with these languages.

Independence from the operating system.   A software product is "operating-system-independent" if it does not call any unusual resource that cannot be guaranteed to have a counterpart on all existing systems. It would seem that this characteristic is almost impossible to achieve, since the resources offered by various systems are much different and more incompatible than those offered by computers themselves, and it could be concluded that true portability is possible only for a program without any communication to the outside. In fact, all that can be guaranteed in any case is that some means of input and output should exist, and these means should allow the transmission of character sequences. The existence of any specific peripheral cannot be guaranteed, and neither can the availability of direct files, or sometimes even of sequential files. Use of a clock, communication with an operator, use of a large number of simultaneously open files, and the ability to reread a file, all may pose obstacles to portability.

Fortunately, most higher-level programming languages provide important help in this area, probably because their designers had encountered the problem of disparity and incompatibility between the various operating systems, and desired to mask it. Since one cannot guarantee that a given resource is provided by any one system, that resource is made a primitive in the language itself, and the implementor has the burden of ensuring a correct implementation of this feature. If the host operating system is cooperative, a simple interface should allow its resources to appear as the primitives required by the language. If the host operating system is hostile, the language implementors will have to encapsulate the implementation in a subsystem, maybe of rather large dimension, that simulates all that is needed for the language. In all cases, portability is clearly increased, but with the unfortunate consequence that system and computer resources may be inefficiently used.

In any case, operating-system independence also necessitates some discipline from the programmer, and the implementor of a portable software product must usually compromise the portability of the product a little by providing a list of the minimal resources that must be provided by any system to which transportation is anticipated. Thus it is generally better to refrain from using other than purely sequential files and to give up the idea of knowing the present date or time, unless the programming language in use contains a particularly precise definition of those operations.

Independence from the programming language.   This property appears to be somewhat paradoxical, since it hardly seems possible that a software product be independent of the language in which it is written. In fact, two completely different types of dependence must be distinguished, depending on whether a computer change without a language change is anticipated or whether the software product is intended to be transcribed into another programming language.

The first case, which is the most frequent by far, implies a change of implementation of the language used. This can occur without a change in the operating system (i.e., a change from PL/1 to PL/1 with the MVS system on an IBM 370, or from Fortran to Fortran with the NOS-BE system on a CDC Cyber), with a change in system but not in computer (i.e., a change from RSX-11M to Unix on a PDP-11), or with changes in both the computer and the system. Normally, a computer change without a system change (i.e., a change from Unix on a PDP-11 to Unix on a 68000) should not cause an implementation change for a high-level language even though the back end of the compiler is changed.

The most important problem, when moving to another implementation of a given language, is that two different implementations never accept exactly the same language, a problem largely underestimated and manifested in four different ways, which almost always occur at the same time:

1. The official definition of the language leaves some important points undefined. If the matter is the order of evaluation of arithmetic expressions, this is rather unimportant; if it is the effect of some statement frequently encountered, it is catastrophic.

2. The official definition leaves several different choices to the implementor, especially the choice as to what exactly must be implemented and what can be ignored.

3. The implementation accepts some extensions to the officially defined language.

4. The implementation, by design or not, does not conform to the official definition.

It should be clear that the existence and contents of the official definition is of central importance. (In the next section, we shall consider at length the most important case of a definition, that of an official standard.) A clear, concise, complete, and coherent definition should be the first concern of any language designer. This definition should be made not only with implementors in mind but also for users, so that all can conform to it.

The second type of dependence occurs when a change of language during transport is anticipated. The process is by definition much more difficult, and the two languages chosen must be somewhat similar: A change from Lisp to Basic would probably be impossible. The most important point is that the software implementors should consciously restrict use in the initial programming language to only those concepts that have a simple counterpart in the language(s) in which the program is to be transcribed.

Higher-level languages provide a fundamental help in this area, since generally they are built upon a very small number of basic concepts. The more a given language is pushed to the best of its capabilities, the more difficult a program will be to transcribe (see Sec. 3.5.1).

4.2.2 Standardization of programming languages

Why standardize?   Standardization of computer science foundations, and especially of programming languages, is a little-known and little-appreciated subject for most programmers. Many have heard of "standard Fortran," sometimes called ANSI Fortran or even ASA Fortran, and they know of the ASCII character set and that it is an American national standard (*not* an international one), but generally their knowledge stops here. Admittedly, the subject is not really exciting, and the slow methods of standardization are often frustrating. However, as Jean Sammet [Sam81a] notes, standardization is probably the activity that has the most profound economic (and even technical) influence on programming languages.

Generally speaking, standardization prevents atomization in the area of programming languages. It provides (or at least it attempts to provide) users with coherent tools. It gives software producers a set of specifications for the products they develop, and it gives software users a set of criteria for evaluating those products. More specifically, standardization of programming languages is a necessary condition for the portability of software products programmed in these languages, as we already noted in the preceding section. It is the only way to gain compatibility of the various implementations of a given programming language, as demonstrated by the contrary examples of widely used but nonstandardized languages, like Lisp and APL, and of languages whose standards appeared too late to be accepted, as is the case with Basic.

Of course, as we shall see in examples to follow, standardization is not a solution to everything, and the existence of a standard is not a guarantee that it will be followed, since it bears no coercive, but only persuasive, strength. In order to be accepted, a standard must obviously be coherent and understandable (which is usually *not* the case); it must be realistic too, i.e., as close as possible to what already exists, since a programming language is normally standardized only after it has proved itself. (An important exception is Ada, but the same situation occurs when standardization committees are metamorphosed into language-definition committees, as was the case for Fortran 77.)

After the standard is accepted, it must then be observed, and here things get sticky: Are there any Fortran compiler producers who withdrew features from their implementation because those features did not appear in the 1966 standard? On the contrary, most language implementations of computer manufacturers have introduced "improvements" and "extensions" to an existing standard, perhaps to prevent the users from subsequently changing to another machine.

In such a context, the time of publication of the standard is crucial; it must not be published too early, when some features of the language have not yet been improved in the light of acquired experience, nor too late, when various dialects have already had time to diverge in irreconcilable directions.

How standardization works.   There is at least one national standardization organization, if not more, in each industrial country; their status varies from that of simple lobby group to national agency. In the United States, several organizations work for standardization. The best known is ANSI, the American National Standards Institute (twice renamed), which has no federal status, in contrast to its competitor, the National Bureau of Standards. The IEEE has its own standardization organization, as does the Army, the Air Force, etc. In Great Britain, the British Standards Institute is a state agency (a "crown agency"). In France, the

Association Française de Normalisation (AFNOR), a private association for public service, holds a monopoly on the approval and publication of French standards.

At the international level, the various national standardization organizations (one per country) are federated in the International Organization for Standardization (ISO), connected to the United Nations in a way similar to UNESCO and of a somewhat similar size (and cost). Depending on the matters considered, ISO is divided into almost 200 "technical committees," of which the ninety-seventh deals with computer science. These technical committees are themselves subdivided into subcommittees; the twenty-second subcommittee of Technical Committee 97 deals with programming languages. Finally, each subcommittee contains "expert groups," which handle matters considered not very important or about which a final decision has not yet been made, and "working groups," each in charge of a precise subject and entrusted with proposing standard(s) for this subject. Thus the second working group of the twenty-second subcommittee of the ninety-seventh technical committee deals with Pascal and is currently revising the 7185th standard of ISO.

The structure of a national standardization organization is similar to that of ISO, but on a smaller scale. If one considers that expert groups and working groups consist of from 20 persons (for the smallest groups) to more than 200 (for the largest), and that all decisions must go up the full hierarchy to be submitted to national and international vote, with at least a three-month delay on each step, it comes as no surprise that the whole standardization process is long, cumbersome, tiring, and frustrating.

Moreover, although every country has one vote within ISO, the economic weight of the United States is so great that a standard must always be approved by the American member (ANSI) in order to be of any influence, whatever the opinion of any other member country.

The special case of programming languages raises additional problems. First, a programming language is probably the most complex object for which standardization has ever been attempted. Ordinary standards in other fields most often amount to tables of sizes, tolerances, materials, etc., and are printed on a few pages. By comparison, the shortest standards for programming languages need at least 50 pages (Algol 60), but may easily occupy four to eight times more space (PL/1). Second, one is not really sure of what should be standardized: When it is decided that a sheet of A4 format shall be a rectangular piece of paper, 210 by 297 mm, it is the specification of a physical object, for which it is easy to judge compliance, within some tolerance. When one states that in Pascal the effect of the procedure call statement shall be to create a new activation which shall . . . , one is specifying the working of a language implementation and not specifying the Pascal language itself, which would be meaningless. In fact, the standard of a programming language should give the "definition" of this language, then specify that a processor for this language is in conformance with the standard if . . . . The problem is that standards themselves must be presented in a standardized form, in which the definitions are given in alphabetic order. Defining a language by presenting all the terms used in alphabetic order would make the definition completely unreadable.

These problems have been progressively overcome, if not entirely solved, but they were embarrassing for the first standardizers. Their starting point was that, just as another group had to choose a standard, from among several formats, for a sheet of paper, so it seemed clear that they should choose, from among several programming languages, *the* standard language. Much time and many discussions were needed before everybody finally agreed that a standard definition had to be given for *each* important language.

Some language standardizations.   The way in which a standard is produced, officially and technically, varies widely from one language to another [HiM80]. The initiative may come from a member of ISO; from ANSI for Fortran, Cobol, Basic, and PL/1; from BSI for Pascal; from AFNOR for APL. It can also come from elsewhere: from IFIP for Algol 60 and Algol 68, from the U.S. Department of Defense for Ada. The standardization document may be a simple arrangement of an existing document (Algol 60, Pascal, Ada), the compilation of numerous documents (Fortran, Cobol), or a large, formal construction (PL/1). The standardization committee may even transform itself into a language-definition committee (Fortran 77, Basic). The standardization process may lead to important modifications of the language, or it may leave it basically untouched, sometimes to the language's detriment. A standard may be a single monolithic document, or it may describe embedded and disjoint subsets. The problem of formalisms is generally a point of dissension among standardizers, and attitudes may reflect either a fierce avoidance of any formalism or the unconditional acceptance of formalization. A standard may be revised from time to time, and an important political and economic decision is whether this revision should birth a new language, maybe incompatible with its predecessor, or whether, on the contrary, the revision should maintain compatibility at any cost. Finally, some standards are accompanied, officially or not, by validation tools to measure conformity to the standard of a given language implementation, to reveal deviations and extensions, to show how the points left at the implementor's disposal are defined, etc. (This is the case at least for Cobol, Pascal, and Ada.)

We shall summarize here the standardization process for some of the most important programming languages.

Fortran.   Fortran has been standardized three times already. The first two standards were published in 1966 by ANSI, and in 1972 by ISO. They define the language presently known as Fortran 66, and its basic subset. The third standard was published in 1978 by ANSI, and in 1979 by ISO. It defines the language known as Fortran 77, which includes in its own definition the basic subset. The key concern in the whole standardization process has been that of compatibility; the first standard has been described as a catalog of all implementation mistakes in existing compilers. John Larmouth needs more than 50 pages to describe how one can program in Fortran and still strictly follow this standard [Lar73]. Although almost all existing compilers claim to conform to this standard (while adding numerous "improvements"), it has been suggested that the only statement actually processed in the same way by all compilers is CONTINUE. It is unfortunate that standardizers were too timorous, that, worrying about invalidating any existing compiler, they did not immediately remove from the language constructs that were already obsolete. However, the net effect of this very first standard has been extremely positive on the portability of programs written in

Fortran, even if some of the standard's features are completely unknown to most programmers. (For example, this standard does not specify that local variables of a subroutine retain their value from one activation to another; thus it does *not* preclude a stack implementation. Who knows that?)

The first revision of the 1966 standard quickly turned out to be a definition of a new language, which kept the name of Fortran and retained the preceding standard as a subset, in order to allow programs written in 1960 to run unchanged in 1980. It is well known that languages defined by committees do not have the same qualities as languages defined by small teams or, even better, by a single person. Fortran 77 is not an exception: It is a complicated, hybrid language that contains constructs of a very low level, together with so-called structured constructs. John Larmouth needs 46 pages to explain how to write portable programs in Fortran 77 [Lar81].

The X3J3 committee of ANSI, responsible for the development of Fortran, is presently working on the next revision of the standard. This language will still be called Fortran, but will be even larger and more complex than its predecessor. Thus it is anticipated [BrA80] that modules will be defined in addition to a kernel, in order to distinguish (1) new features, (2) features that should disappear in the next revision, and (3) features specialized for some applications.

With some extrapolation, one may anticipate that the next revision will be completed in 1986, with another following in 1994. At that point, some features will at last disappear from Fortran: the arithmetic IF statement, assigned and computed GOTOs, and statement-defined functions. Still, the new-features module seems to be growing, and the Fortran of 1994 may be bigger and more unwieldy than any language built before now.

Cobol. Cobol too has been standardized twice, in 1968 and 1974 by ANSI, in 1972 and 1978 by ISO. A third standard is under study and is expected in several years. In contrast to Fortran, in standardizing Cobol, compatibility was not a priority, and the standard is not monolithic. It is made of 12 independent modules, of which three are mandatory, each having two levels, and the remaining nine are optional—one of those having one level, the others two. Between minimal Cobol, with only the three mandatory modules at the lower level, and maximal Cobol, with the 12 modules at the upper level, there is as much difference as between Basic and PL/1, yet both are called Cobol. In fact, this technique of defining a standard as a "kit" has led to 104,976 official distinct variants of the same language and constitutes the main obstacle to portability of any software programmed in Cobol [HoH79]. One aid to portability we shall mention is the set of validation and certification tools for Cobol implementations that was developed by the U.S. Navy for internal use, but whose results are in the public domain.

Algol. In the case of *Algol 60*, ISO's role was only to endorse the existing report and its subsequent revisions and modifications. The reader may be surprised to know that there is still, in 1986, an ISO experts group dealing with Algol 60, working on the last additions to be made to the "modified" version of the "revised" version of the standard. However, IFIP is trying to obtain ISO's endorsement for the *Algol 68* definition report, though the endorsement is problematic, since ISO is less than convinced of its usefulness.

PL/1. The PL/1 standard is dated 1976 by ANSI and 1979 by ISO. This is a special case, in the sense that the language is considered to be IBM property. Even so, standardizers did not fear to modify the language, and they embarked on a fully formal definition, different from that already done in IBM's Vienna laboratory. The standard definition is consequently both huge and of little use, since the implementations of PL/1 are generally limited to IBM computers. However, a language subset has been defined too, and its standard was completed in 1981. A revision of the main standard should be completed in the next few years, but it is not expected to change the language.

Pascal. The Pascal standard was the first case dealing with a language of limited initial ambitions and designed by one person. It is the first international standard established by an organization different from ANSI (in this case, BSI) and represents one of the most quickly developed standards for a programming language. The work was completed in 1981, simultaneous with the publication of the British standard. The international standard, as well as the national standards of those countries that found it useful to establish one (especially the United States and France), dates from 1983.

Two important conflicts arose during the standardization process, mainly because of the uniqueness of the process. On one hand, it was very difficult to decide whether the standard document should clarify, revise, or extend the existing documents. The result is a document that clarifies and specifies, but which also makes two precise and limited extensions. The second conflict was political—pitting ANSI against the other member bodies of ISO—resulting perhaps from the fact that for the first time a standard was presented by an organization other than ANSI. There is still no international agreement, and although ANSI finally accepted the ISO draft standard, the American standard differs from the international one.

Ada. The Ada standard is the first example of a standard dealing with a language not yet fully implemented. It is also the first standard established using the method, proper to ANSI, of the so-called canvass, where the technical work is done outside ANSI and later approval is based on the competence and composition of the committees and individuals who participated in the definition process. This method is uncommon for programming languages, and it raises obvious problems, as demonstrated, for example, by the negative vote of an organization as respected as ACM [Ske82]. The publication of the ANSI standard for Ada, in 1983, is an example, the first, of a standard document that is vague and yet was hastily approved. But the weight of the U.S. Department of Defense prevailed over the opinion of individuals, however respected they may have been [Hoa81, LeS82]. Within ISO, the work on Ada is only beginning; problems with a trademark promise trouble. If the experts group (or working group) does not feel obliged to follow the form and contents of the ANSI standard exactly, there is little chance of having an international standard before 1987, which should leave some time for the language to be developed and for full implementations to multiply.

4.2.3 Comparison of the main languages
used for writing portable software

Some general observations. A full comparison of higher-level programming languages will not be attempted here. First, those that are used for programming portable software are relatively few, and we shall exclude those that are not widespread enough to have seen frequent use—for example, Algol 60, PL/1, Simula 67, Algol 68, Fortran 77, and Ada—whatever their intrinsic qualities may be in other respects, including even their portability. Maybe in a few years, we could add Fortran 77 and Ada to the languages we are going to consider, and exclude some of those we consider here and now.

Not all the characteristics of programming languages affect portability—far from it. Control structures, for example, play no special role. The most important aspects are described below.

Data types, especially numeric. The precision of operations is the most important aspect in portability, especially the means provided by the language for controlling this precision. Available structured types affect portability only if a language change during transportation is anticipated; here there is the risk that the same means of expression is not everywhere available. Otherwise, data types intervene only in a very indirect way, in the sense that they make software building more or less easy, and consequently they affect the qualities that make software transport more or less desirable—i.e., reliability, fault-tolerance, adaptability, and efficiency.

Text-handling features. The character set has a direct effect on portability, and in this case the best choice is that of a character set defined by the language itself, even if it should be simulated on some computers. No designer of an important language has made this accommodation, although several have used existing sets like EBCDIC (PL/1 and Snobol4) or ASCII (Ada). The presence of character strings in the language itself and the presence of a catenation operator are important only in that they provide expressive tools, in the same way as do structured types.

Access to data representation. Such means are often needed in order to build software implementations of reasonable efficiency, especially for dealing with very large complex structures. If the language itself provides some means of access, the level of access has a great influence on portability: With low-level means, one must redefine that part of the software product in order to adapt it to a new implementation, while with higher-level means this adaptation is done automatically. The most unfavorable situation, of course, occurs when the language provides nothing at all. A first solution for the software implementor is to choose to simulate the means of access by deterring the natural use of some language features, which may lead to an extremely inefficient implementation, may prevent portability for very subtle reasons, or may do both. Another solution is to use subprograms in machine language, which at least has the advantage of encapsulating the unportable parts of the implementation.

Input-output. The first point is that input-output should be completely defined: A given implementation should not have the ability to implement some aspects of input-output in an ill-defined way because of their omission from the language. Another problem is the expressive power a language provides, since it varies widely. Direct or indexed input-output are not frequently found in programming languages, and if an implementation adds them, programs that use these features will not be portable. Finally, an important part of the format of the printed results is often imprecisely defined, mainly in case of error, overflow, or default choice, and this is one of the areas most prone to modification during transport, even without any language change.

Access to host-system resources. Much remains to be done if the various concepts implemented by operating systems are to be compatible; we cite here particularly the calling conventions. The most important matter not linked to the implementation of a language itself in this respect is that of file access. The very notion of a file differs in meaning from one operating system to another, and the file name is presently an entirely unportable concept. For some systems, the name is only a link between the internal object of the program and its external descriptor. For others, the name describes the access mode, the device, and all file characteristics, and consequently it avoids the use of a descriptor. For still other systems, the name denotes a node in a hierarchical directory, which provides for accessing all files defined in the system. Aside from this problem, other utilities provided by the system raise fewer difficulties, in the sense that they are generally inaccessible from within programs. The persons who install the software product in a new system have to struggle with the link editor, the file-handling system, the batch monitor, etc., but they should not have to modify the programs themselves.

The languages themselves

Fortran. Fortran 66 (i.e., Fortran IV, or simply Fortran) is probably the programming language most frequently used in writing portable software, to the extent that one often hears such statements as "My program is written in Fortran, so it's portable." The advantage of Fortran is, of course, that it is the only language whose availability can be hoped for on almost any computer (*not* including personal computers). But Fortran has two major disadvantages that necessitate huge efforts from numerous implementors of portable software and have even defeated many transportations, some after several months of work.

The first disadvantage is the poverty of the language, which makes the building of any nonnumeric software product a tedious and delicate operation: There is no data-structuring mechanism other than the array; no characters, no strings; no constant definitions; no structured control statements. There is complicated, clumsy, and inefficient input-output; insecure communication between subprograms, be it via parameters or common blocks; insecure access to arrays; and so on. This being so, building a portable program in Fortran is a discouraging task, especially if one wants to conform strictly to the standard, which is as it should be for a program that is to be portable.

The second disadvantage is a consequence of the first: There probably are no two Fortran implementations that process exactly the same language. This is obvious in the case of the various extensions provided by every implementor, but even more troublesome is the fact that features included in the standard sometimes take different meanings in an implementation. The standard is incomplete or contradictory in places, and it is not always made clear what a correct implementation should do. Anyway, one is often forced to use extensions—for example, to detect an end-of-file while reading or even to handle characters.

For those who want to use Fortran at any cost, two solutions are available: The first is to use tools for automatic verification or conversion (as we have seen in Sec. 3.2), which attempt to enforce the use of a Fortran subset found everywhere or to convert an "extended" construct accepted by one implementation into a construct accepted by another implementation. The second solution is to use Fortran only as the base language of a language pyramid, either by the telescopic-generation method (see Sec. 4.1) in which Fortran is used for programming the most basic, thus the simplest, tool; or by use of a preprocessor (see Sec. 4.4), which converts the additional constructs into basic Fortran. Several examples of these solutions will be shown in Chaps. 6 and 7.

Compared with Fortran, the other languages used for writing portable software still play a minor role, but the situation seems to be changing, and five other languages are used more and more often in certain applications.

Cobol.   Cobol is still the only language most programmers think of as suitable for business applications. And it is a language most hope to find on any computers intended for use in business. The disadvantages of this language are similar to those of Fortran: The subset common to all implementations conforming to the standard is pitifully small, and the tools provided by the language itself are relatively cumbersome and insufficient. The situation is further complicated by the existence of two successive, incompatible standards [Tri78a]. Techniques used to get around these difficulties include voluntary limitation to the smallest usable subset and the use of tools for the automatic conversion and verification of programs. Since the difficulties in Cobol are even greater than in Fortran, and since the language is even less suited for writing programs outside of its normal area of application, Cobol is not, to our knowledge, presently used in building portable programs. Its main use is in turnkey systems that are programmed to work on a given machine and system.

Basic.   Basic was for a long time the only language that could be guaranteed available on personal computers, and it has been used for writing portable software only for those machines. Difficulties encountered are much the same as those we described in the case of Fortran, compounded by the fact that the language is more impoverished in its common version than is Fortran and the various implementations are more incompatible. (It is often said that there are as many forms of Basic as there are implementations.) The present standard (ANSI 1978, ISO 1980) describes a language that no longer has much resemblance to what was designed 19 years ago. The standard describes a language that is no longer simple, and is implemented nowhere; ironically the standard preserves all the design shortcomings of the original language. The next standard, expected in a few years, is unlikely to improve the situation, and it seems that Basic will be superseded by Pascal, except maybe in such applications as computer video games, which must run on extremely small microcomputers.

Lisp. In the special area for which it is suited, Lisp has often been used as a tool for writing portable software. Difficulties encountered do not come from the expressive power of the language, which is flawless (if one likes it, of course), but from the complete lack of any standard. Lisp software implementors cannot rely on anything, and they are generally not afraid to write (in Lisp, of course) an automatic conversion tool (see Sec. 3.5.1). The conversion work is made considerably simpler by the identity of notation and representation between programs and the data they process, one of the most original and useful characteristics of the language.

Pascal. Pascal is one of the two languages whose usage is increasing in portable programming. Its advantages are that it provides a large part of what seems to be needed for many types of software, while still remaining simple, and that it is now almost as ubiquitous as Fortran. Its standardization came relatively fast, and software builders tend to conform to the standard. (One thorny problem we might mention is the discrepancy between the ANSI and the ISO standards.) The weaknesses of Pascal are the lack of powerful tools for string processing, the lack of any nonsequential input-output, and the fact that the language is not really suited for writing anything other than nonmodular programs—weaknesses that BSI and ISO are in the process of addressing. Except for the last point, Pascal's advantages over Fortran and Basic are obvious. Since languages as unsuited as Basic and APL have been used in office data processing, Pascal should have its chance too.

C. The second language whose usage is increasing is C, but the reasons are less its own intrinsic qualities than the qualities of the Unix system, which it helped to build. This system itself is rather portable, as we shall see in Sec. 7.2, and the C language is the privileged tool for writing any software product intended to work within this system. Inconveniences of the language are the almost complete lack of error checking by C compilers (this is generally considered a feature of the language) and the "fuzziness" of the official definition. The best solution to any problems is to use the Lint filter (see Sec. 3.3.3), which flags all dangerous or unportable constructs, thus going through the checks the compiler itself does not make. The influence of the language was minimal until recently. Although its use is clearly spreading, as evidenced by the fact that some operating systems for microcomputers are being rewritten in C, nothing can be stated with certainty about its future use, and opinions differ widely about its suitability for writing portable system software [FeG84]. (This is the only subject dealt with in the book upon which the authors have divergent opinions.)

4.3 The use of extensible languages

4.3.1 Some general observations

The idea of an extensible language is one of the solutions proposed for dealing with the general problem raised by the multitude of applications of the computer: Either one defines a new and different language for every new application area or one defines a universal language. The latter solution led to PL/1, Algol 68, and Ada, which are large, complicated languages, extremely costly to implement.

If one defines and uses a multitude of specialized languages, the cost of their independent implementation on every computer becomes obviously unaffordable, and three solutions may be considered: (1) automate the production of an implementation for a new language on a new computer (see Sec. 4.4); (2) facilitate the transportation of the implementation from one computer to another (see Chaps. 5 and 6); or (3) allow the definition and implementation of the new language by the users themselves, using an existing core language. This last idea is the subject of this section.

According to Solntseff and Yezerski [SoY74], an extensible language must provide for the introduction of new data types, new operations on objects of these types, new modes of flow control for primitive or extended parts of the language, and new statement types and syntactic forms.

All these capabilities do not necessarily occur at the same time; i.e., the boundary between an ordinary language and an extended one is very fuzzy. Any language that contains the concept of the subprogram could be considered extensible, since it provides for the definition of new operations. In fact, some pseudolanguages have been defined as sets of subprograms to be included in host language, and thus they are extensions of these languages. But all languages that provide type constructors, like Pascal, and all those that allow the definition of new operators or the overloading of existing operators, like Algol 68, Ada, and even Snobol4, can be categorized as extensible languages. Thus, the custom is to call "extensible" only those languages that provide mechanisms for the programmer to change both syntax and semantics. It is revealing that no really important language belongs in this category.

Five categories of extensible languages may be distinguished, depending on the phase of the translation process where the extension occurs [SoY74]:

- Category 1: The extension occurs during lexical analysis (scanning) with textual macroprocessing, coming back to the base language, as in PL/1.
- Category 2: The extension occurs during syntax analysis (parsing), with syntactic macroprocessing, also coming back to the base language, as in some preprocessors.
- Category 3: The extension occurs during intermediate-language generation, with the addition of a subtree to a syntax tree, as when using subprograms defined in the program.
- Category 4: The extension occurs during intermediate-language analysis, with

the transformation of extended subtrees into unextended ones, as in some optimization phases of ordinary compilers.

- Category 5: The extension occurs during object-code generation, where the extensions are defined in terms of the object language, in contrast with all the other extensions, which come back to the base language or to one of its representations.

4.3.2 Examples

Extensions of the first two categories distinguished by Solntseff and Yezerski can in fact, from the user's point of view, be grouped together. They are more-or-less sophisticated means, included in, or overlaid on, the base language, which always allow the same thing: to define, for one program, new notations expressed in the base language. The best-known example is provided by PL/1, and it exhibits the limitations of this idea: One can parameterize a program, define numerous, and more-or-less convenient, abbreviations, but one can never add any new expressive power to the language.

The most frequent use of such a method occurs outside the frame of extensible languages. It is seen in the numerous preprocessors that convert a text, written in a so-called structured extension of Fortran, into simple Fortran (see Sec. 4.4). One could call this extensibility if users could, at the beginning of a program, define the new constructs they wanted to add to the language, and the equivalent constructs in the base language. This mechanism has often been proposed as a way for doing anything, while avoiding the definition of new programming languages. Such claims have largely been abandoned, and it is clear that despite extensions of this type a language can provide only what it already contains.

Two simple examples may be used to show both the capabilities and the limitations of extensions made by lexical or syntactic macroprocessing. For instance, one can add the complex type feature to a language without complex values. It can be done by replacing any reference to a complex variable with references to a two-component array, and any access to the real and imaginary part with access to elements of this array. The expansion of arithmetic operations may be more difficult, and the relative convenience of extension definitions depends greatly on the capabilities of the mechanisms that are provided. Unfortunately, the mechanisms of extension are generally very primitive, and not well integrated with the programming mechanisms of the language. This means that the work needed for programming extensions is not trivial and that the benefits the programmer is supposed to obtain from extensibility are at least partly obliterated by the supplementary work needed to provide it.

Another idea of an extension is to add a generalized repetitive statement, similar to that of Algol 68, for example, to a language that provides only an iterative statement:

```
while condition do statement-list done
```

To program such an extension necessitates great expressive power, since it is necessary to generate some text fragments, written in base language, only if some parts of the extended statement are present. It may be also necessary to generate local variables or labels. Several remarks may be made about this example:

1. The repetitive statement usually is found in programming languages, and the compiler is thus able to generate code using the best capabilities of the target computer, especially registers and specialized instructions (decrement, test and branch, for example). Those benefits are lost in the present case.

2. An extensible language is, in theory, useful as a means for allowing users to define a language well suited to their needs. But are the forms of repetitive statements really so very different, suited to such different domains, that programming important applications becomes unfeasible if one form is available instead of another?

3. Another advantage of an extensible language is to allow the implementation of a very simple base language, easing the building and transportation of this implementation. But we just saw that the mechanisms of extensibility must be complex and efficient in order to be of any interest.

Extensions of category 3, which are processed during the phase of the compiler that generates intermediate language (preferably in tree form), correspond rather well to what is done in a limited fashion in nonextensible languages. To add new data structures necessitates mechanisms very similar to those provided by all languages with type constructors, like Algol 68, Pascal, and Ada. New operations, on the other hand, are added by defining new syntactic constructs that call subprograms, while in ordinary languages the syntactic form of the subprogram call is frozen, and is generally very restricted.

Coming back to our two examples, it can be seen that, in an extensible language of category 3, the definition of the type complex would be done in a way very similar to what is done in Pascal. Defining operators on objects of type complex would activate overloading and "genericity" mechanisms similar to those found in Algol 68 and Ada, two languages not well known for their ease of implementation. The definition of a generalized repetitive statement can be done more easily than in extensible languages of the first two categories, by calling a procedure with a variable name, three expressions, and a statement sequence as parameters. Extensible languages of this category generally provide, through macroprocessing, a choice between the call to a closed subprogram and the in-line expansion of the call. Anyway, the limitations are the same as before, in the sense that complex mechanisms of extension allow the expression of the new constructs only in terms of the base language.

Extensions of category 4, which use methods of pattern matching and macro-substitution in the intermediate language, differ, from the user's point of view, only marginally from extensions of the third category. The means for defining extensions are very similar, and the capabilities and limitations are the same.

Extensions of category 5, which are processed during target code generation, are the only ones where the semantics is defined using the target language and not the base language. In order to define the meaning of an extension, the user, instead of providing its equivalent in base language, must specify what instruction sequence will be generated by the compiler. Of course, such a mechanism is the only one that allows an actual increase in the expressive power of the language. It is possible, for example, when defining the generalized repetitive statement, to use the most appropriate instructions of the target computer.

On the other hand, extensions of this category demand from the user a high-level competence in the area of language definition, which is not within everybody's reach (but this is true of any extension), as well as in the area of object-language generation. It appears that the work of defining extensions should be entrusted to a professional implementor, and should not be done by every programmer in front of every program. Moreover, the mere idea of a base language loses much of its appeal: Since one can define some constructs in terms of the target computer language, why not do this for all constructs? It becomes clear that the idea of an extensible language blends into that of a compiler-writing system, as we shall see in Sec. 4.4.

4.3.3 An assessment

The concept of an extensible language suffers from several fundamental limitations, which were revealed in the preceding section and are summarized below:

1. The extension modes generally available are only means for abbreviating or paraphrasing constructs of the base language. They cannot really increase the expressive power of the language, and they run the risk of lessening the implementation efficiency. They have no power to add new primitives to the base language.

2. Extension mechanisms, which are similar to those used by macroprocessors (see Sec. 3.1), are generally very costly, both in time and storage. The cost of compiling a program that uses many extensions may become prohibitive, and the object program generated by the compiler is generally of very poor quality.

3. Designing a new programming language is one of the most difficult tasks in all computer science. Thus it seems rather absurd to expect a programmer to redesign a part of the language in front of each program. Of course, one could imagine that some set of extensions could be defined once and for all, for some problem category and some user group, but this leads to a rather cumbersome and very inefficient way of defining a new special-purpose programming language.

This being considered, it comes as little surprise that, after flourishing as a seemingly promising area of research about 10 years ago [ChS69, Sch71], extensible languages today seem to have almost completely disappeared. Some of the ideas they contained have been reused in languages like Algol 68 and Ada, but that is the only trace of them left. As Jean Sammet remarks [Sam81a], the claims for extensible languages were so great, compared with the actual achievements, that the viability of the whole area of research was destroyed, perhaps permanently.

Extensible languages could conceivably make the production of portable software easier in two ways. First, one must assume that it is possible to define by extension a special-purpose programming language especially suited to writing the intended software product. In order for this product to be portable, one of two conditions should be satisfied: (1) the base language is implemented on many computers or (2) the base language is not fixed, and one can choose any of those available on the target computer. Moreover, it is necessary for the extension mechanisms themselves to be implemented on many computers or to be built in a portable way.

In order to circumvent these conditions, which would be very difficult to satisfy, and in practice are false, mechanisms very similar to those described in the preceding section are used. The basic difference is that, instead of being integrated into the exaggerated idea of an extensible language, they become parts of compiler-writing systems, or they constitute general-purpose tools, or they are defined in an ad hoc way, in order to make some specific software product portable.

4.4 The use of augmented languages

4.4.1 Some general observations

The concepts of an augmented language and of a preprocessor bear some relation with those of an extensible language and a macroprocessor, respectively. Thus it is necessary to establish a clear distinction between these concepts, and this section will attempt to do so.

In the case of an extensible language, the implementor provides a base language as well as mechanisms of extension, and it is left to the user to define the language he or she wants. Thus two individual users may well use different languages descended from the same base language. It is even possible for a single user to define several different extended languages for different applications.

In the case of an augmented language, the implementor provides a single language, implemented using a preprocessor, which transforms the augmented language into an existing base language. Thus all users are given the same language. The benefits of this approach are that it makes the implementor's work easier, since a preprocessor is much simpler to use than a compiler, and at the same time it makes the user's job easier, since the augmented language presents only a small number of new concepts to be learned and added to a language already familiar. Moreover, a program written in the base language is normally accepted by the preprocessor, which does not transform it, thus providing upward compatibility with existing programs.

The preprocessor of an augmented language is an incomplete translator. Its source language is a mix of constructs from the base language and new constructs. Its object language is the base language itself. Moreover, the translator is frequently written in the base language, as we shall see below, thus yielding a translator of the form [AL + BL, BL, BL] (see Sec. 5.1.2 for explanation of the notation). All constructs which are not recognized as parts of the augmented language are left untouched and simply copied.

The preprocessor may be implemented using a macroprocessor (see Sec. 3.1), if the constructs of the augmented language have a simple enough syntax, but this is not necessary. On the other hand, constructs included in the augmented language may provide macroprocessing capabilities, in which case the preprocessor, among other functions, plays the role of a macroprocessor.

Because of the dynamic state of our terminology, the term "preprocessor" has come to be used to describe two other things that have nothing to do with augmented languages. This term serves to denote the initial—and optional—macroprocessing phase that exists in some compilers—for example, for PL/1 (see Sec. 4.3.2) and for C. Here the idea is closely related to that of an extensible language. On the other hand, some automatic conversion tools (see Sec. 3.2) are also called "preprocessors." They allow, from a source that contains constructs suited to several different variants of the same language, the extraction of those that suit a specific variant. One cannot pretend that the source is written in an augmented language, which would serve to hide the differences between variants, since here the existence of all the variants must be anticipated by the user.

4.4.2 Examples

In most cases, the base language, extended using a preprocessor, is Fortran. When structured programming became fashionable, a dubious approach was used, adding a few control structures to an old language with many problems. It was supposed that preserving prior programmer training and compatibility with old Fortran programs was more economical than using a new language. This led, in the early seventies, to the proliferation of "structured Fortrans," hastily defined to allow programmers to avoid GOTOs, which would automatically yield "structured", i.e., better, programs. Several dozen preprocessors were built for this purpose, and some have been very heavily used. Most have fallen into oblivion, though many of the ideas they tried to add to Fortran have carried over into Fortran 77.

One of the most successful of these preprocessors—probably the best known since it is the best described [Ker75]—is called "Ratfor," an abbreviation of *rational Fortran* (which implies that Fortran itself is not a rational language). The name is used for denoting both the preprocessor and the language it implements. It has twice been used as a portability tool: for a set of various software tools [KeP76] and for the first implementation of the language Icon (see Sec. 6.3). One may note that Kernighan and Plauger rewrote their book, using Pascal in the new edition [KeP82], and that in the present Icon implementation, Ratfor has been replaced by C, which leads one to suppose that the experimentation with Ratfor as a portability tool has not been a complete success.

Some of the additions to Fortran by Ratfor are of interest when discussing portability. Those that add control structures (inherited from the language C) have only an indirect effect, in the sense that they can improve a program's readability, and consequently its reliability and adaptability. The addition of definition capabilities, used mainly for constants, allows easy parameterization of the programs. Fortran input-output, although still usable, is, in fact, replaced by something reminiscent of Pascal's textfile handling. Moreover, a type character is added, with a standard internal representation, the conversions to and from the external representation being handled by input-output on textfiles.

The Ratfor preprocessor is a program of moderate length (1500 lines), distributed in Ratfor and easily transported thanks to its Fortran version. Its performance, however, is unfortunately very poor, in part because of Fortran, in part because of poor programming [CoK78], and the transported version must be immediately improved (see in Sec. 6.3 the case study of the language Icon). Ratfor served as a basis for an experiment in software adaptation [Han77] that yielded another preprocessor [Ratsno + Snobol4, Ratfor+Fortran, Snobol4] (see Sec. 5.1.2 for explanation of the notation). This later preprocessor does not seem to have been used in any significant way.

Among other preprocessors, used in order to augment base languages other than Fortran, we may mention MAP [Com79], whose base language is Pascal and which is written in Pascal. This preprocessor, which adds several disparate capabilities to Pascal (expression-defined constants, environment inquiries, conditional compilation, inclusion of fragments external to the program, and macro-substitution), is a portable tool rather than a tool of portability.

4.4.3   An assessment

The idea of using an augmented language and its associated preprocessor to make software portability easier comes from the basic idea of programming this software in a widely implemented language, combined with the observation that the most widely used languages are imperfectly suited to the construction of large, general-purpose, easily parameterized software products.

It is a much less ambitious idea than that of extensible languages, but it might be called naive: A language such as Fortran is unsuited to programming applications other than those for which it was designed, i.e., numeric applications. Its insufficiency for business applications and systems programming, to mention only two cases in which portability is especially efficacious, stems above all from its lack of facility in handling data types and data structures (see Sec. 4.2.3).

As for the preprocessors, since their object language is nothing less than the base language, they cannot make up Fortran's shortcomings in the area of data structures. Even the addition of one new basic type is not easy, as demonstrated by the Ratfor experience. The positive effects of augmented languages are consequently limited to the areas of control structures, parameterization, and program structure.

The help that a preprocessor provides in portability thus centers on two points:

1. Programs written using a preprocessor can be of better quality than if they were written in the base language, since they can be better structured, more modular, and better parameterized. This improvement, however, is not automatic, and takes a conscious effort on the part of the implementor of the portable software product.

2. The preprocessor may possibly be provided in several compatible versions that accept the same source language, but translate it into different variants of the same base language, for different implementations. Thus it can do the work of an automatic conversion tool (see Secs. 3.2 and 3.5.1).

   By adding a few features to an existing language, most efforts in establishing augmented languages have tried to avoid the bottom-line fact that redesigning a language is an extremely difficult task. There have been some modest successes, but the limitations of the base language, and the imperfect fit between features of the augmented and the base languages, are problems that have never been entirely overcome. Consequently, augmented languages play a minor role in portability.

4.5 The use of compiler-writing systems

4.5.1 Some general observations

It is not very easy to state precisely what is meant by the term "compiler-writing system," where "compiler" is often replaced by "translator," and where the entire term itself is often replaced by such other terms as "compiler generator," "meta-compiler," and "compiler-compiler." The subject of compiler-writing systems, although vast, complex, and of current interest, is partly or entirely neglected by textbooks on compilation, even the most recent ones (see Aho and Ullman [AhU77], Cunin et al. [CGV80], Berry [Ber81], and Waite and Goos [WaG84], for example). The first and only survey paper on the topic dates back to 1968 [FeG68], even though an entire issue of *IEEE Computer* was more recently devoted to it [Aho80]. Although relatively ignored by the current literature, compiler-writing systems are the focus of much research and development, often successful, and specialized papers describing certain aspects or some specific systems appear frequently.

The concept itself of a "compiler-writing system" has never been realized. A compiler is a program, written in some writing language WL, which serves to translate any program, written in some source language SL, into an equivalent program, written in some object language OL. The most general system should be able to generate the compiler [SL, WL, OL] automatically with the only data being the descriptions of the three languages SL, WL, and OL. The existing systems are only rather distant approximations of this general idea.

Another way to consider the question is to draw a parallel: A compiler is a software system which, given the description of a program in a suitable language, is able to translate it into runnable form for a given computer. By analogy, we can call the "compiler-compiler" a software system which, given the description of a compiler in a suitable language, is able to translate it for running on a given computer. The term comes from Brooker et al. [BMM63] and has been used mainly in British literature.

The two terms introduced here serve to show that there can be several very different ways to consider the problem. The first way is to emphasize the characteristic languages of the compiler that will be generated (see Chap. 5), as well as the descriptive aspect of the data provided by the compiler writers. The second approach is to emphasize the language used for writing the description and its operational aspect. The boundary between these two approaches is not as sharp as one might believe, especially since the first one must accommodate numerous compromises with respect to its basic idea.

The first aspect of a completely general compiler-writing system to be abandoned by all systems is the parameterization of WL, the writing language of the generated compiler. Some systems, generally very incomplete, may allow the parts of the compiler description that are expressed in some programming language to choose the language. Most often, however, the choice is made from the start by the system implementation, since the generated compiler is very often a predefined program driven by system-generated tables.

More general systems, which are at present experimental, are consequently used for accepting as data the descriptions of languages SL and OL and for generating a compiler [SL, WL, OL], where WL is always the same. The major problem, then, is the means of description for programming languages. The general theory of phrase-structure grammars, and especially the simpler cases of regular grammars and context-free grammars, has been used for more than 20 years to provide satisfactory formal notations for describing lexical and syntactic aspects of programming languages [HoU69]. Intensive searches in this area have led to satisfactory methods for automatically generating lexical analyzers and syntactic analyzers from formal descriptions. We now know how to generate efficient analyzers of adequate scope, and the corresponding techniques have progressed to production quality (see Secs. 3.4.2 and 3.4.3). It would be unusual today to program a parser by hand, unless it were a recursive descent parser [DaM81]. The processing and recovery of syntax errors is the only area where progress remains to be made [GHJ79].

Difficulties are much greater, and research is much less advanced, in the domain of semantics, to the point that the boundary between syntax and semantics has often been referred to as that which we know how to formalize versus that which we must program directly. For a long time, compiler-writing systems have been used for automatically generating only the scanner and the parser, the remaining parts of the compiler being provided as semantic actions, expressed in some specific programming language, which the system (or even the user) inserts into the compiler at the proper places. In such systems, only a part of SL is described, the remainder of SL and all of OL being described only implicitly. Only during the last few years have real approaches been made toward the ideal system we mentioned at the beginning of this section. Systems are now being designed where the descriptive aspect of data prevails over the operational aspect.

First, semantic formalisms as satisfactory as those that exist for syntax are necessary. At present, we are far from this goal, and compiler-writing-systems designers are choosing between several competing methods [Jon80]. The formal definition of the semantics of a programming language may be done according to numerous methods [MLB76], of which the three most common are given here:

1. "Operational semantics," which describes the meaning of language constructs in terms of an abstract machine, being itself described in natural language. The most accomplished example is the Vienna development method [BjJ78].

2. "Axiomatic definition," which consists more in giving the fundamental properties of constructs than in actually defining them [Hoa69, HoW73].

3. "Denotational semantics," which associates with each language construct the abstract mathematical object that is its meaning [Gor79].

The first method of semantic definition has not been used much in compiler-writing systems, other than in the very ambitious MUG1 system of the Technical University of Munich. The second method does not seem to define completely enough to be useful here. The third is beginning to be used, and it is the only one for which experimental compiler-writing systems have been built with purely descriptive data. Finally, a very popular method generally serves to formalize and simplify the relations between lexical and syntactic descriptions and the programmed semantic actions. This is the method of affix [Kos71a] and attribute [Knu68] grammars, already mentioned in Sec. 3.4.4 and used in several operational compiler-writing systems.

4.5.2 Examples

The techniques that are used in the generators for the various parts of a compiler, generators that together constitute a compiler-writing system, have been described—somewhat superficially—in Sec. 3.4. Here we will take the point of view of a user of such a system in order to show, in some simple examples, the work that must be done by the user and the extent to which the system helps in building portable software. We distinguish three different systems, categorized according to the increasing help they provide for building compilers. We avoid the use of the term "compiler-compiler," since it is a poorly understood term, used for describing almost anything—a compiler-writing language, a portable compiler, an actual compiler generator. . . .

Compiler-writing languages. By "compiler-writing languages" we do not mean medium- or high-level programming languages well suited to programming compilers (for example, BCPL, Bliss, XPL, Pascal, or C), but languages that are more descriptive than imperative, that already contain some very specific operations as primitive operations, and that often cannot be used for any applications other than compiler construction.

Floyd-Evans productions [Eva64] are an old but complete example of such a language. A production is a statement of this language, which can be labeled and whose first part represents a configuration of the parser stack. If this configuration occurs at the top of the stack, actions described in the remaining parts of the production are executed, otherwise control falls to the next production. Possible actions include modifying the stack (pushing or popping elements), generating object-text components according to various rules, calling the scanner (the symbol just obtained is stacked), or transferring control to another production. All these actions, as needed, may be combined in the same production.

A sequence of Floyd-Evans productions can therefore constitute a compiler or, more precisely, the first phase of a compiler, since the actions provided are not powerful enough to allow semantic analysis and code generation. The language they define is both primitive and undisciplined: It is easy to write a sequence of productions; it is difficult to assert that this sequence will analyze all of a given source language. While the main advantage of parser generators is precisely that they guarantee, by their construction, that the generated parser conforms to the described language, a language such as Floyd-Evans productions leaves its user without this guarantee.

The compiler-writing languages designed later have mainly dealt with what follows parsing: semantic analysis, intermediate-code generation, table handling, more-or-less complex tree handling, semantic attribute handling, etc. Thus they are used as a complement to systems like those covered in the next section, and when scanning and parsing are supposed to be automatically processed, they make the programming of semantic actions easier. Programming semantic actions necessitates the expressive power of a higher-level programming language; this means that compiler-writing languages are very close to conventional languages. Differences occur in the primitive actions that are included and in the relative closeness of the actions to the parsing part. The language Jossle, for example [WhP73], is simply a programming language with very restricted control structures, special-purpose data structures, and a set of predefined procedures oriented toward compilation. The systems-writing language provided by the RCC system [NaF80] has an unusual design, mainly because of its very tight links with the system in which it is included. The grammar of the language to be compiled creates high-level control structures, and the various components of the compiler are already mirrored in the true structure of the writing language. The difference between these systems and the systems considered in the next section is mainly a difference of philosophy.

Systems for assisting in compiler writing. In this category we place those systems which, while automating the production of a part of the compiler, leave the burden of programming the remainder entirely to the user, though they might provide some tools to help. Some of these systems constitute relatively well-integrated systems, while others are loosely gathered collections of components.

The best documented in this category of systems is certainly XPL [MKH70]. It is at one and the same time a systems-programming language, a self-compiling compiler for this language, and a parser generator, again programmed in the language. The XPL compiler serves as a model for the generated compilers by providing their skeleton: scanner and parser, both driven by tables that represent the corresponding aspects of the language to be compiled, table housekeeping, error handling, and various utility procedures.

In order to build a compiler for a given language SL, the user must:

1. Define the contents of the scanner tables, if the lexical structure of SL is similar to that of XPL. (Otherwise, the only solution is to rewrite the scanner.)

2. Provide a grammatical description of the language syntax, feed it to the parser generator, and change it until it is accepted (since the parser generation algorithm is somewhat restrictive).

3. Program the semantic actions in XPL.

4. Incorporate the tables generated by the generator, those built by hand, and the semantic actions into the compiler skeleton.

The tools available in the Unix system [Joh80] exhibit a somewhat different approach. They are two independent generators, Lex for scanners and Yacc for parsers. The first relies on regular grammars, the second on LALR grammars. The user provides a formal description of the tokens and grammar of the source language to be compiled, associating actions, programmed in the language C, to each grammatical rule. The use of these tools provides more flexibility than does the use of XPL, and compilers that are more general in scope and more efficient can be generated. On the other hand, the assistance provided the user is rather restricted, since all the rest of the compiler must be programmed by hand. The generated compiler can be rather efficient, but it is not very portable, of course.

The Montreal compiler-writing system [LeB74, BoW78] aims at providing more assistance, in a more flexible framework. It contains a scanner generator, two parser generators (one using the bottom-up method of weak precedence, the other using the top-down method of recursive descent), and a test-program generator. These three generators get their common data from an integrated description of the language to be compiled, in which the semantic actions, programmed in Pascal, can refer to semantic attributes found in the syntax rules. The scanner generator, less general than Lex, chooses from a set of predefined lexical tools, which allow it to describe all languages with keywords or reserved identifiers. Additional tools could be easily integrated into such a system—an error-handling generator, primitives for code generation, constraints on attributes—while maintaining the basic philosophy. However, as in all systems of this category, it is left up to the user to program the whole back end of the compiler.

Compiler-production systems. Systems in this category are much more ambitious than the ones discussed above, since their goal is the complete automation of compiler production. Thus they must address aspects that the other systems ignore entirely. With reference to the construction of the compiler, it is necessary to generate several phases or modules automatically—semantic analysis, intermediate-language generation, global and local optimizations, and machine-code generation. With reference to a user of the system, it is necessary to design formalisms or notations for defining language semantics.

Two different categories of compiler-production systems are the subject of active research at present: those that emphasize the efficiency of the generated compilers and those that stress a formal definition of the source language. Several experimental systems already exist, but it does not seem that any have attained the status of an industrial product.

In systems that stress efficiency of the generated compilers, the compiler phases of main interest deal with optimization and machine-code generation. The generated compilers are produced in several phases, and users must provide descriptive information to generators for each phase. The most important part of the description—and, surprisingly, the least dealt with in the literature—is the complete description of the target-machine language, the properties of its instructions, unusual instruction sequences, etc. Generally, users themselves must provide the instruction sequences that correspond to the various constructs of the source language, a rather informal way of defining semantics.

Among various representatives of this category, we can cite the MUG2 system of the Technical University of Munich [GRW77] and the PQCC system of Carnegie-Mellon University [LCH80], which emphasizes the performance of the generated compiler and the possibility of changing the object language without losing this quality.

In contrast, the systems that are mainly interested in generating a compiler from a formal definition of the source language generally neglect any idea of efficiency. Their aim is to accept as input a combination of the customary syntactic definition and a semantic definition, making use of the known formalisms. Most of these systems give up any idea of describing the object language and generate compilers where this language is decided beforehand. [A general intermediate language (see Sec. 5.2) or even a higher-level language is typically used.] Among these systems we cite NEATS of Aarhus University [Mad80], which uses "extended attribute grammars"; HLP of Helsinki University [Räi80b], which also uses attribute grammars; SIS of Oxford University [Mos75], which relies on denotational semantics and in which the users have nothing to program; and Paulson's system, from Stanford University [Pau82], which combines denotational semantics and attribute grammars.

4.5.3   An assessment

Compiler-writing systems have constituted a flourishing area of research for about 20 years. After having dealt almost exclusively with syntactic aspects, where great success (and industrial-quality products) has been achieved, research has been focused for several years on semantic aspects, optimization, and code generation. It is still too early to predict exactly when the research in the last three areas will bring results of equal quality. But just as the syntactic design of current programming languages takes into consideration the anticipated class of parsers, it is likely that advances in the semantic and generative aspects of compiler-writing systems will impinge on the corresponding aspects of future programming languages.

This does not mean, however, that the implementation of a new programming language, or even of an already well-known language, has become a trivial task. If the most tedious and repetitive aspects of compiler building are now handled by the compiler-writing system, its main contribution is that it guarantees conformity to the user's description of everything it generates. This means that while the most important work in implementation has shifted from the programmer to the language designer, the difficulty of the work, and the care involved, have not diminished much.

From the point of view in which we are interested here—i.e., software portability—the assistance provided by compiler-writing systems is rather limited, except where they are themselves portable. It is not imaginable, for example, for software implementors to choose a programming language not widely available and claim that their product is portable simply because this language can be implemented on other machines using a compiler-writing system.

On the other hand, if this system is portable, it's conceivable that a software implementor might supply possible installers with the software product and a compiler-writing system, as well as the description—suitable to the system—of the language used for programming the product. To install the whole, of course, would be a rather cumbersome operation, warranted only for a very large software product of very great interest. Moreover, interesting side effects might be achieved, since the installer would also benefit from the compiler-writing system and the writing language.

Compiler-writing systems, however, especially complete ones, are not very often portable. In fact, they necessarily refer to a specific object language that will be changed during the transport operation. Moreover, because language descriptions given to the system must themselves refer to the object language, they are not generally portable either. In any event there are no special techniques used; recall those that were briefly mentioned in Sec. 4.1.

In contrast, compiler-writing systems are often used as tools in software portability; they may be involved during a specific phase of the original implementation operation or during a phase of transportation to a new environment. We shall see several examples in Chaps. 6 and 7.

Chapter

5

Language-Implementation Methods

5.1 Introduction

The preceding chapters described the tools, means, and techniques used in transporting software. In this chapter we shall examine how they are used—that is, we shall present the major methods used to implement and install portable software, particularly language translation software. We will first give some definitions and present the formalisms that will be used in this chapter and in the subsequent case studies. We will then discuss some elementary methods of producing language-implementation systems, with a distinction made between translators and interpreters, and conclude the chapter with examples of these methods in use. The case studies of Chap. 6 will further develop the examples and show how the various methods of language implementation may be combined.

5.1.1 Definitions

In the preceding chapters we have already used most of the keywords you will find in this chapter. However, it seems useful to recall their definitions here and to introduce a few new words at the same time. We will not attempt to give really rigorous definitions, and we will assume that it is unnecessary to repeat some of the most basic definitions.

We shall use the term "language-implementation system," or simply "implementation system," to denote any software system that provides a given programming language on a given computer, allowing programs written in the language to run. In the simplest cases—for example, in a compiler that directly generates executable machine language—this system may comprise only one module. We do not take into account here the possible existence of a linkage editor, and we do not consider the specific problems that may be encountered with systems that provide for separate program compilation.

A "translator" takes a program written in a source language as input and translates it into a program having the same meaning but written in an object language. If the source language is a higher-level one, the translator is a "compiler." This definition excludes all assemblers, as well as preprocessors (see Sec. 4.4), and decompilers (see Sec. 3.5.2) from the category of compilers, but it does not exclude, for example, a hypothetical translator from Ada into Basic.

An "interpreter" directly executes its source language, without first translating it into an object language. Some Lisp or APL implementations could be considered to be almost pure interpreters. Most Snobol4 implementations consist of a compiler and an interpreter. The former translates the source language into an interpretable intermediate language (see Secs. 5.2 and 6.3).

It is interesting to notice that what is referred to as a "compiler" is, in fact, very often an implementation system that includes an interpreter. This elementary combination of a compiler and an interpreter will be examined in Sec. 5.4.

A "macroprocessor," as explained in Sec. 3.1, is a text-substitution program, which might be characterized as a specialized interpreter whose purpose is to execute the program represented by the macro calls that occur in its source text.

We have previously (in Sec. 4.2) given the definition of a higher-level programming language (called at times simply a "programming language"), and we shall define auxiliary languages in Sec. 5.2. "Auxiliary languages" will be divided into "writing languages" and "intermediate languages." Note that an intermediate language, which occurs between two phases of an implementation system, is an object language for the first phase and a source language for the second phase. In the rest of this chapter, we shall frequently encounter similar situations, where the same language plays several different roles.

5.1.2 Formalisms

In order to describe specific implementation systems and to facilitate our study of the methods used in these systems, we will need a formal, graphic notation to show the similarities and differences between implementation strategies, the role of each system component, the operations accomplished, and so on, at a glance.

The most frequently used formalism for describing implementation systems is that of Earley and Sturgis [EaS70], called "T-diagrams," derived after several intermediate steps [Bra61, SFR68] from the formalism proposed in 1958 for the Uncol project [SMO58]. We shall use it as is, although we augment it with illustrative arrows to clarify the role of components that might be reused and the processes they undergo. Moreover, we shall use nested elementary schemes as often as possible.

This formalism can be extended to represent compiler-interpreters (in which the compiler is only an auxiliary of the interpreter, and the interpretable intermediate language is invisible from the outside) and to clarify situations where programs are incomplete [Pel80]. These extensions will be used in the next chapter; Fig. 5.1 shows all the notations that will be used in this chapter and the next. In the body of the text, we shall use a linear notation, already seen in Chap. 4; [SL, WL, OL] denotes a translator from SL to OL, written in WL, and

[IL, WL] denotes an interpreter of IL, written in WL. These abbreviated notations will not be mixed.

Note that no specific schema exists for macroprocessors, which are represented as interpreters, for reasons developed in Sec. 3.1. When a set of macro definitions is used for translating an intermediate language consisting of macro calls into machine language—e.g., Janus [HaW78a, Wai77b]—we represent this situation as the interpretation, by the macroprocessor, of the macro definitions. This is demonstrated in Fig. 5.1.

A completely different formalism has been proposed more recently by Rosin [Ros77]. We consider it to be less well adapted to our purposes than T-diagrams,

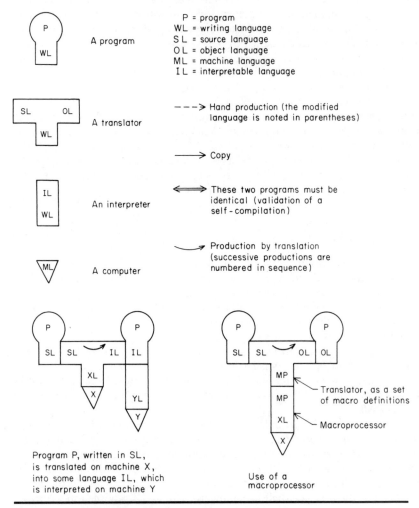

Figure 5.1 Formalisms for describing implementation systems.

and we shall not use it. Both formalisms serve to describe a specific translation or interpretation module, as well as a specific implementation system, perhaps one including multiple combinations. Both representations are used in Fig. 5.2 for the same example, the initial implementation of the BCPL language [Ric71]. This comparison makes the reasons for our choice clear: The Rosin formalism is one-dimensional, and it does not show clearly whether successive translations deal with the object language or the writing language. By contrast, once one is familiar with T-diagrams, the overall structure of an implementation system and the

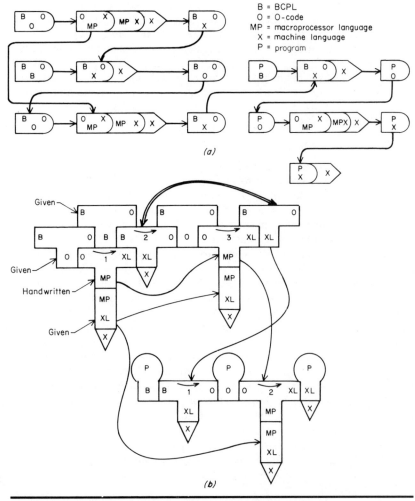

(a)

(b)

Figure 5.2 Comparison of descriptive formalisms: (a) Rosin's formalism; (b) Earley and Sturgis' formalism (T-diagram)

actual work needed for its realization become clear. This results from the fact that T-diagrams are two-dimensional, contrary to Rosin's diagrams. Moreover, they often allow a single compound diagram to describe the full set of operations, thus avoiding many repetitions.

T-diagrams are therefore an invaluable tool for describing language-implementation systems: On the one hand, they provide for the complete description of actual examples of implementation (see Secs. 5.3 and 5.4); on the other hand, they show clearly both the elementary combination operators and the more complex combinations that occur in various implementation systems (see Sec. 6.1).

However, one of the purposes of this chapter is to classify implementation methods for programming languages, and T-diagrams are not suitable for this, mainly because an implementation system may be defined as a sequence of applications, recursive or not, of elementary methods. Thus we need a new formalism, drawn from syntactic diagrams that ordinarily serve to describe the syntax of programming languages. In fact, this formalism is a sort of disciplined flowchart, which allows recursive processes to be described. Figure 5.3 presents the conventions we use, while Figs. 5.4 and 5.5 set forth the various situations to be considered.

5.1.3   Chapter contents

It is difficult to classify elementary methods for translator and interpreter production, since the classification must rely on very different criteria. We finally chose to rely on the basic components of T-diagrams. One may decide at once whether the final product, considered as a whole, should be presented as a translator or as an interpreter. Moreover, all implementation systems can more or less be reduced to complicated combinations of translators and interpreters.

Since these elementary methods are based on the nature of both the writing language and object language involved in the translation, the set of programming languages put into play constitutes the main classification criterion. Other secondary factors intervene in the implementation of a given higher-level programming language on a given computer. We do not consider these other factors separately, and we have not chosen them as main classification criteria, but their importance should not be underestimated.

The next section (Sec. 5.2) describes in detail the idea of an auxiliary language, a concept that plays a central role in the rest of the chapter. The two sections thereafter (Secs. 5.3 and 5.4) consider the elementary methods for producing the two basic components of all implementation systems, the translator and the interpreter, by examining all the possible cases, with the help of the diagrams seen in Figs. 5.4 and 5.5.

Chapter 6 then will demonstrate with actual examples how several elementary methods can be combined into almost any possible implementation system, beginning from any situation. Self-compilation is a special combination that will be considered separately.

It must be noted here that the elementary examples given in Secs. 5.3 and 5.4

will make use of several combinations that will be presented later. The less complex cases are set forth first in order to facilitate an understanding of the cases presented in Chap. 6. Because the subject matter is recursive, it may sometimes be necessary to reread earlier sections in order to understand later ones.

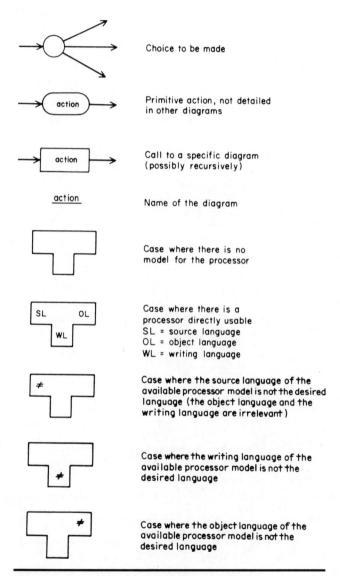

Choice to be made

Primitive action, not detailed in other diagrams

Call to a specific diagram (possibly recursively)

Name of the diagram

Case where there is no model for the processor

Case where there is a processor directly usable
SL = source language
OL = object language
WL = writing language

Case where the source language of the available processor model is not the desired language (the object language and the writing language are irrelevant)

Case where the writing language of the available processor model is not the desired language

Case where the object language of the available processor model is not the desired language

Figure 5.3 Formalisms for classification of methods.

5.2   Auxiliary languages

5.2.1   Introduction

The main goal of an auxiliary language is to facilitate the installation of a given language-implementation system. An auxiliary language is, in general, independent of the source and target languages. It is designed to be much easier to

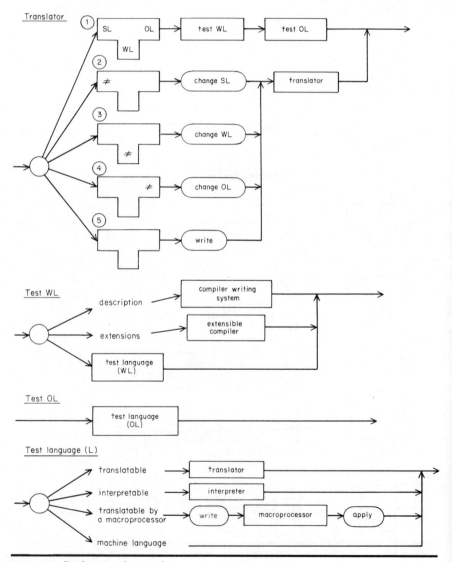

Figure 5.4   Production of a translator.

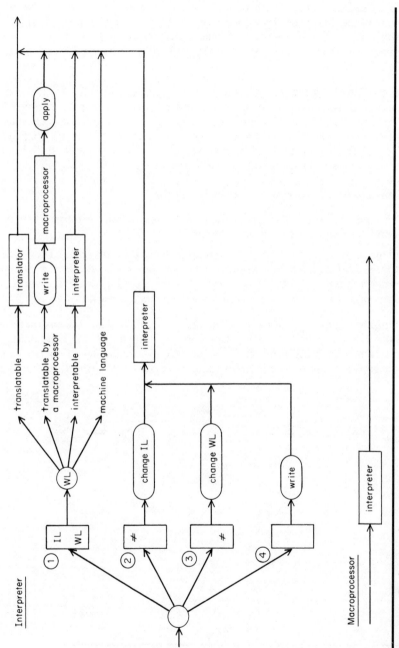

Figure 5.5 Production of an interpreter.

117

implement on a new computer than is the initial language. Two categories of auxiliary languages may be considered: intermediate languages and writing languages. While their uses differ, their form and implementation are often similar. In the case studies presented in Chaps. 6 and 7, we shall see that auxiliary languages occur, in most examples, across different contexts in which translators are built.

Intermediate languages.   A compiler is a large piece of software, which by nature is tightly bound to both a language and a computer. Compiler writers may divide their work into two or more independent phases, using one or more intermediate languages as the interface between the phases. This is advantageous because each individual phase is smaller and more manageable than the compiler as a whole and because one of the phases may be reusable later in another context.

Thus intermediate languages satisfy two needs:

1. The compiler is easier to build, since each phase is simpler, compared with the initial task represented by the compiler.
2. (This is the point in which we are most interested in this book.) They make the resulting product more portable. Only one part will have to be rewritten in order to install the compiler on a new computer (see Fig. 5.6b). The simplest form of a compiler that uses an intermediate language is shown in Fig. 5.6a.

Writing languages.   The main advantage of an auxiliary language is that it is usually of a lower level than the language to be implemented. Thus nothing prevents it from being used, in the same way as a higher-level programming language is used, to write a portable compiler or interpreter, with the additional

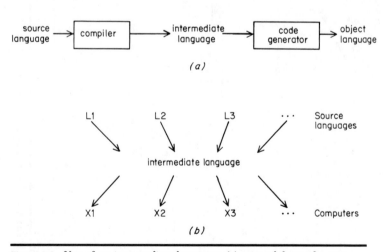

Figure 5.6   Use of an intermediate language: (a) general form of a compiler; (b) the Uncol diagram.

benefit that the auxiliary language will be much easier to implement, if it is not already available on the new target machine.

Here again, a writing language may be of any level:

- It may be of a high level, close to the source language. This is frequently the case when the source language contains unusual features that are difficult to express with different means (e.g., the generators of SL5 [Gri77e]; see Sec. 6.3.3).

- It may be a low-level language, perhaps the assembly language of a fictitious or a real machine.

All implementation systems use a writing language. In many cases, it is a high-level language, perhaps the source language to be implemented. In the same implementation system, one may find a writing language and one or more intermediate languages. It should be noted that the writing languages are used only during the transport or installation operation, while intermediate languages are used in the final product, each time the compiler is run.

The design of an implementation system may include the definition of a new writing language that is specific to the system, to avoid using other ill-suited high-level languages. The design and use of a specially tailored writing language can facilitate the task of writing, as well as of installing. Choosing the best writing language is especially important in the case of an interpreter, since, in contrast with a compiler, an interpreter's writing language does not disappear when the interpreter is installed.

5.2.2 Forms of auxiliary languages

Intermediate languages represent internal interfaces in the compilation process, and consequently they can take any suitable form: trees, triples, quadruples, etc. Writing languages, of course, are constrained by the fact that their use is in the writing of large programs (at least one). They therefore have conventional forms and resemble either an assembly language or a medium- or high-level language.

Trees. A tree is a more-or-less direct representation of the intermediate form generated by the various phases of analysis, and it seems to be a natural interface between two translator phases, especially when the grammar describing the language is an attribute grammar (see Sec. 3.4.3).

The intermediate tree is typically different from a syntax tree, which would explicitly represent all the derivation rules used and would include purely syntactic elements such as delimiters, parentheses, and nonterminals that describe operator priorities. Often each node is decorated with attributes. These attributes give all the information needed for each elementary operation, if the node represents an action, or for each object, if the node represents an object. Thus the tree structure includes data semantics and context information, as well as a definition of the execution order, which is taken from a canonical traversal.

For example, the Ada statement of Fig. 5.7a is translated into Lolita [RTM82] according to Fig. 5.7b. The tree form is used only for intermediate languages.

```
if A (I)  = 0 then
   B : = 3;
elsif A (J) = 0 then
   S2; S3;
else
   S4;
endif;
(a)
```

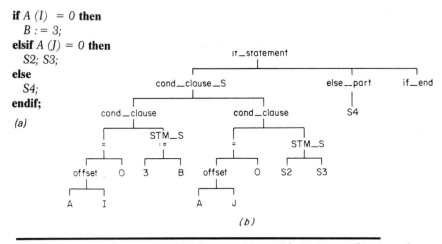

(b)

Figure 5.7   A tree-form intermediate language: (a) an Ada statement; (b) its translation into Lolita.

Assembly languages.   In this notation, a program is represented as an instruction sequence to be executed sequentially. Each instruction contains an operator field and one or more operands. Instruction sequences may be grouped together in procedures.

For example, the Pascal statement of Fig. 5.8a is translated into P-code [NAJ75] (see Sec. 6.2.4), according to Fig. 5.8b.

Assembly-level languages are also, of course, used as writing languages; for example, see the language Flub in Secs. 5.2.3 and 7.4.2, or Minimal in Sec 5.2.4.

Higher-level languages.   Of course, the writing language may be a higher-level language. Most often, it is an already existing language, or, in the case of a

```
if T[J] = 0
  then B : = 3
  else begin
         S2; S3
       end;
       (a)
```

```
         LODA   0   24   /   load address of T (24)
         LODI   0   32   /   load value of J (at address 32)
         IXA    0        /   load contents of T, indexed with J
         LDCI   0        /   load constant 0
         CP              /   compare two values at top of stack
         BNZ    L1       /   branch if not equal
         LDCI   3        /   load constant 3
         STO    0   36   /   store into B (at address 36)
         B      L2       /   branch to L2
  L1     S2
         S3
  L2
```

(b)

Figure 5.8   An assembly-form intermediate language: (a) a Pascal statement; (b) its translation into P-code.

translator, the language to be compiled (see Sec. 6.1). In some cases, the writing language is specially defined for one implementation system, for example, Sil/2 (see Sec. 5.2.4). However, a higher-level language may also, if infrequently, be used as an intermediate language. For example, Fortran has been used as an intermediate language for Icon (see Sec. 6.3.4).

5.2.3 Related abstract machines

Every auxiliary language is more-or-less clearly related to an abstract machine. In the case where the language depends on a specific machine or on a family of machines, the abstract machine is well-defined, since it is simply a generalization of several actual machines. In other cases, there may be a wide range of possibilities. The abstract machine may be fictitious or hidden, simply sketched out or perfectly defined. We shall see several examples later.

The usefulness of an abstract machine stems from the fact that it allows the majority of the compilation process to be isolated from dependency on a specific machine. To obtain an actual implementation, the abstract machine must then be transported to the actual machine. Various solutions may be used:

- The base operations of the abstract machine could be implemented using a macroprocessor (if the auxiliary language resembles an assembly language). If the macroprocessor is not a very powerful one, the resulting code is usually rather inefficient.

- A specialized translator could be built.

- An interpreter could be programmed or microprogrammed, which would amount to direct execution of the abstract machine's instruction set. Although this method is an important one, we shall not consider it in the following presentation. It constitutes the basis of "language machines" specifically built for higher-level language execution. An interesting example is the Western Digital Pascal Micro-Engine, with microprogrammed P-code execution, which has recently been adapted for Ada. This method may also be used for less advisable purposes, like the simulation on a new machine of an obsolete machine whose software is not portable. In very unusual cases, this method is actually used for transporting a language implementation, if a machine's microcode is accessible [Sno78a].

It is often possible to use a very general tool, which is itself almost immediately portable, as a first step toward abstract-machine implementation. If the resulting efficiency is unsatisfactory, the first simulation of the abstract machine may be replaced by another more specialized and more efficient implementation, one that depends on the environment and on the context of its use. (One might, for example, microprogram the abstract machine.)

Another benefit of abstract machines is that they allow an implementation system to include several utilities that would normally be machine-dependent: program analysis, debugging aids, optimizers, etc. The abstract-machine approach allows such tools to be constructed in a way that depends on the source language and not on the target machine.

Examples of abstract machines. The abstract machine associated with Pascal-P [NAJ75] (see Sec. 6.2.4.) is very conventional and rather flexible. It is a stack computer with five registers: top of stack, base of global variables, top of heap (used for dynamic variables), base of local variables, and instruction counter. Figure 5.8 gives an example of P-code. A model very similar is used for O-code and Intcode in the case of the BCPL language [Ric71]—and in many more recent examples. ("P-code" has almost become a household word!)

The EM-1 machine [TSK81] is also similar to this model, with a stack of local variable areas whose top is used as an execution stack, a heap, a global variable area, and a program area. Its language, however, is more sophisticated and is closer to actual assembly languages than is P-code. It contains about 130 instructions (P-code has only 60), plus a dozen pseudoinstructions. Its intended usage is more ambitious than that of P-code (see Sec. 3.4.5). Figure 5.9 shows the translation into EM-1 of the Pascal statement.

> **for** I := 1 to 100 **do** A[1] :=I*I;

Slightly different abstract machines are often used for string-handling languages (e.g., SIL or Stage2). Memory is divided into descriptors, allowing characters and pointers to character strings to be kept in a reserved area of the machine storage. Figure 5.10a shows an example of a program in Flub used for implementing Stage2 (see Sec. 7.4.2). A program in Flub is a linear sequence of instructions, without functions or procedures. The only programs written in this language are the Stage2 macroprocessor and some test programs. Figure 5.10b shows the macro definitions needed for translating some fragments of the Flub text into Fortran.

The abstract machine associated with the intermediate language Janus (see Sec. 7.4.4) has a memory that is divided into several independent areas that are organized as tree structures. It uses an operand stack for expression evaluation, a processing unit to execute Janus instructions, and three specialized registers: condition code, instruction counter, and index register. The Fortran program of Fig. 5.11a is translated into the Janus code of Fig. 5.11b.

```
loc   1      constant 1
stl   2      i is the first local variable, on two bytes
2            label
lol   2      load i
dup   2      duplicate stack top (two bytes)
mul          i x i
lal   18     base of array a
lol   2      load i
sar   .2     a [i] := (.2 is the array descriptor)
lol   2      load i
loc   100    constant 100
beq   3      branch if equal
inl   2      increment i (two bytes)
brb   2      branch
3            label
```

Figure 5.9 The EM-1 intermediate language.

5.2.4 Other examples

In this section we shall show other examples of intermediate languages that will be used in the case studies presented in Part 2. The three languages—SIL, Sil/2, and Minimal—are used for writing compilers or interpreters implementing string-processing source languages.

SIL is associated with Snobol4 [Gri72, Gri77d]. The only program written in SIL is the Snobol4 compiler-interpreter, from which the example of Fig. 5.12 is

```
get    a=x.              put into registers a and b two words
get    b=y.              whose addresses are in registers x and y
to     l1 if val a=b.    if their value fields are equal, go to l1
sto    b=z.              else store b at address stored in z
to     l2.               end
loc    l1.               label
sto    a=y.              store a in place of b
loc    l2.               label
end    program.
```

(a)

```
.#$'0.     definition of special characters
get #=#.   definition of macros for generating Fortran
        jf'10=1(jp'20)$
        jv'10=1(jp'20+1)$
        jp'10=1(jp'20+2)$

$
sto #=#.
        1(jp'10)=jf'20$
        1(jp'10+1)=jv'20$
        1(jp'10+2)=jp'20$

$
loc ##.
'10'20 continue$

$
to ## if ### #=#.
        if(j'30'60.eq.j'30'70)goto'10'20$

$
to #=#.
        go to '10'20$

$
end program.
        stop$
        end$

$$        end of macro definitions
```

(b)

Figure 5.10 The Flub writing language: (*a*) a program in Flub; (*b*) some Stage2 macros for translating Flub instructions.

```
SUBROUTINE IRES(I)
COMMON /BLOCK/ J,K(2)
DATA L/1/
I = L + J - K(2)
RETURN
END
```

(a)

```
begin nonrec Pl.                        non-recursive procedure
param addr nonrec I5.                   reference parameter
parend nonrec Pl.
array D15 align Fl(2).                  unpacked array K
record R2.                              common block
field Fl align Jl.                      J
field D15 align K4.                     K
recend R2.
common R2 intern (S23) block5.          definition of global name "block"
space Fl static L2 V Fll.               L
fldv int static Flll A int 1.           L=1
vend Fll static Fl.
load int static 2 Flll.                 get L .
add int intern S(23) Jl Flll.           add J (from common)
sub int intern S(23) K4 Fl Flll.        subtract K(2)
base addr param I5.                     access parameter I
store (N) int based Flll.               store into I
return nonrec Pl.
end nonrec Pl.
```

(b)

Figure 5.11 The Janus intermediate language: (*a*) a program in Fortran; (*b*) its translation into Janus.

extracted. Procedure INVOKE serves as a switch to the beginning of the suitable function.

Minimal is associated with Spitbol [DMC77], a variant of Snobol4. The example of Fig. 5.13 is a subprogram of the Macro-Spitbol implementation. This code-generation procedure is called during compilation.

```
INVOKE  PROC                            procedure entry
        POPD    INCL                    get the function descriptor
*                                       on top of stack
        GETDC   XPTR,INCL,0             get the link descriptor
        EQLTT   INCL,XPTR,INVK2         test on argument number
INVKL   BRANIN  INCL,0                  if equal, branch indirectly
*                                       to function body
INVK2   TESTF   XPTR,VFLG,ARGNER,INVKL
*                                       test if function accepts a
*                                       variable number of arguments
*                                       return to invkl if OK
*                                       else call error procedure argner
```

Figure 5.12 A program fragment in SIL.

```
*           CDGNM   :   code generation
*           recursive procedure generating code for operands
CDGNM       PRC     R,0             entry point, recursive procedure
            MOV     XL,-(XS)        save XL
            MOV     WB,-(XS)        save WB
            CHK                     test if stack is full
            MOV     (XR),WA         load type
            BEQ     WA,=B$CMT,CGN04  branch to 4 if blank
            BHI     WA,=B$VR$,CGN02  branch to 2 if variable
*           constant
CGN01       JST     ERRPR           raise an error signal
            ERR     syntax error: value used where name is required
*           reference to variable
CGN02       MOV     =OLVN$,WA           call to variable load
            JSR     CDWRD           generate code
            MOV     XR,WA           copy VRBLK pointer
            JSR     CDWRD           generate a new value
```

Figure 5.13 A program fragment in Minimal.

Sil/2 is associated with SL5 [GRI77e]. It is a much higher level language than either SIL or Minimal and can be used as a general-purpose language. The example of Fig. 5.14 is not a part of the SL5 compiler.

5.2.5 Comparison of auxiliary languages

Objects handled.   Most auxiliary languages have the usual simple higher-level-language data types: integer, real, boolean, and character. When an auxiliary language is dependent on a source language, only the types needed for translation are present. For example, in O-code or Intcode, all objects have the single type "value," like in BCPL. By contrast, in an auxiliary language that is less dependent on a specific source language other types are necessary:

- The address type, for representing pointers or for standardizing parameter passing

```
#  This procedure searches a symbol in a table
#  The table is organized as a binary tree

routine    lookup (table,symbol):
begin
#  Traverse the binary tree
while   table  ≠  nil do
    begin
        if table ! entry = symbol then
            return (table,1):
        test table ! entry ≤ table ! rightling
end;
```

Figure 5.14 A program fragment in Sil/2.

- The procedure type, found in Janus, which allows a procedure to be passed as a parameter (This is not present in P-code.)

- The type "program address" (or code address or instruction label), found in Janus and Minimal

The structured types of higher-level programming languages are almost always transformed in their auxiliary language representation. Arrays and records are typically linearized, as in P-code, SIL, Minimal, O-code, Intcode, etc. However, even if linearization is appropriate for a large number of conventional machines, it still seems advisable that the auxiliary language contain some of the source language's declarative information, to take maximum advantage of each target machine [KKM80].

The structured types that still occur in auxiliary languages usually reflect the associated source language: Strings in P-code, for example, are all of a fixed length, while in SIL they are the basic elements of Snobol4. A similar situation occurs with Pascal sets. The representation of these types is too machine-dependent to be fixed in advance, as is usually done for arrays and records.

In all auxiliary languages except Janus, objects are represented in linear memory. Only an object's value, with no type representation, is present. An object is directly accessed, using its name (in SIL) or its address, which is most often computed with specialized registers: base of local areas (in P-code, O-code, and Intcode) or index registers (Intcode and Minimal).

In contrast, Janus relies on a tree-structured memory. The reference to an object is in fact a path in a subtree, whose starting node represents the category of memory to which the object refers. A compound object is itself a subtree. Various elements are accessed with the base register and the index register. Such a structure is supposed to map onto any computer architecture.

Program structure.   Procedure handling in the auxiliary language depends on its role in the transport operation. In a writing language, procedures have little relation to those of the source language, unless the source language contains some features that are difficult to express in other ways. For example, SL5 coroutines exist in its associated writing language, Sil/2. In other cases, such as SIL and Minimal, procedures are used for structuring the program but are not independent execution units.

In contrast, the structure of programs in intermediate languages is much more dependent on the source language. For example, Pascal procedures and functions may be found in P-code; BCPL procedures are found in O-code and Intcode. In order to be more source-language-independent, Janus also contains blocks and modules. Thus it is able to represent Pascal procedures as well as Fortran subroutines, Algol 68 blocks, and BCPL segments.

In writing languages, the structure of source programs has no effect on the associated abstract machine. By contrast, in P-code, O-code, and Intcode, source-language procedures need a stack organization of memory to allow the implementation of the visibility rules for local variables found in Pascal and BCPL.

In a similar way, the memory of the Janus abstract machine is handled as a tree, in order to allow the representation of the various program components and of the associated visibility rules.

External form.   The syntax mainly depends on the way in which the auxiliary language is translated. If it is interpreted, like P-code or Intcode, statements are short and operands are often implicit, because of postfix notation, or are denoted only by their address in memory, thus making the program difficult to read.

When the auxiliary language is translated by a macroprocessor, instructions usually are in a fixed format, and the number and types of operands vary depending on the operation. The instruction syntax depends on the macroprocessor chosen: The choice of Stage2 for translating Janus, for example, results in redundant definitions, avoiding costly table searches. In contrast, the specialized translator for Minimal maintains global information, which allows simplified notation and semantic verification.

The character set used in auxiliary languages is generally distinct from that of the abstract machine. Auxiliary languages usually need only a very limited character set in program texts—at most a dozen characters, in addition to letters and digits. In contrast, the character sets of abstract machines are generally fitted to those of actual machines, either by using a parameterized number of characters or by parameterizing the characters themselves.

5.2.6   An assessment

Most of the auxiliary languages already mentioned have the common property of being associated with a given source language. This is the most frequent case, because the choice of the auxiliary language best suited for the translation of a given source language facilitates the building of the translator.

Some languages, however, have more universal purposes—for example, EM-1, which has been used for translating C as well as Pascal, is designed for the translation of most Algol-like languages. In the same way, Janus could be used in the translation of very different languages, but currently its only use is with Pascal and Algol 68 [HaW78b]. Minimal and Sil/2 could also be mentioned in this category; though broadly designed, to our knowledge they have been associated only with Spitbol and SL5, respectively. In fact, they are rather independent of these languages and are complete enough to be usable in other contexts, although they are of different levels.

There are very few examples where an intermediate language depends on the computer and not on higher-level language. However, there is an attempt to standardize microprocessor assembly languages [Fis79], which could converge on an actual language and, if really used, could be employed in developing tools for all microprocessors, especially machine-independent compilers.

5.3   The production of translators

5.3.1   Introduction

A translator, as its T-diagram shows, puts three programming languages into play: its source language SL, its object language OL, and its writing language WL. As already seen, we shall often denote it [SL, WL, OL] in the body of the text. The descriptive diagram of Fig. 5.4 shows some tests on these three languages that allow us to distinguish the various steps of translator production, whether the objective is to produce a compiler or an auxiliary translator needed somewhere in the implementation process or in the system to be built.

Meaning of the diagram.   The diagram shown in Fig. 5.4 should be considered as simply a description of the situations that may occur. It does not describe in what order the various operations must be done nor how to make the choices that lead to one solution rather than another one. The recursive nature of the diagram allows pieces to be combined, with no limit on complexity.

When exiting the main part of the diagram, the desired translator [SL, WL, OL] is available; when entering the diagram, five different cases must be distinguished, depending on the nature of the available translator [SL', WL', OL']. However, after recursive or iterative applications of this diagram and of the diagram relating to interpreters (see Fig. 5.5 and Sec. 5.4), all cases reduce to the first one. In fact, one should always end with a translator whose three languages are usable. Perhaps these three languages are not those of the desired translator, but in any case they appear somewhere in the sequence of operations that produces it.

Cases 2, 3, and 4 deal with situations where one of the three languages is not the desired one but is independent of the other two, and where, as a consequence, the available translator must be modified. If several languages do not fit, they are considered one after another, in any order. Thus it may be necessary to modify the translator several times before the starting conditions are satisfied. These modifications may be of very different nature and amplitude, and the notation "modify xL" (where x is either S, W, or O) is sometimes incorrect; in fact, modifications do not deal with the language, but rather with the translator itself.

In case 2, we consider those situations where the modifications to be made to the source language are only extensions, restrictions, or minor changes to the same language—for example, when changing from one version to the next. In fact, to change the source language completely would mean changing all the analytical parts of the translator (scanning, parsing, and semantic analysis), which would amount to a full rewrite, without actually using the original translator.

In case 3, modifications of the writing language may range from a simple version change of the language to a complete rewriting of the translator into an entirely different language. In the latter situation, in contrast with the former, the algorithm of the translator does not change, only its expression in a given language.

In case 4, the change may be a version change for an intermediate object language or the production of an object language for a different computer (actual or virtual). In the latter case, the modifications to be made to the translator are major but still feasible, especially if the model translator was designed to be modifiable in this way.

In case 5, no translator is available, except perhaps as a model. One must therefore begin by writing one from scratch without special help (except, of course, the help that may be provided by a compiler-writing system; see Sec. 4.5). We now return to the first case.

Tests and conditions for the languages.   The testing of the writing language and the object language of the final translator occurs in all cases in branch 1 of the diagram (Fig. 5.4). It is important to note that this diagram is not a decision diagram: One does not wait until some translator is built in order to ask oneself whether the object language is the desired one. On the contrary, the object language is chosen at the start. This fundamental fact explains why some situations cannot occur; they are either impossible or absurd.

Thus, if WL is a machine language, this is necessarily the desired language; otherwise branch 3 would have been used and no more work would be necessary.

If WL is a translatable language, a translator for WL is needed, which leads to a recursive use of the diagram to build this new translator (which will not appear in the final implementation system). (This will be shown in Fig. 5.18a.)

If WL is an interpretable language, an interpreter for WL is needed, which leads to the use of the diagram of interpreter production (see Sec. 5.4). This interpreter will appear in the final implementation system. (This will be shown in Fig. 5.19a.)

If WL is a language that is translatable by macroprocessing, one must write the corresponding macro definitions, then "interpret" them using the macroprocessor. This constitutes a very special case of a translator, and again leads to the use of the diagram for the production of an interpreter (Fig. 5.4). The macroprocessor will not appear in the final implementation system. (This will be shown in Fig. 5.20a.)

The testing of the object language leads to the traversal of the same branches of the diagram, but this time the translators or interpreters appear, in all cases, in the final implementation system.

If OL is a machine language, it is necessarily the desired one (otherwise one would have chosen branch 4), and nothing more is needed.

If OL is a translatable language, a translator for OL is needed. In this case, the generated translator is necessarily in two passes, with OL playing the role of an intermediate language. The second translator necessitates another (recursive) use of the diagram. (This will be shown in Fig. 5.16a.)

If OL is an interpretable language, an interpreter for OL is needed, or more precisely an interpreter for the object program generated by the translator. (This will be shown in Fig. 5.16b.)

If OL is a language that is translatable by macroprocessing, one must write the corresponding macro definitions, then use the macroprocessor. The generated translator is in two passes, the second one processing the macros. (This will be shown in Fig. 5.16c.)

Elementary cases of translator production. We begin with the following hypothesis: In order to decide how a translator must be generated, one considers both WL and OL at the same time. Sections 5.3.2 and 5.3.3 examine all possible elementary cases, using simple examples when necessary. Combinations of elementary cases, those where another translator or an interpreter is needed, will be considered in Chap. 6, where we use complete examples.

When a machine language is used, either as a writing language or as an object language, one must examine whether it is the language of machine X (the target machine of the desired translator) or the language of another machine Y. We shall call their machine languages XL and YL, respectively.

The diagram in Fig. 5.4 is complicated to read because of its lack of parameterization: The languages of concern do not appear explicitly. This is because, as already explained, it is not a diagram for making choices between different solutions, but only a description of the various combinations of solutions available.

The main classification of the various elementary cases of translator production is made according to the nature of the writing language, depending upon whether it is a machine language. If it is not a machine language, another component, whether a translator, an interpreter, or a macroprocessor, may be involved. The same division into two categories occurs with the object language.

5.3.2 Writing the translator in machine language

1. WL = XL. The writing language is the language of machine X. In this case, the translator runs directly on X (Fig. 5.15a).

    a *OL is a machine language.*

       (1) OL = XL. In this case, the desired translator is obtained, since the programs are translated into the language of machine X and can run directly on X. Examples are so numerous that it is useless to mention any specific case (Fig. 5.15b).

       (2) OL = YL. This case cannot occur, as explained in the preceding section. If the object language is the language of a computer other than the target computer, one chooses branch 4 of the diagram in order to change the object language.

    b *OL is not a machine language.* The object language is an intermediate language IL, and at least one more phase is needed to translate or to interpret the object language generated by the translator.

       (1) *IL is translatable.* A translator for IL is needed, and in the simplest case a translator in two passes is obtained (Fig. 5.16a). An example is the use of Icon on some computer X, IL being a higher-level language, in this case, Fortran (see Sec. 6.3). Pascal on the Iris 50 [Lec77a] uses the same scheme, IL being a language especially designed for transporting translators.

       (2) *IL is interpretable.* An interpreter for IL is needed, and it is usually

written in XL. The result is a translator that generates an object
language to be interpreted (Fig. 5.16*b*).

(3) *IL is a language that can be translated using a macroprocessor.* A
macroprocessor is thus needed to interpret the macros, as well as a
"translator" consisting of the set of macro definitions used to translate IL into an object language, generally XL. The resulting translator
consists of at least two passes (Fig. 5.16*c*). An example is the implementation of BCPL using O-code [Ric71].

2. *WL = YL.* The writing language of the translator is the language of a
computer other than X. The only important case to be considered is when
OL = XL. Such a translator, which runs on computer Y and generates object
programs for another computer X, is a cross-compiler, which we prefer to
call a "transcompiler" (Fig. 5.17).

The case where OL = YL is impossible, since branch 4 of the diagram would

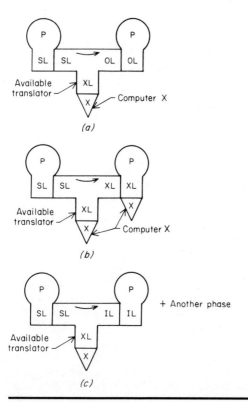

(a)

(b)

(c)

Figure 5.15 Writing a translator in the target machine language: (*a*) WL = XL; (*b*) WL = XL, OL =
machine language; (*c*) WL = XL, OL ≠ machine
language.

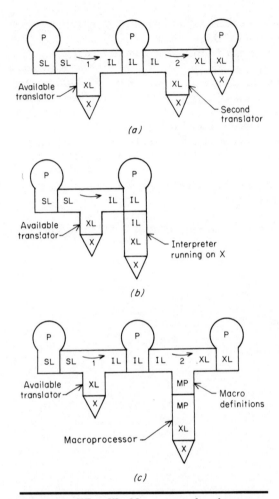

Figure 5.16 WL = XL, OL = intermediate language IL: (a) IL is translatable; (b) IL is interpretable; (c) IL is translatable using a macroprocessor.

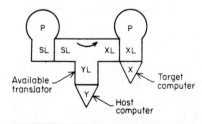

Figure 5.17 Transcompilation.

have been used first in order to change the object language. The case where OL is not a machine language, which corresponds to a transcompiler generating an intermediate language, adds nothing special, and consequently does not have to be considered separately.

5.3.3 Writing the translator in another language

One more step is needed in order to translate or to interpret the writing language, since the translator cannot be executed directly. This step concerns only the translator, and it adds a level of vertical nesting to the representation with T-diagrams, while a supplementary step dealing with the object language extends the representation horizontally.

The writing language, whatever its level, is thus an auxiliary language (see Sec. 5.2), and we shall refer to it as AL in the following section. We shall now examine the different possible cases, each case based on the nature of the writing language (translatable, interpretable, or translatable using a macroprocessor), and examine each case according to the nature of the object language.

1. *WL = AL is translatable.* At least one more translator is needed to translate the first one (Fig. 5.18a). The simplest case occurs when the second translator generates an object program written in OL' = XL; this reduces to the situation already described in Sec. 5.3.2 (WL = XL). If OL' = YL, this comes down to the other situation described in Sec. 5.3.2 (OL $\neq$ machine language). If OL' is not equal to ML, we are in the exact situation we are considering.

   a *OL is a machine language.* The desired translator is obtained, and it uses only one pass (Fig. 5.18b). An especially interesting case, which will be considered again in Sec. 6.1.3, occurs when AL = SL, i.e., when the translator is written in the language that it has to compile, and hence is a self-compiling compiler [LPT78]. The second translation, which appears in Fig. 5.18c in the case of a Pascal compiler for the CDC 6600 (see Sec. 6.2.1), is a validation step, as we shall see in Sec. 6.1.3.

   Identical schemas may be encountered when a compiler is written in another language—for example, a Pascal compiler for the IBM 360 was first written in PL/1 [RuS76]—or in another version of the same language—as in "telescopic generation" (see Sec. 4.1) using a subset of the source language or a version change in the source language—and when production steps are followed until a self-compiling compiler is obtained.

   b *OL is not a machine language.* A compiler with at least two passes is obtained, and OL is an intermediate language IL. The schema of Fig. 5.18d corresponds to the case where IL is translatable. If IL is interpretable, an interpreter is needed for object programs written in this language. If IL is translatable by a macroprocessor, we return to the schema of Fig. 5.18d augmented by a macroprocessor, which interprets the macro definitions that constitute the third translator. In all cases, this reduces to the various cases already seen in Sec. 5.3.2. This is a situation where the

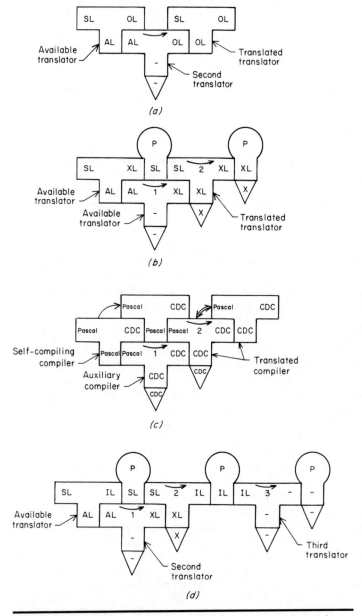

Figure 5.18 Writing the translator in a translatable language: (*a*) the general case; (*b*) OL = machine language; (*c*) self-compilation; (*d*) OL ≠ machine language.

combination of elementary methods allows the construction of complex examples, such as those that will be considered in Chap. 6.

2. *WL = AL is interpretable.* The translator must be interpreted, using an interpreter normally written in XL, in order to run on computer X.

   a *OL is a machine language.* An interpreted one-pass compiler is immediately obtained (Fig. 5.19a). This is a very uncommon case, although it occurs in the "translator" (in fact, a pseudoassembler) of Lap, which is needed to compile Lisp.

   b *OL is not a machine language.* A second pass is needed in order to translate or to interpret the program generated in OL. Once again, this is a situation where elementary methods can be combined, and we shall give only a few examples here:

   (1) *OL is translatable.* This is the case for the already-mentioned Lisp compiler. By applying the resulting translation schema to both components of the translation, one can eliminate interpretation, but two passes are still needed.

   (2) *Ol is interpretable.* This is the case for the portable Pascal compiler known as Pascal-P (which will be considered again in Sec. 6.2.3), and

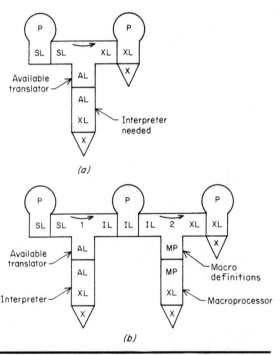

(a)

(b)

Figure 5.19 Writing the translator in an interpretable language: (*a*) OL = machine language: (*b*) OL is translatable using a macroprocessor.

for all compilers derived from it. In this precise case, the translator was produced by self-compilation, which is why OL and WL are identical.

   (3) *OL is translatable using a macroprocessor (Fig. 5.19b)*. This schema could be used, for example, in an implementation of Pascal-J [HaW78b] that would use Pascal-P, Janus, and Stage2. But this might lead to an extremely inefficient result, which would only serve as an intermediate step during the production of something better.

3. *WL = AL is translatable using a macroprocessor*. The structure of Fig. 5.20a is obtained. The right part of this schema varies depending on the nature of OL, and we again find the same cases considered in Sec. 5.3.2. For example, in the implementation of BCPL using O-code [Ric71], OL is itself translatable using a macroprocessor: The translator is thus in two passes, of which the second processes the macros (Fig. 5.20b).

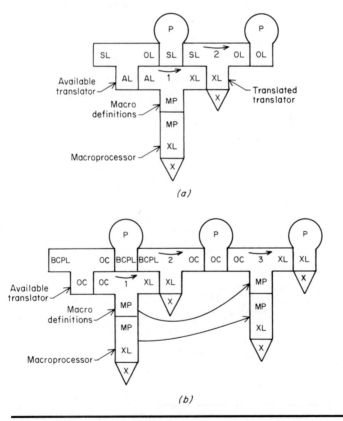

Figure 5.20 Writing the translator in a language translatable using a macroprocessor: (*a*) the general case; (*b*) OL = WL (BCPL's case).

5.4   The production of interpreters

5.4.1   Introduction

In the case of an interpreter, the production methods depend essentially on the writing language, since there is no object language. For this reason, the possible combinations are much less numerous. An interpreter for a given (interpretable) source language is built either for a given computer or, in order to be portable, for a family of computers. In the first case, it is written in assembly language, or sometimes in a higher-level language, but still taking into account the characteristics of the particular computer on which it must run.

The various methods are thus related to the nature of the writing language:

- It may be *compilable,* in which case it is usually a higher-level language, for which a compiler already exists on the target computer or for which a compiler can be (more or less easily) implemented.

- It may be *translatable,* in which case it is usually a special-purpose language, specially designed to build this interpreter.

- It may be *translatable using a macroprocessor,* in which case it is most often a lower-level language, here again specially designed.

- It may be *interpretable,* though this occurs very seldom—on the one hand because of the appalling performance of the resulting product, and on the other hand because this does not help in generating (automatically) a more efficient version, since there is no generation of machine language.

- It may be a *machine* or *assembly language.*

These various cases will be considered in more detail, using examples, in the subsequent sections, without separating the case of a compilable (higher-level) language from that of a translatable (low-level) language. The corresponding elementary methods are represented in the diagram in Fig. 5.5, which should be interpreted in the same way as was Fig. 5.4. These methods may be combined, with each other or with other methods, to produce translators, as we have already seen in Secs. 5.3.2 and 5.3.3.

We shall assume in the subsequent sections that we are dealing with the case where one wants to implement, on machine X, an interpreter that already works on another machine, and that the interpreter is written in a language WL that is usable on X; that is, WL is either directly available on X, or WL can be implemented using an auxiliary operation.

Thus we shall ignore branches 2 to 4 of the diagram seen in Fig. 5.5, in the same way as we ignored branches 2 to 5 of the diagram in Fig. 5.4. For this step to make sense, SL must either be the desired language, a language of the same family, or a prior version of the desired language. It is necessary to change the code associated with each instruction to be interpreted, and to add the code corresponding to the new instructions. The nature of an interpreter, together with the fact that interpretable languages are often of a low level, makes these changes relatively easy.

If WL is not available on computer X, the interpreter can be rewritten, provided the interpreter used as a model does not depend too much on the language in which it is written. In most cases, however, the writing language only passes from one version of an already available language to the next version.

Of course, if no interpreter is available, it will be necessary to write one, and we are finally brought back to branch 1 of the diagram, just as we were in the two cases given above.

5.4.2   WL is translatable

The translator must be obtained, whether by using one of the elementary methods of Secs. 5.3.2 and 5.3.3 or by combining several methods. This is the case, for example, with Pascal-S [Wir75] and with Prolog, whose interpreter can be written in Fortran [BaM73] or in Pascal [Bru76].

Example: Pascal-S is a subset of Pascal that is used in introductory computer science courses; it represents a case where an interpreted implementation is preferable to a compiled one. In this precise case, it is a compiler-interpreter that uses an internal intermediate language; we shall assume that it interprets the Pascal-S language directly. This compiler-interpreter is itself written in standard Pascal, for which a compiler is assumed to be available on computer X. Thus [Pascal-S, Pascal] and [Pascal, XL, XL] are available, which leads to the schema of Fig. 5.21a.

The implementation method of Macro-Spitbol [DMC77] is another example of such a situation. Despite its name, this method does not use a macroprocessor, but rather a specialized translator written in Fortran or in Snobol4, whose source language is the assembly language of an idealized computer.

5.4.3   WL is translatable using a macroprocessor

It is necessary, in this case, to have a macroprocessor available; moreover, it is necessary to write the macro definitions that carry out the translation. The macroprocessor may be general or specialized, and it may be obtained using a previous implementation, possibly a computer-aided one.

Example: In the so-called standard implementation of Snobol4 [Gri72], a compiler-interpreter is available, written in SIL, a low-level language especially designed for this purpose. This language can be translated using a general-purpose macroprocessor or a macroassembler; a set of model macro definitions for the IBM 360/370 macroassembler is provided along with the compiler-interpreter. The schema of Fig. 5.21b represents the compiler-interpreter as a simple interpreter and demonstrates the case where the general-purpose macroprocessor Stage2 is used.

5.4.4   WL is interpretable

As we already discussed in Sec. 5.4.1, very few implementations use this method, since the lack of an object language prevents an efficient product from being obtained.

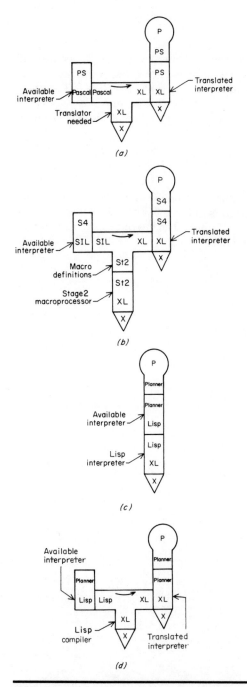

Figure 5.21 The production of interpreters: (a) WL is translatable; (b) WL is translatable using a macro-processor, (c) double interpretation; (d) compilation of the interpreter.

Example: The language Planner [Hew69], a higher-level language for artificial intelligence, includes characteristics that make its interpretation compulsory. Its interpreter is written in Lisp, which allows an interpreted version of Lisp to be used when debugging and tuning the interpreter or the programs written in Planner (see Fig. 5.21c). Later, a compiled implementation of Lisp may be used (Fig. 5.21d; see Sec. 5.3.3).

5.4.5 WL is a machine language

This machine language can only be that of computer X, otherwise one would have first traversed branch 4 of the diagram in Fig. 5.5. The idea of transcompilation has no equivalent in the case of interpreters. The interpreter can run directly on X, but is not usable on other computers.

Case Studies

In Part 1 we enumerated the problems encountered during the design, construction, distribution, and use of portable software, and then described, in a somewhat abstract manner, how these problems can be solved. We presented in succession the software tools, the linguistic means, and the implementation methods that can be used for portability. Although we referred as often as possible to precise examples, they were not always adequate models of the real world.

The purpose of Part 2 then is to demonstrate how what was described in Part 1 can be used in actual situations, on real-size problems. This will allow us to demonstrate how elementary techniques can be combined and how they can be used in the presence of certain constraints. We will also point out qualities and weaknesses of the resulting software products.

The case studies are presented in two separate chapters, according to the nature of the transported software products: Chap. 6 deals with language processors, Chap. 7 with operating and programming systems. The first set of case studies (Chap. 6) constitutes an important class of examples, since every software product must in the end be written in a programming language: If the language is implemented in a portable way, an important step has been made toward portability of the software product itself. In the system examples of Chap. 7, we will find again some portable language processors, as parts of these systems.

6

Translators and Interpreters

6.1 Some general observations

6.1.1 Introduction

This chapter presents some case studies of "language processors," those pieces of software used to implement a given programming language on a given computer. Such processors are often called compilers, but that term lends a restrictive meaning to the concept, since true compilers translate only from source program to object program.

We therefore make the distinction in the title of this chapter between translators and interpreters, just as it was made in Chap. 5 where we noted that the methods used were different for these two kinds of processors.

There are a lot of examples of more-or-less portable translators and interpreters that use various techniques. We have chosen some of them which are especially significant, having one or more of the following characteristics:

- They give a clear indication of the problems and their solutions.
- The techniques they use are different from the others.
- They often represent the first use of a particular technique.
- They are successful; i.e., the resulting processor is now commonly used, which is proof of a valid solution. (Or on the contrary, they proved that some theoretically valid solutions lead to unusable results.)
- They are relatively recent models.

The first two sections describe what is actually a family of related examples. Section 6.2 considers a set of solutions used by Pascal portable implementations; the specific techniques represent one of the main reasons for the success of the language. The solutions we present are the most characteristic and the most successful.

Section 6.3 considers a family of three programming languages and the implementation of these languages, which was designed by the same main author. It is particularly interesting to see that new techniques were used for each language.

Section 6.4 considers only one of the solutions currently used to implement Ada. The language itself, as well as the solution described, is too big to allow the study of more examples, especially since most of them are not yet publicly described. Anyway, the solution shown is a combination of several techniques.

The choice of some examples leads inevitably to the exclusion of others. We can mention here some case studies we considered and then discarded, either because they did not show anything new, they were too old, or the documentation describing them was not precise or detailed enough:

- BCPL [Ric73, RWS80] has been implemented with the use of a common-level interpretive language and again with a much lower level language. In the first case [Ric71], a multiple-step self-compilation is used; as for Pascal-P, see Secs. 6.2.3 and 6.2.4. In the second case, a macroprocessor is employed instead of the interpreter, a technique also exemplified in Chap. 7 in the implementation of Stage2 (see Sec. 7.4.2).

- Lisp [MCA62] is usually implemented in a nonportable way, but the very first compiler, run on an IBM 7090, used an original technique described in Lecarme and Peyrolle-Thomas [LPT82a] and discussed in Sec. 6.4. On the other hand, Griss and Hearn [GRH81] describe another method for portable implementation of this language.

- Prolog is usually implemented by programming a minimal interpreter in another language, and then extending it. However, Kanoui and Van Caneghem [KVC80] describe an abstract-machine superposition technique of implementation, known as "telescopic generation" (see Sec. 4.1), which is also cited in an example in Sec. 7.4.

- C will be treated only in its use as an implementation tool for Unix (see Sec. 7.2). The techniques used are similar to those described in this chapter.

6.1.2   Combination operators

The elementary methods described in Chap. 5 do not usually yield a directly executable compiler generating a directly executable object code. Most often several elementary methods have to be combined, in order to build a new processor from one or more existing processors. This means traversing once or several times the branches of the diagrams seen in Figs. 5.4 and 5.5. We shall distinguish three ways of combining elementary phases of implementation, according to the auxiliary languages used; we call them "combination operators."

Combination operators linked to the object language.   When a translator generates an object language that is not a machine language, an extra translation may be necessary. Depending on the type of object language, these combinations correspond to one of the schemas shown in Fig. 6.1a. Note that this translation phase will appear in the final product.

Combination operators linked to the writing language. Unlike the previous case, these operators are used only during the construction phase and do not appear in the final product: The first translator is modified. They correspond to the schema seen in Fig. 6.1*b*.

A combination operator using interpretation. Interpretation may be used for the object language as well as for the writing language. The former case is shown in Fig. 6.1*c*. In both cases, the schema cannot be extended (see Sec. 5.2). Thus the corresponding operator can only be used once; it is a terminal step appearing in the final translator.

6.1.3 Self-compilation

Self-compilation is a common combination of elementary methods: The compiler is written in its own source language and can compile itself [LPT78]. To start the bootstrap, one has [SL, SL, MX] (the same "triple" notation as used in Chap. 5 to denote a translator *of* source language SL, *in* language SL, producing machine code MX for machine X) and then the compiler [SL, MX, MX]. The latter compiles the former on machine X. For a new machine Y, the code generator of [SL, SL, MX] must first be modified (branch 4 of Fig. 5.4) in order to generate code for Y. Two successive translations of this compiler are then needed on the machine Y, as shown by Fig. 6.2*a*.

Here the first step corresponds to the application of combination operators linked to the writing language: [SL, SL, MY] becomes [SL, MX, MY]. In the second step [SL, MX, MY] becomes [SL, MY, MY] by a new application of the same operator.

To validate the compiler produced, an extra phase is needed, this time on Y. The same operator is applied again to [SL, MY, MY]; the results obtained by the last two steps must be perfectly identical, for they are both translations of the same program [SL, SL, MY] by two different programs with the same semantics.

The complete schema of self-compilation is shown in Fig. 6.2*b*. It must be noted that the same method can be used on one machine only.

6.2 Implementation of Pascal

6.2.1 Introduction

Pascal was designed in 1969 by Niklaus Wirth. The author intended to design a language that could be used as a teaching support for systematic and structured programming—in other words, a language that could present fundamental concepts of programming in an easy and natural way and that could be easily and efficiently implemented on the existing machines. Its first implementation, on the CDC 6600 [Wir71b] was realized before the language definition was published. This definition was revised slightly by its author in 1972 [Wir73], and again during the definition of an international standard between 1978 and 1981 (see Sec. 4.2.2). The language has been remarkably stable for the last 15 years, however (as compared with Fortran, Cobol, and PL/1, for instance).

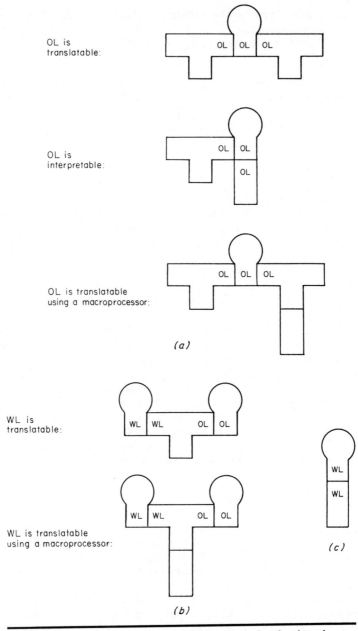

OL is
translatable:

OL is
interpretable:

OL is translatable
using a macroprocessor:

(a)

WL is
translatable:

WL is translatable
using a macroprocessor:

(b)

(c)

Figure 6.1 Combination operators: (*a*) operators linked to the object language; (*b*) operators linked to the writing language; (*c*) combination by interpretation.

Pascal can be considered a small language—much simpler than Cobol, PL/1, Algol 68, Fortran 77, and Ada; a little easier than Fortran 66; and a little more complex than Algol 60. Although it includes various control structures and very complete structures, it still is a simple language, with data declarations only at subprogram level and visibility rules inherited from Algol 60. Its syntax was designed to allow a recursive descent parsing, which means it can be described by an LL(1) grammar. Declaration and name definition rules—especially the very strict order of their appearance in a program—were designed to allow one-pass compilation, or at least a complete resolution of all references in a single sequential survey of the source program.

The first implementation, under the control of the language designer, was realized simultaneously with the language definition in order to guarantee the implementability of each new idea. It is fairly certain that this conception had an effect upon the language: On the one hand, all mechanisms that appear in the language were included only after they had been proved efficiently implementable; on the other hand, the first real compiler (see Sec. 6.2.2) used self-compilation, which meant that it contained in itself all that was necessary for the boot-

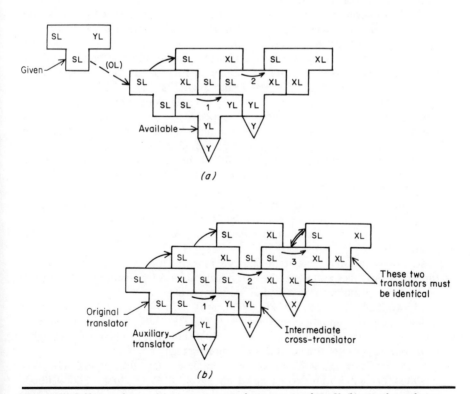

Figure 6.2 Self-compilation: (a) successive translations on machine Y; (b) complete schema with validation step.

strap of other Pascal compilers. This implementation proved to be the model used by most implementations that followed.

A study of Pascal implementations is interesting since it shows various methods, generally well described, which do not differ in the compiler structure or internal working but in the combinations of methods used. All the implementations described in this chapter are one-pass compilers (at least until the production of an intermediate language), using a recursive descent method and having no special code-optimization phase. It is also important to note that one of the main reasons Pascal is now found in almost all computer systems is the portability of its implementations.

6.2.2 The first implementation on a CDC 6600

This implementation is the only example [Wir71b] where no other Pascal compiler existed when the first compiler on a CDC 6600 was to be implemented. There were two possibilities: It could be written in a high-level language or in the target-machine assembly language.

The first alternative was chosen since it is both easier to write in a high-level language and easier to port a program written in such a language. All the compilers in the following examples are also written in high-level languages. Whenever the writing language is an auxiliary language, the translator was obtained after a first translation; this is not true, of course, for interpreters, as is shown in the cases of Macro-Spitbol (see Sec. 6.3.2) and Stage2 (see Sec. 7.4).

At first Fortran was chosen as the writing language for the Pascal compiler, but it proved to be poorly adapted and was dropped after a year of work. The compiler was then written in Pascal (an almost complete subset) and translated by hand into a medium-level language closer to the machine language [Amm81].

Since no prior product existed, branch 5 of the diagram in Fig. 5.4 had to be traversed. There was a single machine, the CDC 6600, and a need to produce the compiler [P, 6600, 6600].

The first step consisted in writing by hand a compiler for a subset of Pascal; the compiler was also written in this subset [PO, PO, 6600] (branch 5). Then the source language was modified in order to compile a full Pascal [P, PO, 6600] (branch 2).

After these two iterations in the diagram, branch 1 was traversed with Pascal as the source language and PO as the writing language. A translator for PO was then necessary and the diagram was entered recursively.

The available translator [P, PO, 6600] must be modified to [P, 6600, 6600] (branch 3) to be executable on the CDC 6600. The object language is the right one. This translator is applied to [P, PO, 6600] to obtain [P, 6600, 6600] through a combination operator linked to the writing language.

In a second step, the self-compiler [P, P, 6600] was desirable. [P, PO, 6600] was modified (branch 3) in order to take advantage of full P. The first [P, 6600, 6600] was then used to implement the self-compiler. (Note that one of the steps of Fig. 6.2 is unnecessary because the source and target machines are the same.)

The complete schema of this implementation is given in Fig. 6.3. The third translation corresponds to the validation step.

The fact that self-compilation was used to implement Pascal had several consequences:

- The language itself was affected, being modified to some degree in order to allow the programming of its own compiler.

- The compiler was affected, being much more reliable than a compiler written in an assembly language; moreover, self-compilation necessitated the generation of good-quality code in order to ensure satisfactory compilation performance.

- The quantity of work entailed was affected, because two compilers were written and several successive translations were needed to obtain the final product.

This compiler was used as a basis for the implementation of most other Pascal compilers.

6.2.3   The construction of Pascal-P

We outline here the construction of an implementation system [NAJ75] that the reader will see used in the next example. The goal in this case was a compiler for an abstract machine easily simulated on an actual computer; the reference compiler of Pascal's first implementation (or rather its successor for a revised Pascal) was to be used. Moreover, the same CDC 6600 was available. Two important design choices were the definition of the abstract machine, taking into account the characteristics of the real machines onto which the compiler was to be ported, and the definition of a simple mapping of the abstract machine onto the actual one.

The first choice was to write the compiler in its own source language. The compiler would generate code for an abstract stack machine, which was in turn adaptable to most existing machines. Most abstract machines are stack-oriented: P-code, Janus, O-code, Intcode, etc. (see Sec. 5.2). This allows a simple instruction set, since a single operand is necessary for most instructions. And it has another consequence, each instruction being more easily interpreted, which was the method chosen to implement the abstract machine.

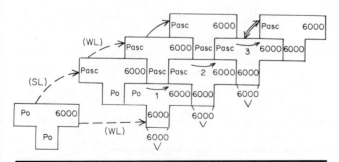

Figure 6.3   First Pascal compiler, on the CDC 6600.

The goal was to have a compiler for an abstract P-code machine: [P, PC, PC]. As noted above, the CDC 6600 with [P, P, 6600] and [P, 6600, 6600] was available. One may follow the course of the development by reference to Fig. 6.4.

In a first step, the object language of [P, P, 6600] is modified to have [P, P, PC] (branch 4). The writing language is Pascal, since its compiler existed on the CDC 6600. The object language is P-code, the desired result.

A second application of the writing-language operator leads to Fig. 6.4b, which is a self-compilation. The result must then be validated in a third step. P-code being an interpretable language, an interpreter is needed, one written by hand (Fig. 5.5, branch 4). The complete schema of this implementation is shown in Fig. 6.4c.

This is another Pascal implementation using self-compilation. The resulting

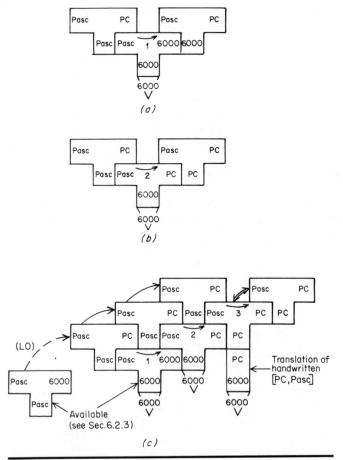

Figure 6.4 Construction of Pascal-P: (a) first WL combination; (b) second WL combination; (c) complete schema with validation step.

compiler is written in the abstract machine language and generates code for this same machine. Hence the compiler itself must be interpreted. This takes place in two passes: The first one translates Pascal into P-code, the second one interprets P-code. Consequently, performance (at least, timewise) is not very good. (This judgment applies where the compiler is run on ordinary computers, because on personal computers the user is so accustomed to direct interpretation of Basic that an interpretable intermediate language yields a spectacular gain in performance.) Yet it is relatively easy to write a new interpreter for a new machine, a quick way to have new Pascal implementations. This kind of implementation is a principal reason for the rapid diffusion of Pascal to so many machines.

6.2.4   An implementation using the Pascal-P system

To implement Pascal on the DEC PDP-10 [GLN76], only this machine and the two compilers of the previous example were available. Several methods could have been chosen:

- Implementing only an interpreter for Pascal-P (This is what has since been done on many microcomputers.)

- Rewriting the compiler in a language available on PDP-10, using [P, P, PC] as a model

- Changing only the code generator in [P, P, PC] and finding another compiler to compile this one

The first solution was not satisfactory for a timesharing computer because the two passes of the compiler both had to be themselves interpreted. On the other hand, this compiler could be used as an auxiliary compiler. [P, P, PC] was then usable, PC being simulated by an interpreter. To implement the actual compiler, the code-generation phase of [P, P, PC] then had to be rewritten.

In the first step, the object language of [P, P, PC] was changed to generate code for the PDP-10. [P, P, PDP] was obtained by branch 4 of Fig. 5.4. The writing language being Pascal, [P, PC, PC] was needed, written in PC. The necessary interpreter was obtained by modifying the writing language of [PC, P], which becomes [P, PDP] (branch 4 of Fig. 5.5). Its object language is also PC, but the interpreter has now been produced.

A Pascal compiler is now available; the complete schema of its implementation is given in Fig. 6.5, with two interpretation operators on the writing language and a self-compilation. In the first two steps of self-compilation, the support machine is the P-machine, implemented on the PDP-10 by an interpreter. The third step is a classical validation step.

In this example, Pascal is again implemented by self-compilation. Since the compiler is written in Pascal, it is easily modifiable, and only the code generator must be rewritten, something that has often been done and for many machines. A disadvantage of this approach is that restrictions and some small errors from the first compiler are now found in many existing implementations.

152   Software Portability

6.2.5   Other Pascal implementations

We have just described in some detail three specific implementations of Pascal,
but many others deserve to be cited; they would compose a good, if partial,
anthology of combination methods. We will cite here only those that are particularly interesting. A more complete comparison is made in Lecarme and Peyrolle-
Thomas [LPT78].

The second Pascal compiler [WeQ72] was for the ICL 1900. This compiler [P,
P, 1900] was obtained by a change of [P, P, 6600]. It was then translated into the
cross-compiler [P, 6600, 1900] by [P, 6600, 6600]. A second translation of [P, P,
1900] by [P, 6600, 1900] led to [P, 1900, 1900]. As this work was done in Zurich,
the result was tested by a simulator of the ICL 1900 on the CDC 6600 [1900,
6600], obtained by translation of [1900, P] by [P, P, 6600, 6600]. The result was
then physically ported to Belfast, North Ireland.

The second compiler for the CDC 6600 [Amm74] was not an adaptation of the
first one, but a completely new construction adapted to the revised language. Its
installation was made from the first compiler [P, 6600, 6600] and [revised Pascal,
P, 6600]. The resulting compiler was capable of self-compilation on a single
machine.

The Pascal-S implementation [Wir75] was a unique case because it was not a
self-compilation: Since Pascal-S is a subset of Pascal, it is not sufficient to write
its own compiler. Its implementation is a compiler-interpreter, written in Pascal
and implementable on any machine on which there is a complete Pascal.

Several implementations used self-compilation with two separate machines—
for instance, the implementation for an Iris 80 and one of the many for the PDP-
11 [BdV76], which was interrupted after the cross-compiler [P, PDP-10, PDP-11]
was obtained.

Other implementations use the "trunk-compiler" technique, where the compiler is written but the parts that generate code for a given construct are left

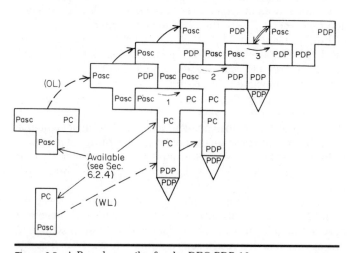

Figure 6.5 A Pascal compiler for the DEC PDP-10.

blank, to be filled in for a given target machine. This method was used for a second implementation on the ICL 1900 [Wel81] (self-compilation on a single machine and from the first implementation), on the ICL 2900 [Wel81] (self-compilation with two machines), and on the Hitachi 8000 (self-compilation on a single machine by Pascal-P).

Among the many implementations on the IBM 360/370, one is especially interesting [RuS76]. It uses the same method as the first implementation on the CDC 6600, with a translation by hand of the compiler into a language already available on the machine, in order to obtain a bootstrap tool that is abandoned as soon as the actual compiler is able to compile itself. The auxiliary language chosen was PL/1.

More recent Pascal implementations are not described in detail here—on the one hand, because they use similar methods, and on the other, because they are commercial products, which precludes a detailed description. However, we want to cite the Pascal-UCSD success. The system is based on the first version of Pascal-P and is installed on many personal computers by a simple rewriting of the interpreter.

A Pascal machine has also been microprogrammed to execute P-code; it is enjoying commercial success. On the whole, P-code, which was the result of a study by students from the Technische Hochschule of Zurich, has enjoyed extraordinary acceptance in industry.

Let us finally cite, among the most recent implementations, the one at the Free University of Amsterdam [TSK81]. It relies on a semiuniversal intermediate language, EM-1 (see Sec. 5.2). The first part of this compiler generates EM-1, which can also be used for Algol 68, C, Ada, and other languages. The second part is either an interpreter or a specialized translator and optimizer (see Sec. 3.4.5 and Tanenbaum et al. [TSS82]). An exemplary implementation was done on the PDP-11, where the object program can be either interpreted or translated into machine language.

6.2.6 Conclusion

As we have noted, the study of Pascal implementations leads to a remarkably large inventory of self-compilation methods. Results are of several kinds; there are

- One-pass compilers, monolithic, compact, and fast: CDC 6600, PDP-10, ICL 1900 and 2900, Iris 80, Hitachi 8000, IBM 360/370, etc.

- Compilers followed by an interpreter, of small size and low implementation cost, usable on personal computers: Pascal-P and all its more-or-less derived implementations

- Two-pass compilers, the second performing optimizations: implementation at the Free University of Amsterdam and many other commercial implementations.

All compilers that are derived from the two made on the CDC 6600 (Pascal-P included) are notable for their compactness, but they have been criticized for their monolithic structure and their use of a recursive descent analysis, which yields poor separation between the analytic and synthetic parts of the compiler [WaC81].

For purposes of comparison, the different methods of obtaining new implementations of Pascal can be split into several categories:

- Methods that imply a lot of manual programming: the first implementation on the CDC 6600, the first on the ICL 1900 and the IBM 360/370

- Methods that are relatively routine, benefiting from self-compilation, since it already is a part of the compiler: the second compilers built on the CDC 6600 and the ICL 1900 and the further evolution of all self-compiling one-pass compilers

- Cases where the entire work is done on the target machine: the DEC PDP-10 and the Hitachi 8000 implementations

- Cases where the entire work is done on the source machine: construction of Pascal-P and the first implementation on the ICL 1900

- The most frequent cases, where the work is split between the source and the target machines, front end on the source machine and back end on the target machine

6.3 Implementations of Snobol4, SL5, and Icon

6.3.1 Introduction

Pascal is a relatively simple language where all variables are typed at declaration time. Such a language is well adapted to an implementation by a real one-pass (or more) compiler, generating machine language.

In the present section we shall present the case of very different, rather powerful languages having many operators, where data types are not linked to variables. This last characteristic generally prevents determination at compile time of the operand types of a given operator. Generation of machine language is impossible, at least in the general case, and implementation of such languages is often made by a compiler-interpreter, where the compiler is smaller and simpler than the interpreter. Even if the two phases are separated, very few semantic treatments can be done at compile time.

We are grouping in this section three languages of the same family, successively designed under the direction of the same main author, Ralph E. Griswold. They all represent successive states of the same philosophy of programming-language design. They use implementation techniques very different from the ones we saw for Pascal, and also very different from each other, despite their design continuity.

It is impossible to present each language in detail in this chapter. We refer the reader to the documentation cited in the references, and more particularly to

Lecarme [Lec81b], which discusses the three languages and compares them. We shall be content here with a very brief summary of each language.

Snobol4 was designed in 1967 [GPP68], at the same time as the implementation method called "standard," which we shall describe in Sec. 6.3.2. It is a general programming language, but with powerful facilities for string manipulation. Program syntax is very primitive, and there are no control structures or static visibility rules for identifiers. The language provides many data types, operators, and predefined functions, as well as important debugging facilities. Pattern matching in strings is made by complex and powerful mechanisms that form a kind of sublanguage inside Snobol4, with backtracking possibilities (not controlled by the programmer). The language has been widely diffused because of its implementation portability and in spite of its very low efficiency in execution.

SL5 is a transition language [GRH77], a temporary successor of Snobol4, designed to provide new semantic mechanisms. Structure and syntax of programs are quite classical, close to those of Algol 68 and Pascal, but semantic aspects are numerous and original. For example, the classical procedure call is split into three successive operations, which allows easy definition of value generators and coroutines. Many extensions may be added to the basic mechanisms, sometimes such that one extension is incompatible with another. The fact that it is a purely experimental language explains why it has been implemented, but not distributed nor definitively described.

Icon is the official Snobol4 successor, using the SL5 experiment results [GHK79]. It is a more concise and a simpler language, though still powerful and original; Icon, like Snobol4, has been widely diffused. Implementations have also been distributed and a reference book has recently been published [GrG83]. Program structure and syntax are quite strongly inspired by the C language. However, various data types of Snobol4 and SL5 are kept in the language, and there are some new and very powerful computation mechanisms: a mechanism for coexpression, which leads to a very efficient implementation of coroutines, the use of generators, etc.

6.3.2 Implementation of Snobol4

Use of the macrolanguage SIL. The standard Snobol4 system uses two superposed intermediate languages, one of which is invisible during transport, while the other is the basis of system portability. The Snobol4 system includes a very simple compiler (mainly because of the rudimentary syntax of the language) that generates an interpretive language, and it includes also an interpreter for this language. These two components share a memory manager (with a garbage collector) and a run-time system. The compiler can be called by the interpreter like a subprogram for converting a string into code.

The interpretive language is a Polish prefix notation, which is uncommon, but it makes the treatment of the unusual notion of success or failure of expression easier. The use of an interpreter is justified by the extreme difficulty of producing machine code directly, data types being known only at execution time. Moreover, it has a very positive effect on system portability since the object language is completely independent of the computer.

The second intermediate language is the writing language SIL, already presented in Sec. 5.2. The system is a large, monolithic program (6400 lines) written in SIL. Though it is organized in a very disciplined way, it cannot be split into modules. It is a very slow program and uses a lot of memory, but, fortunately, is very reliable.

Actual implementation. The implementation kit includes detailed documentation and the Snobol4 system. There are no example sets or test programs for SIL itself, and the abstract-machine instruction set does not clearly distinguish between what must be directly translated into machine language and what should be a run-time system call.

The implementor's work includes the following procedures:

- Read the documentation (large but well done)
- Determine the correspondence between the abstract machine and the real one (the crucial step)
- Using a macroassembler for the target machine, define a set of macros to translate SIL into machine language
- Write the run-time system, mainly input-output routines
- Make the system acceptable to the macroassembler, which almost always means making systematic modifications to the shape of SIL instructions
- Assemble the system
- Try the result and correct the bugs in the macros or the run-time system

This is the basis of the schema of Fig. 6.6. We have made explicit the fact that it is a compiler-interpreter and we have demonstrated the necessity of writing the run-time system by hand, using the conventions described in this figure.

An assessment. The main problems encountered during implementation can come from several sources:

- There is no macroassembler on the target machine, which forces the use of a general macroprocessor such as Stage2.
- The limitations of the macroassembler can lead to difficulties in writing the macros or in modifying the source text.
- There are limitations in the assembler itself, which cannot always treat such a large monolithic program. (Porting Snobol4 has led to the detection of major bugs in many assemblers!)
- The memory limitations of the target machine can make the realization impossible in actuality, even if it is possible in theory.
- There are difficulties in writing the run-time system both because of the lack of clear delimitation and because of target system defaults.
- There is no way to test the work in progress.

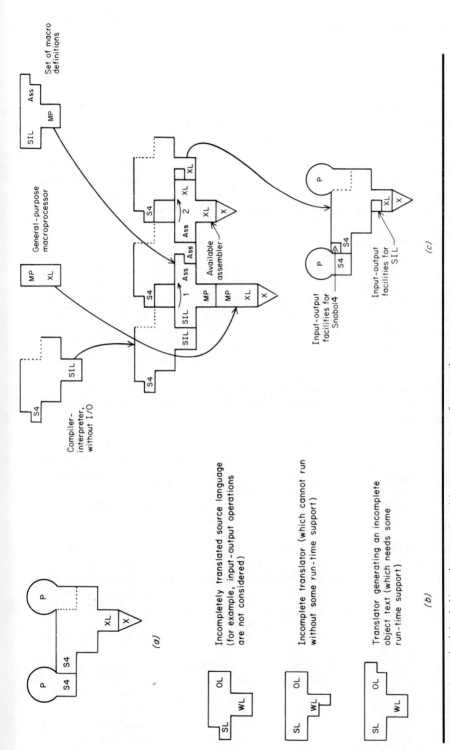

Figure 6.6 A standard Snobol4 implementation: (*a*) representation of a compiler-interpreter; (*b*) representation of incomplete processors; (*c*) standard implementation of Snobol4.

• The total cost, mainly of the assemblies, is prohibitive; cost in time is also a consideration, for the implementation can take from one to six months.

To summarize, the characteristics of the standard Snobol4 system prompt a slow and cumbersome implementation, which is not feasible on small or medium-sized computers. But it is extremely flexible, corrections are easy, and the system has evolved along with the language. The system is largely machine-independent, but this is the main cause of its inefficiency. As a system-writing language, SIL is of very low level; this makes the work of the initial implementor very difficult, but at the same time it discourages local deviations. Programs written in standard Snobol4 are among the most portable.

Other Snobol4 implementations.   There are several implementations of Snobol4, generally written in machine language, which are specific to a given machine and thus not portable. CAL Snobol [Gas70] on a CDC Cyber and Sitbol [Gim74a, Gim 74b] on a DECSystem-10 both use an interpreter, with algorithms very different from the ones used in standard Snobol4 and much more efficient. The first treats a relatively small and arbitrary subset of the language. Fasbol [San71, SaM70] on a Univac 1100 and Spitbol [Dew71, DeB77] on an IBM 360 370 are two very different, tentative attempts to avoid interpretation and to generate machine code, which obviously must use a lot of run-time routines. Fasbol imposes a major deviation from Snobol4 in requiring the declaration of variables. On the contrary, Spitbol stays very close to the standard language, but a major effort has been given to efficient implementation, using all possible target-machine features.

Macro-Spitbol [DMC77, MCD77], on the contrary, is a portable implementation with an interpreter. Profiting from their standard Snobol4 and Spitbol experiments, its authors succeeded in achieving a much more efficient result, in time and in memory use, which is still relatively easy to port. The two main reasons for this success are a simplified interpreter, which is made faster by the use of indirect threaded code [Dew75], and a new low-level system-writing language, Minimal (see Sec. 5.2).

Minimal is yet another abstract machine language, but, as opposed to SIL, it has registers, a parameterized memory, and a large set of simple instructions. Minimal is translated into the target machine language by a special translator (with Fortran and Snobol4 versions), which makes many verifications of validity in the source. The implementor, who must write a large program in Minimal, is constrained to a relatively structured programming style; hence the resulting program is likely to be correct. This is unusual because most low-level implementation language translators are relatively lax in their enforcement of programming rules.

Documentation given with the implementation kit is detailed and includes a lot of test programs for the final product. However, test programs for Minimal itself and for the run-time system are lacking. The schema of Fig. 6.7 shows the implementation steps with the same conventions as used in Fig. 6.6.

Macro-Spitbol has proved to be an easily and cheaply portable implementation; it allowed the first implementations of Snobol4 on microcomputers.

6.3.3   Implementation of SL5

The writing language Sil/2.   Like Snobol4, the only SL5 implementation uses
an interpreter, which is even more indispensable here: Notions such as environments and filters make generation of machine language impossible. Like Snobol4, the SL5 system is written in a portable language, Sil/2 [Gri77e], which is
very different from SIL and Minimal, for it is not an abstract machine language
but a well-structured, high-level language (or perhaps medium-level), with modularity and coroutines.

Sil/2 is an expression language inspired by BCPL [Ric71], and by SL5 itself. It
has a nested-block structure with static visibility rules of the Algol family. Sil/2
programs are made up of separately compiled modules, themselves consisting of

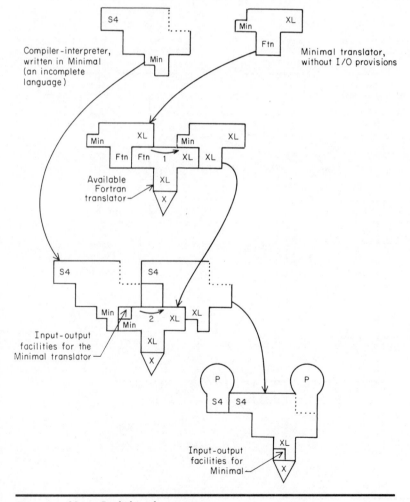

Figure 6.7   Macro-Spitbol implementation.

procedures. Although it is a high-level language, it relies on an abstract machine model, the Sil/2 machine, which is much closer to actual computers than is the SIL machine. Its memory is linear and made of descriptors (without qualifiers). These descriptors are less cumbersome than those of SIL, because an integer no longer has to be in one of the fields, and the use of 24- to 36-bit words is now possible. The abstract machine includes an operand stack easily matching actual machine registers, and a set of only 35 simple instructions.

Since Sil/2 is a high-level language, an ordinary macroprocessor is not enough to translate it into a machine language. This is done in two passes, as shown in Fig. 6.8. A compiler translates Sil/2 into the Sil/2 assembly language (IL), then this intermediate language is translated to the target machine language. The compiler and the translator are written in Snobol4, which is used as a portable

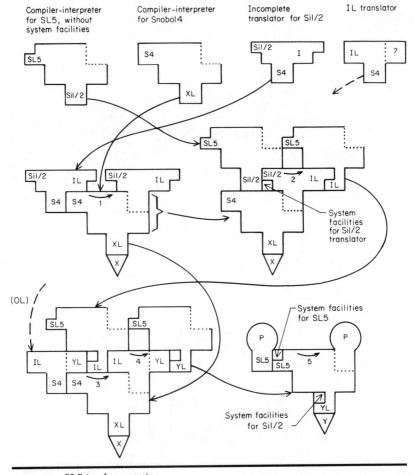

Figure 6.8 SL5 implementation.

system-writing language. The compiler is independent of the target computer, which means that the translation of the SL5 system into the Sil/2 machine assembly language can be done only once. The translator is itself conceptually divided into two parts: The first one, again independent of the target computer, works as if code were generated for a "universal target machine," close to an actual machine because it includes registers (for communications between procedures and stack simulation); the second one is made of final object-code-generation procedures from the universal machine.

The schema of Fig. 6.8 shows the different steps of the SL5 implementation system. It involves two interpretation operators on the writing language, and two combination operators linked to the object language. On the whole, this implementation involves not less than five programming languages (not counting SL5 itself): two writing languages—Sil/2 and Snobol4—and three intermediate languages—the SL5 interpretive language, the Sil/2 machine assembly language, and the universal machine language. And that does not count the target machine language that has to be produced and in which the run-time system routines must be written.

Actual implementation.   Unlike the Snobol4 standard system, the interface between SL5 and the host system is clearly defined, because of the concept of "system functions." In order to port SL5 to a new computer, an efficient Snobol4 implementation must be available (either on the target machine or on another machine used to cross-compile the SL5 system written in Sil/2). Code-generation functions must be written in Snobol4 and the system functions in the target machine language. Some of these functions, like input-output operations or string manipulation, are necessary for Sil/2, whereas others belong only to SL5. These system functions can very often be written in Sil/2, at least for temporary use, which reduces the initial work. Other functions are given in Fortran and can be used as is in a first step (if communication between the different languages is feasible). To allow the easy replacement of a function written in one language with the same function in another language, without recompiling the whole system, a uniform procedure calling mechanism is used.

Sil/2 is machine-independent and is designed to be quite portable, but the transport of the SL5 system, i.e., of a particular program written in Sil/2, is the critical factor. The port may be done at any of three levels, each one more ambitious (and consequently more costly). The easiest method is to redo only the translator's code-generation routines. Translation of the SL5 system (from the Sil/2 machine language) is then done only once—on the source computer, the target computer, or even an intermediate computer.

A more expensive method consists of remaking a new translator for the Sil/2 machine language; this is necessary if the source computer is not accessible and no usable Snobol4 implementation is available on the target or the intermediate computer or if the universal machine step results in an inefficient object code. The use of a general macroprocessor is sufficient for this translation.

The most expensive method consists of porting Sil/2 itself using Snobol4, which means writing a new Sil/2 compiler. If a first implementation has already been done, it can be tempting to write the compiler in Sil/2.

Because SL5 has not been distributed, we do not know what is given to the implementor or how long it takes to do the work. Though the method seems attractive, it was abandoned by its authors. We do not know what their conclusions from the experiment were, but they do not seem very positive.

6.3.4   Implementation of Icon

Description of the method.   Like that of SL5, the first implementation of Icon was designed at the same time as was the language itself, and was immediately used on a DECSystem-10 and a CDC Cyber. But that is the extent of their similarities, for the Icon system implementation relies entirely on a single programming language, which is used to write the compiler and the system functions, and is the language of the code generated as well. This principle is viable, of course, only if the language can satisfy all these needs, and only if it is available on all computers: At implementation time, the authors chose Fortran as the language.

As an object language, even though it is somewhat clumsy and restrictive, Fortran can be considered acceptable, since most of the generated code consists of procedure and function calls. As a compiler- or system-function-writing language, it is really not convenient, and the Icon system relies on Ratfor [Ker75]. Ratfor adds disciplined control structures and the concept of constants and characters to Fortran (see Sec. 4.4.2); it is translated into Fortran by a preprocessor (itself written in Fortran).

Therefore Icon is translated by a compiler written in Ratfor into a Fortran program calling a lot of system functions, themselves written in Ratfor. These system functions avoid the explicit use of an interpreter, but they have the same role. The whole Icon system relies exclusively on Fortran, aside from six simple functions (mainly bit manipulation) that must be written in machine language. The schema of Fig. 6.9 shows the different steps of this implementation.

However, an implementation using only Fortran would be so inefficient that it would be almost unusable. Therefore at least the input-output operations and the character manipulation routines must be rewritten in the target machine language. This must be done for Ratfor itself [CoK78] (for compilation of Icon programs) as well as for Icon system functions. Thus the long-standing reputation of Fortran for efficiency is shown to be ill-deserved in nonnumeric domains.

Actual implementation.   A potential Icon implementor receives an especially detailed implementation kit [GrH79]. A dozen documents, of from 10 to 100 pages, describe Icon itself as well as Ratfor and Icon implementation techniques. For both languages, documents give examples from the DECSystem-10 and CDC Cyber implementations. The tape contains more than 400 files representing about 33,000 card images, divided into 11 subsets, such as:

- The Ratfor preprocessor, written in Fortran, needed to initialize the Ratfor implementation: [Ratfor, Fortran, Fortran]

- The same preprocessor, written in Ratfor, which is the reference version: [Ratfor, Ratfor, Fortran]

- The Icon compiler, written in Ratfor: [Icon, Ratfor, Fortran]
- The Icon system functions, also written in Ratfor
- Test programs, written in Fortran, for the system functions the implementor has to write in machine language
- A Fortran translation by the Icon compiler of test programs (to test the compiler)
- Input data for these programs and the results that should be produced
- Three cross-reference indexes, showing how system functions are used

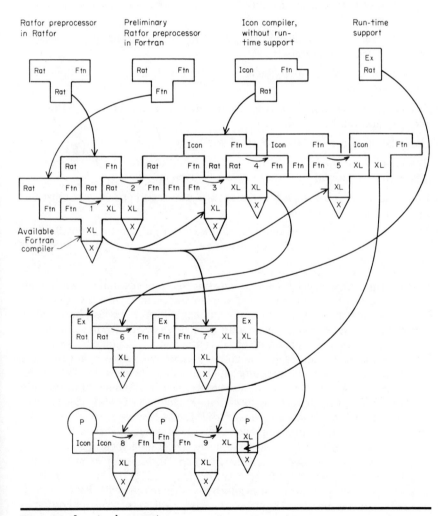

Figure 6.9 Icon implementation.

The implementor's work may be split into the following steps:

- Documentation study.

- Tape reading, some files being printed and most others being stored: This implies writing utility programs to split files into subfiles and to build large libraries. (There are more than a hundred system functions for Icon alone.)

- The first implementation of Ratfor: The preprocessor can usually be directly compiled and run for at least a few lines.

- Improvements to Ratfor to make it actually usable: Input-output routines need to be rewritten in machine language; they are extremely slow (character decoding is done through a linear search in a table on both input and output) and very restrictive.

- Construction of the "cruising" version of Ratfor, by recompiling a possibly improved Ratfor preprocessor.

- Implementation of machine-language system functions and their verification by the test programs.

- Choice of suitable values for machine-dependent parameters, which describe memory and word structure.

- Compilation of the Icon compiler (via Ratfor then Fortran).

- Testing of the compiler on the test programs and checking of the object code, which must be exactly identical to what is given on tape.

- Compilation of Icon system functions (via Ratfor then Fortran) and construction of a library for the linker.

- Compilation (from Fortran into machine language) of test programs, linkage with the system-functions library, execution with given data, and checking of results.

An assessment.   A crucial point is that the Icon implementation relies on an excellent Fortran compiler. From the implementor's point of view, the main difficulty is the manipulation of the large number of files on the distribution tape. Even though, in theory, no actual programming is necessary, the implementor in fact must write a large "program" of operating-system commands. Variations between command languages are sometimes greater than between programming languages, and this leads to communication difficulties between the first implementor and the others. It is this difference that led R. E. Griswold to invent a hypothetical operating-system pseudocommand language [Gri82]. The Icon installation manual is written in terms of this pseudolanguage, which is implemented nowhere but ensures that everybody understands the same thing.

The authors did not evaluate the time necessary to implement Icon on a new machine. The resulting performance, particularly in terms of memory, is described as satisfying. But the authors were not prepared for the fact that Fortran and Ratfor portability in most cases caused many more problems than expected. The use of Ratfor as a writing language is far from ideal, as is the use of Fortran as an object language.

These serious drawbacks caused the authors to change their implementation strategy completely for the third and following versions of Icon [GrG83]. The writing language is now C. The object language is an intermediate one that can either be interpreted or translated into the target-machine assembly language. The interpreter and the translator are themselves written in C. The performance of the generated code is much better, in memory as well as in time. There are now several implementations using these more classical techniques, but the gain in efficiency has been paid for by loss of portability.

6.4 Implementation of Ada

6.4.1 Some general observations

We shall describe in this section a multitarget-compiler implementation method for a very large language. The techniques are therefore particularly complex and represent several combinations of the elementary methods described in Sec. 5.3.

The language.   Ada is a language designed for the needs of the U.S. Department of Defense, and its last and standardized version appeared in January 1983 [ARM83]. Its design was proposed through international competition, in response to very constricting written requirements; many proposals were offered. The language was to be particularly suited for embedded systems, but it was also to be the unique language used in the defense establishment, which means it had to solve the classical problems. The goals gradually evolved toward a "universal" language such as PL/1 or Algol 68.

Ada is a "strongly typed" language, with various structured types. It also includes generic subprograms, packages, separate compilation, tasking, exceptions, and implementation specifications.

Concepts that were previously only separately available are gathered here in one language, and both high-level concepts and machine dependencies can be expressed. Each of these programmer conveniences leads to specific implementation difficulties: Genericity and name overloading make identification very complex, etc.

The project in context.   CII-Honeywell Bull, Alsys, and Siemens are collaborating in the development of a portable compiler root for European industry. The development work is being done simultaneously on a CII-HB DPS-7 and a Siemens 7700. However, portability is a major goal in the project, and the range of target machines is wide and dissimilar. The implementation system must be compatible with different machines and different systems.

The solutions posed.   The size of the language and the necessity of several compiler passes immediately exclude a monolithic architecture. Moreover, compiler complexity imposes a solution that splits the task into several subtasks.

For a multitarget compiler, the split between front end and code generation is natural, but introducing machine dependencies can be done in different ways: We could have one code generator per target, a single generator and an interpreter per target (which would be detrimental to the efficiency of program execution), or a single generator generating a multitarget intermediate language and then a generator per target. The later the introduction of machine dependencies, the less the work in retargeting. We shall see that the solution chosen is very close to the last alternative posed above, although the separation between the target-independent and target-dependent parts is not so clear.

Among intervening languages, the most important choice is that of the writing language: The source language must be full Ada (with no subset allowed); the object language is necessarily a machine language, possibly preceded by an intermediate language. The writing language is almost necessarily a high-level language, for the compiler itself must be portable. Among the widely used languages, few are satisfactory. Self-compilation is a seductive idea, but it raises the problem of bootstrapping.

6.4.2 The solution chosen

The choice of a compiler with two independent parts, one for analysis and the other for code generation is not entirely satisfactory: Too much work would be left to the code generator, and the rewriting of this part of the compiler for each new target machine would be too difficult.

Therefore an extra step is introduced, called the expander, which is an intermediate phase between the analyzer and the code generator. The compiler must also include some tools, such as a prelinker and a context-manager to manage separate compilation of programs.

The compiler has the structure shown in Fig. 6.10. All the modules constituting the front end of the compiler (the analyzer, expander, and optimizers) and its environment (the context-manager, prelinker, and virtual memory manager) are written in Ada in a completely portable way. Although the code generator and the run-time system are written mostly in Ada, the back end would have to be largely rewritten for a new machine. The input-output module includes compiler and memory-manager input-output, and its interfaces with the rest of the compiler are system-independent.

The analyzer. The first of the three major parts of the compiler is itself split into several phases:

- Syntax analysis generating a syntactic tree, the AIL (*a*bstract *i*ntermediate *l*anguage)
- Identification
- Semantic analysis

Each phase communicates with the others via the AIL tree and a symbol table, which are filled in at the same time. The analyzer generates a standardized, decorated tree that includes generic instantiations. Each node includes its type, links with its father, its right brother, and its first son. Terminal nodes also have reference to the symbol table.

A detailed description in the symbol table corresponds to each variable, type, or program unit declared in a given program.

Figure 6.11*a* shows a program fragment; Fig. 6.11*b* shows its translation into AIL.

The expander. This part of the compiler is introduced so that the interface between the portable part of the compiler and the code generator can be of low level, allowing the generation of good-quality code. One of the unique characteristics of the expander is a mechanism of parameterization that allows, at this level, some implementation-dependent choices.

The expander's work consists first of allocating data depending on information in the symbol table produced by the analyzer and some parameters (the addressing mode, the allocation mode for local arrays, etc.). The fact that data allocation is made at this point allows complete expansion of all access paths to objects in a low-level intermediate language and optimization of these accesses, usually a large part of the program code.

The most important task of the expander is to translate the AIL tree into the low-level language Lolita: AIL constructions are broken into more elementary ones, accesses are expanded, run-time checks are explicit. Also, the symbol table is transformed into a low-level table of more compact form, containing only those objects the program effectively refers to. Like AIL, the low-level language has a tree form. We have already seen an example of it in Sec. 5.2.

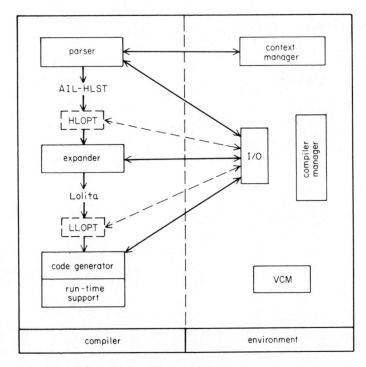

Figure 6.10 Structure of an Ada compiler.

Figure 6.12 shows how an access path can be expanded depending on the addressing mode: static link (Fig. 6.12a) or display (Fig. 6.12b). The expander can therefore produce different trees for a same source program, depending on parameterized implementation-dependent choices.

The optimizers.   The expander also includes two optional phases, the optimizers. One of them works at the AIL level and does the analysis of the program (call graph, flow graph, and recursivity analysis). It can also modify the source tree by in-line inclusion of small subprograms, by check optimization, by replacement of variables with their value, etc. The other, the low-level optimizer, works on the low-level tree produced by the transformation phase of the expander and deals specifically with expression reduction (i.e., reorganization, replacement of variables with their value, propagation of constants and values, reduction of operators, etc.). These two optimizers are independent of the target language.

The code generator and run-time system.   From the low-level tree and symbol table, the code generator generates an executable translation of the source program, calling the run-time system to perform input-output, memory management, exception propagation, and task management. Therefore this part of the compiler is mostly target-machine-dependent and must be rewritten again for each new machine.

6.4.3   The construction of the implementation system

Construction.   Since the compiler is written in Ada, a first translator must be available. As no compiler existed yet, a translator for Ao, a subset of Ada, into HPL, a subset of PL/1, had to be written: [Ao, HPL, HPL]. The translator for Ada

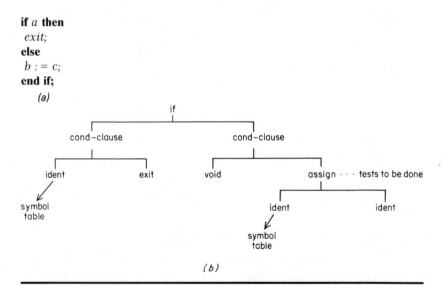

if a **then**
  exit;
else
  $b := c;$
end if;
  (a)

  (b)

Figure 6.11   The AIL tree: (a) a program fragment; (b) its translation into AIL.

into the low-level language for the development machine, LO_x was written next: [Ada, Ao, LO_x]. And then the corresponding code generator was developed in order to have an Ada compiler on machine X, here a CII-Honeywell Bull DPS-7. The compiler for machine X is formed of the two parts shown in Fig. 6.13a, and works in the manner illustrated in Fig. 6.13b.

Retargeting.   On the source machine, [A, A, LO_x] must be modified to become [A, A, LO_y], following Fig. 6.14. Then, to install it on machine Y, either a code generator [LO_y, P, L_y] must be written, P being an available high-level language, working on Y, or a new code generator [LO_y, Ada, L_y] must be developed on machine X, after which the compiler is compiled on X and transported in binary form onto Y. For the first case, where the code generator is developed on Y, we obtain the final compiler, Fig. 6.15b, by the schema seen in Fig. 6.15a.

6.4.4 An assessment

Some choices have been made that have a strong influence on the final product. The most important choice certainly is the fact that the compiler is a self-compiler. This is demanding for the language as well as for the implementation system, but it has the great advantage of making portability easier and more reliable by virtue of the validation phase (see Sec. 6.1). Writing in Ada also allows

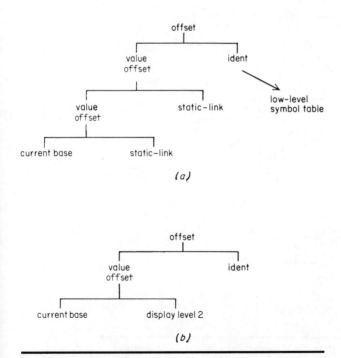

Figure 6.12 Access path to a nonlocal variable: (a) using static links; (b) using a display.

easy modification of the source text in order to adapt it to new machines, which certainly is an advantage but can lead to incompatibility between different versions or to a multiplication of local versions. The subsequent validation of the compiler may be a solution to this problem.

Another unusual choice is the introduction of machine dependencies in the

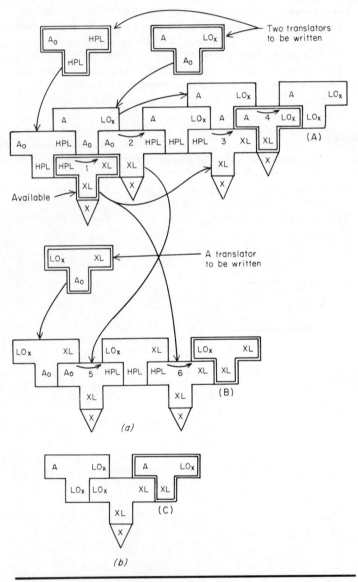

Figure 6.13 Implementing the compiler: (*a*) producing the compiler components; (*b*) using the components.

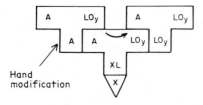

Figure 6.14   Modification of the first compiler.

front end of the compiler, which improves its adaptability to the detriment of its compilation speed. On the other hand, the generated code should be of better quality, for it is better adapted to the target machine.

A part of the installation on a new machine should be done on the source machine, at least for the first ports, because an Ada compiler must be available. The first intention was to leave the entire responsibility of the port to the implementor, by providing an interpreter for the low-level intermediate language. This interpreter would have been written in another high-level language, probably

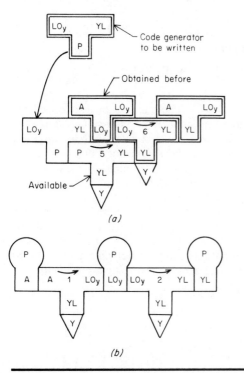

Figure 6.15   Production of the final compiler: (*a*) production; (*b*) use.

Pascal. But with the current configuration, adaptation of translators from Ada to the low-level intermediate language for the target machine must be done on the source machine.

6.5 Conclusion

The examples we have given in this chapter have allowed us to describe in detail seven methods of implementation for portable language processors and to mention about 15 others. Though each of them is different, they clearly have some aspects in common. It is tempting to try to establish a clear classification of these methods, but the choice of criteria is not easy. We could cite some major distinguishing characteristics:

- The nature of the languages
- The program models used for the construction of the implementation system (by translation, modification, or completion)
- The possibility of using a compiler-generator tool
- The characteristics of the source machine (if it intervenes), of the target machine (including its operating system), and of machines eventually used for the port
- The qualities wished for in the final product: efficiency of compilation or of object programs, ease of use, reliability, etc.
- The time and personnel constraints: time limits, team size, experience and availability of programmers, etc.

Any system of classification could conceivably help in the choice of a method. Unfortunately, it seems impossible to establish such a classification, simply because it is impossible to decide which criteria must be taken into account and how to weigh the criteria. Therefore all we can do is to provide a descriptive tool, not too constraining and not too rigorous, for clarifying the main characteristics of each method. We have proposed such a tool in Chap. 5, and we have used it here to illustrate the most important methods used in practice.

This should allow the reader to better understand the description of a particular implementation he or she might have seen elsewhere, to imagine new combinations, and to use known combinations in all situations where he or she has to choose a specific implementation method. There are not many methods of choosing an implementation strategy; we made a rather exhaustive presentation of them in Chap. 5.

Operating and Programming Systems

7.1 Some general observations

In this second chapter of case studies we present software systems that are usually much larger than the programs mentioned before. A compiler, even for a complex language, can still be designed as a single program or as several programs working together and communicating through files. But operating systems are made of a set of modules tightly linked to each other but still self-governing, working in parallel and in cooperation, with severe constraints on memory, response time, and reliability. In such a system we can no longer clearly distinguish individual programs.

Very large operating systems, such as OS/360 and its progeny or Multics, are certainly among the most complex systems conceived by the human mind. (Some people maintain that the success of such systems is much less impressive than their ambition.) An operating system (OS) may represent the huge efforts of hundreds of people over many years and may comprise thousands of modules and hundreds of thousands of lines of programming. The cost of such huge programs, and their strong ties to a particular machine architecture, exerts a negative influence on the definition of new OS architectures. (The user's software investment is a factor here too, of course.)

However, we are beginning to develop the expertise to write portable operating systems—or rather to make actual operating systems portable. We are no longer constrained by the toy or experimental systems we began with 15 years ago. This tendency to portable systems seems to have grown with the proliferation of micro- and minicomputers; it has not yet affected the market for mainframes, and it is still impossible to say if it ever will.

The two case studies we present in this chapter concern two very different but significant systems. The first, Unix (Sec. 7.2), is an operating system that has become popular very quickly; its popularity is easily explained by its original characteristics, though it has some weaknesses in both design and construction and though portability was not at all an initial concern. The second system,

MUSS (Sec. 7.3), has had no commercial diffusion (to our knowledge), and yet here portability was a main goal, rather than a feature added after the design was completed.

Unix and MUSS constitute, for our purposes, an adequate sample of existing portable systems. Among the others we might have studied, we can cite the following:

- OS6 [StS72] is a very rudimentary system, designed for a single user in order to demonstrate the possibility of writing an operating system in a high-level language, in this case BCPL. It has been ported [Sno78a] to a machine permitting microprogramming of the interpreter of the intermediate language O-code. The result is a single programming language system, for O-code is too specific to BCPL to be easily adapted to any other language.

- Solo [BrH76] has the same kind of philosophy as OS6, but it uses sequential and parallel Pascal. Compiler object code is interpreted. The system kernel and the interpreter are written in machine language, in a way very dependent on the initial computer, a PDP-11. This part must be reprogrammed to port the system, which for Powell [Pow79] represented the work of two students for six months.

- Pascal-UCSD [Bow78] is also a Pascal system implemented by interpretation. The interpreter must therefore be rewritten for each new machine, but already compiled programs can supposedly be ported as they are. This system is still rather primitive, very limited, and fairly inefficient, which has not prevented its success in use with personal computers.

- Tripos [RAB79], like OS6 and Solo, is only an experimental system, although much improved. It is also written in BCPL, but the kernel and device drivers are written in machine language (1500 lines), and BCPL programs are actually compiled. In this case, a system port is estimated to take two people six months' work.

- CP/M [Kil81] deserves to be mentioned for its popularity, even though it is not exactly a portable system. First written for the Intel 8080 microprocessors and their derived microcomputers, it was programmed in machine language, and completely reprogrammed when it had to be installed on incompatible micros. System interfaces, rather than implementations, are portable, in itself a positive accomplishment [Pec83].

- Thoth [CMM79, Che82] resembles MUSS in several ways. It is a large academic project (done at the University of Waterloo over six years) and the source of several theses. It is a multiuser system for minis, written in Zed, a remote descendant of BCPL. Its port consists mainly in redoing the code generator of the Zed compiler [BGM79] and in reprogramming about a thousand lines of machine code. System portability was a basic goal of the design and is well described in the book dedicated to it.

The third case study of this chapter (Sec. 7.4) does not concern an operating system, but a set of processors and utilities grouped under the presumptuous term, "programming system." Though it is quite an old development, it seemed interesting as a demonstration of some original techniques. In the conclusion (Sec. 7.5), we shall briefly describe several other portable utilities.

7.2   The Unix system

Unix is a multiuser timesharing operating system developed at Bell Laboratories. It consists of a kernel (a reserved, permanently resident module) and a large library of nonkernel tools.

Unix has traditionally been used for program development and text processing in universities and research centers, although it has more recently been used as a general-purpose system in a wide scope of applications and environments.

Some of its principal tools are suited to program development (compilers, linkers, debuggers, a configuration manager), text processing (editors, formatting programs), electronic mail, and file management. Unix advances the idea of a minimal kernel and maximum tool flexibility. Things typically seen by a programmer as being part of the "system," e.g., the command processor and the log-in program, are, in fact, only tools and are independent of the kernel.

Unix's user interface shows its research/university origins. Its style offers a user great freedom and power. The standard interface is oriented more toward the experienced user than toward the beginner, and the former's wish for abbreviated syntax often takes precedence over the latter's desire for explicit dialog and a lot of help in every step.

7.2.1   Unix portability

The first version of Unix was written in assembly language for a Digital PDP-7 computer by Ken Thompson, a programmer who wanted an agreeable programming environment after his Multics system at Bell Laboratories had been removed. As the system became popular for different users at Bell, different versions were made, and Thompson and Dennis Ritchie quickly realized that version control and modifiability were reasons for writing an operating system, like any other software, in a high-level language. The system was rewritten in C [KeR78], a language invented by Ritchie to be low level enough to efficiently interface with hardware but still of a much higher level than assembly language.

The first serious transport of the system, described in Johnson and Ritchie [JoR78], occurred in 1977 from a PDP-11 to an Interdata 8/32, a 32-bit machine. Many parts of the system were rewritten to be more portable, and nonportable parts were isolated into identifiable subprograms. The portable C compiler was developed.

Unix has since been transported to over 20 machines, ranging from the early PDP-7 through Interdata to the current generation of microprocessor-based, network-connected graphics work stations such as SUN and others. The machines have ranged in power from 16-bit micros, through the 1970s generation of minicomputers by DEC, Honeywell, and others, to the current generation of 32-bit "superminicomputers" like the VAX and the Perkin-Elmer. It has even been implemented as a "virtual operating system" on top of two other systems: the IBM VM/370 and the VAX VMS.

To transport Unix is perhaps easier than to transport any other operating systems, but the job is still very nontrivial; typically it takes about 1 to 3 person-years of work. Most of the kernel, and all the standard tools, are written in C. So transporting Unix to a new machine consists of (1) making a C compiler for the new machine, (2) transporting the kernel, and (3) transporting the tool set.

Transporting the C compiler.   Different strategies have been used for moving the C compiler to a new machine, but by far the most popular has been the portable C compiler, PCC [Joh79, Joh80], a compiler that has a machine-independent preprocessor for the C macros INCLUDE and DEFINE; a mostly machine-independent front end that does lexical, syntactic, and semantic analysis; and a table-based code generator. The front end has also been rewritten to analyze Fortran 77 instead of C, retargeting C; hence retargeting the code generator produces new compilers for both C and Fortran 77. The main work in transporting PCC to a new machine is the rewriting of the set of tables that describes the machine's architecture and assembly language, and the rewriting of a routine used for register allocation in the computation of expressions. It is typically about six months' work for one programmer.

The run-time libraries for C are mostly portable. All of the input-output routines are written in C. Some routines, such as auxiliary arithmetic routines that must be done in software on a given machine and the routines that change subprogram arguments from normal C format to a special format for system calls, are in assembly language and have to be rewritten for a new machine.

Transporting the Unix kernel.   The Unix kernel consists of three main parts: a set of machine primitives (about 1000 lines of assembly language on a PDP-11), a set of device drivers (about 3000 lines of C on a PDP-11) and the system executive, including memory management, file system, process scheduling, etc. (about 5000 lines of C on a PDP-11).

The machine primitives directly control hardware such as device registers and interrupts and manipulate memory maps and segmentation registers. These are entirely machine-specific. The system executive is almost entirely machine-independent, using algorithms for such functions as processor scheduling and file access that do not change from machine to machine. The device drivers are specific to a computer and a peripheral device, but still have a logic and an overall structure that is often similar across hardware.

The kernel has an interface with other Unix programs that is small, clean, and well defined. Depending on the version of Unix, this interface is a list of about 50 "system calls" through which programs request services such as input-output, creation of processes, more memory, etc. This small list of system calls is all there is to the kernel, and any Unix program has access to the same limited list of services. Thus, compared with other, larger operating systems where much more is built in to the reserved part of the system, there is relatively little service that a new implementation of the Unix kernel must provide in order to be judged complete. This economy and simplicity of services has been a major reason for the successful transportation of the Unix kernel. Another factor, of course, has been the fact that as much of the system as possible is written in C.

Transporting the Unix tool set.   About 95 percent of the lines of software that compose Unix are outside the kernel, in the tool set. Most of the programs are written in machine-independent C and are theoretically easily transportable to any system with a C compiler, the corresponding libraries, and a correct implementation of the Unix system calls. Nevertheless, a significant minority of the tools require some effort in transport from one machine running Unix to another. One can distinguish tools that are nonportable because of their purpose (e.g., compilers and linkers) versus tools that are nonportable because of their implementation. An example of the latter is the Version 7 Unix Shell (a command interpreter), a program that defines a command language with Algol-like control structures, interprets commands written in this language, and creates processes to execute the commands. The shell should theoretically be immediately portable to any Unix Version 7, but because of the way the C code is written (see the next section), it is in fact very hard to port.

7.2.2 Problems with the portability of C programs

C was designed as a high-level substitute for assembly language to gain some advantages, like control structures and data typing, while keeping much of the power and freedom of assembler. This power and freedom has made C popular for systems programming, but it has caused problems in portability.

There are two problems with transporting C programs: dependence on Unix and dependence on a given machine. Programs may be more-or-less dependent on Unix, according to whether they make direct calls to the operating-system primitives. For example, there are no input-output primitives in C, so a program may either call the lower-level system primitives directly or call the higher-level standard input-output library. C and the standard I/O library might well be transported to another operating system in such a way that C programs that only do input-output through the standard I/O library can run on the other system. But the portability problem is caused by the fact that there is no control: A programmer can choose which primitives to use.

C programs are also machine-dependent because C allows operations that may not be portable. The classic example is the assignment between an integer and a pointer, which is allowed by C (but rejected by the filter Lint; see Sec. 3.3). Much original Unix code included such assignments, which worked on a PDP-11. But in a recent transport [DiC82] of Unix onto a machine where integers, pointers to integers, and pointers to characters are all implemented with different sizes, much of the code, both in the kernel and in the tool set, contained bugs and had to be modified.

Lint helps to eliminate some (but not all) such machine dependencies, but historically only some parts of Unix were written to "pass Lint."

Unix translated into other languages.   It could be argued that reprogramming Unix in another language is a better solution. Project SOL [Gie81] has rewritten Unix in Pascal, with the goals of better portability, use of a European-industry-standard language, and freedom from AT&T Unix licensing. SOL is running in experimental form on a CII-HB Mini-6 and on SM-90, a 68000-based processor. There is debate as to whether C or Pascal is better as a system-programming language. Pascal is defended in *Club SOL Info* [CSI82], and C is preferred by Feuer and Gehani [FeG82].

Unix has also been rewritten in Concurrent Euclid; see Holt [Hol82].

7.2.3   The exchangeability of programs within Unix

An early design choice in Unix was to have one model for all files: a stream of bytes. There is no notion of records, blocks, file headers, or indirect indexes built into any file-accessing method. So a program may operate on a disk file, tape, terminal, or interprocess communication channel ("pipe") without being changed. (Some actions are not possible—e.g., random access on a terminal or a pipe or a read to a printer, but all allowable actions have the same interface.)

Such differences in external file systems have traditionally been handled by the run-time system of a high-level language; for example, a Pascal program gives *writeln* and the run-time system decides which file-system primitive to call with which parameters. Much of the popularity of Unix comes from the fact that a systems-programming language, in which the underlying operating-system primitives are not hidden, can use the same system primitives (open, close, read, write, . . .) without worrying about the type of the external file.

The portability that is available here is perhaps limited, because programs that use the system primitives are only portable to another Unix, while programs using the higher-level standard I/O library may be portable to another operating system. But it promotes portable programming style because programs can be parameterized by their input-output objects, and sometimes exchanged and composed in ways different from the original intention of the program's author. A program can see the objects in its environment as being essentially homogeneous, identifiable by a name that is a string of characters and accessible as a stream of bytes.

7.2.4   Portable programs for terminal-display manipulation: TERMCAP

As has been noted, the successful transport of a program involves more than making it produce the same binary result (i.e., the same string of bits or words) for the same input. It also involves producing the same higher-level objects, such as text or numbers, even though these objects may be represented differently on different machines. The mapping from a correct result on one machine may be exact—e.g., the mapping between character sets for textual data—or approximate—as is the case in some numerical programs.

Transporting graphical software involves still higher-level objective judgment. Comparison of two "correct" implementations of a graphical program has probably very little to do with comparing the data that results from the computation.

For a graphical program to produce a result desired by the author of the program depends inherently on the output device to which the result is displayed.

And transporting the program can often consist of moving it only to a new display device rather than to a new computer or operating system. How, then, is a programmer to write a graphical program that is transportable? We know of one example, TERMCAP (Terminal Capability database [JoH81]), where a set of applications has been programmed for a large variety of video-display terminals, in such a way that once the program runs on one terminal it can run on all. Applications that have been programmed include VI [Joy79], a full-screen text editor, and BRUWIN [MeM81], a window-manager virtual terminal system.

TERMCAP describes in its database the details of how a given terminal is programmed: what output sequences are needed to address and move the cursor, erase and insert text, scroll in different directions, and so on. The database is accessed through a library of routines, TERMLIB, that read capabilities for a given target terminal and write results onto the display. An example of how display algorithms are made relatively portable is its method of cursor addressing. Cursor addressing is a capability that is normally present on a terminal, but in notoriously unportable ways. The cursor can be sent to a position on the screen by giving an (X,Y) coordinate, but on different hardware either the horizontal or the vertical coordinate can come first and the origin of the coordinates can be located at either the lower-left or the upper-left corner. The origin can be either (0,0) or (1,1), the X and Y can be either binary or textual numbers preceded and followed by escape sequences, etc. TERMLIB overrides these discrepancies with a virtual interface that defines a grid with one origin and one order for all terminals. An application program sees its output device as a virtual matrix of characters in which the cursor can be jumped from place to place and groups of characters can be inserted, deleted, moved, or scrolled. The interface is the same for all terminals, with the physical differences described in TERMCAP and manipulated in TERMLIB.

Once an application works on one terminal, it usually works on all terminals described in TERMCAP. Transporting it to a new terminal involves writing a new TERMCAP entry, which typically takes a few hours.

Application programs can be not only portable but efficient. The text editor VI defines many functions that are available in one hardware operation on some terminals but not on others. An example is the editor command "erase from current position to end of line." The availability of this hardware capability is read from the database. If the function is available, the operation is performed; if not, spaces are output to the end of the line.

TERMCAP and TERMLIB represent intermediate software levels between a graphical application and its output device, so that the program can "draw the same picture" on different devices. Such an intermediate level seems necessary if a graphical program is to be written in a transportable way.

7.2.5 An assessment

Programming as much of the system as possible in C, isolating machine-dependent portions of code, and using a table-based "portable" compiler (and, of course, the fact that the Unix kernel has simple and well-defined interfaces with other programs) have aided the portability of Unix. Limits on the portability have come from the fact that C allows nonportable programming constructs and from the fact that no matter how they are written, an operating system and a compiler are programs with large machine-dependent parts requiring significant effort to move to a new machine.

Although Unix was not originally designed to be so, along the way much thought was given to making it as portable as possible. Many factors have contributed to the ease of porting Unix code, but the reason it has been ported so often surely lies more in its popularity among users as a programming environment than in its internal implementation.

7.3 MUSS

7.3.1 Introduction

MUSS (Manchester University Software System) is a general-purpose operating system developed at Manchester University between 1968 and 1977, simultaneous with the conception and development of the MU5 prototype computer [MoI79]. If the system was strongly influenced by the computer it was designed for, it was not a one-way effect, for the MU5 design took into account software needs and imperatives. On the other hand, MUSS is not necessarily tied to the MU5, since it has been ported to very different computers.

In fact, MUSS is a family of compatible operating systems. Its evolution over about 10 years, without concern for commercial and compatibility considerations, permitted the rethinking of many fundamental concepts and thus avoided propagation in the final product of choices made 10 years earlier with less knowledge and experience.

The authors published many articles, and the evolution of the system is well documented. The articles about MUSS can be split into those about MUSS itself [KMR68, MDF72] and those about the languages and tools used [MWC70, MKL71, CMR72]. Finally, five simultaneously published articles [FrT79a, FrT79b, ThF79a, BCP79, ThF79b] describe the total experience, and the summary that follows here comes mainly from those articles.

Compared with large commercial operating systems, MUSS is much less ambitious: The system does not pretend to give the user all that might be desired, but rather attempts to adapt itself to the user's needs and to installation constraints. Compared with Unix, MUSS does not adopt the "tool set" philosophy, where often the user has only to put together elementary pieces of software to realize more complex functions. MUSS is more of a programming system where users build new tools to enrich the existing system.

The characteristics considered the most important during the conception of MUSS were performance, user interface, portability, and adaptability. The last two characteristics are, of course, of more interest in this case study. Here we shall study MUSS structure and organization (Sec. 7.3.2), system portability (Sec. 7.3.3), and compiler portability (Sec. 7.3.4). We shall end with a general evaluation of the system (Sec. 7.3.5).

7.3.2   System structure and organization

The material configuration on which MUSS was first developed is a heterogeneous computer complex. The three main components are

1. The MU5 computer, with 5 MIPS of power; a memory hierarchy consisting of 128K bytes of 250-ns memory, 1M bytes of 1000-ns memory, and a 4.8M byte fixed-head disk; and a pagination mechanism making this hierarchy transparent. Conceptually the computer is a stack machine dedicated to intensive computation.

2. An ICL 1905E, with 0.2 MIPS of power, 96K bytes of 650-ns paged memory, and batch devices (printer, card reader, paper-tape reader/punch).

3. A DEC PDP-11/10, with 0.5 MIPS of power, 32K bytes of 850-ns nontopographic memory, and interactive terminals.

Task distribution between these three machines is based on their characteristics: The MU5 does the computation, fed by the 1905 for batch jobs and by the PDP-11 for interactive jobs.

To this basic set, various computers can be added:

- An MU5, with 1.3 MIPS of power and 64K bytes at 500 ns. It also offers registers. This computer is dedicated to graphics and computer-aided design.

- A Membrain MB 7700, with 0.5 MIPS of power and 96K bytes of 350-ns memory. The Membrain offers base registers; it is connected only to the PDP-11/10, has various devices, and is dedicated to research.

- A DEC PDP-11/20, with 0.5 MIPS of power and 16K bytes of 850-ns nontopographic memory. With several terminals and a printer, the computer is connected to the University Computer Center's ICL 1906A and CDC 7600, and also to the PDP-11/10.

- A DEC PDP-11/40, with 0.5 MIPS of power and 16K bytes of 850-ns memory. It has base registers; with various terminals, it is connected to the PDP-11/20 and is used by undergraduate students.

A single operating system runs these very different and sometimes experimental computers. Each machine has its own version of the system, with necessary adaptations.

General structure of the system.   The general organization of MUSS is one of cooperative processes, communicating by message exchanges. Conceptually the system is split into basic modules, each being a process: device drivers, file-system manager, bookkeeping, user job manager, etc. Several distinct versions of the same module may exist at the same time, depending on the software and hardware environment. Users can add new modules to the system at any time.

In order to make the processes work, the system gives each its own virtual machine. System modules have their own protected virtual machine. Messages between processes are sent through a message manager. This structure can easily be adapted to a distributed system such as the MU5 complex computer net, ensuring maximal protection.

A version of MUSS works on each computer of the complex, though computers without memory protection have only a simplified version of the system. Communication by message between computers is only a special case of interprocess communication. This flexible structure avoids the necessity of distributing the operating system itself.

What the user sees.   For the user, MUSS is a relatively classical operating system, usable in batch or interactive mode, giving at first a rather austere programming environment. However, like many modern systems, it allows the user to add new tools to its environment, either unique or shared with other users, and nothing distinguishes system modules from user-defined modules.

The system's only truly original concept probably concerns the place of the command language. On one hand, nothing distinguishes an interactive command from an internal one; on the other hand, the authors of MUSS made a clear distinction between the command form and the function performed. Functions are realized by library routines from the system library or from the user's library. Language form is determined by the program interpreting it. This interpreter knows nothing about the routines, and the routines know nothing about the command language. To define a new command, one has only to define a new routine.

Apart from this, the only unusual aspect of the command language is in the treatment of files—in particular, in the notion of "current file," which permits simplification of most commands by avoiding repetition of the name of the working file or of a file derived from it.

System adaptability.   The adaptability of the MUSS system comes mainly from its split into many modules. This has been made possible by a technique, using Flocoder, which, because of the obsolescence of the tool, is not likely to be used again.

Flocoder [MKL71] is first of all a flowchart generator. What distinguishes it from the numerous tools of its kind made in the sixties is that, instead of deducing flowcharts from the program, it produces programs from the flowchart descriptions.

This approach is, of course, much more logical, because here one can describe what one wants to do *before* doing it rather than after. Moreover, producing programs automatically from documentation rather than writing them by hand guarantees an equivalence and coherence between them. In the case of Flocoder, all modifications are made through documentation. One can choose the level of expression—for example, produce general flowcharts or more detailed ones—until an actual program language is produced.

Each module is thus described, and in a way, programmed, by Flocoder. MUSS itself is designed as a matrix of modules, of which one dimension is the function being done and the other is the version of the module doing it. To produce a version of MUSS adapted to a given configuration, suitable modules are extracted from this matrix.

Each module is represented by a specification and documentation source file. Generation of a version of the system produces, at the same time and as one of its fundamental components, its description, which includes the statement of the module's mission, the visible interface specifications, any particular information (in natural language), and general and detailed flowcharts, where boxes are MUDL (Manchester University Design Language) instructions.

7.3.3 System portability

Why make MUSS portable?   Insistence on the portability of a system designed for an experimental machine may be surprising, but in fact it was needed for integrating software on the MU5 complex. The system was run on seven computers (two of which were experimental), with many different kinds of connections and peripheral devices, and portable software was crucial to avoid redesigning the system for each machine. Moreover, to build a system so that it can be reused on other computers is a way to make it more cost-effective.

Rather than building a specialized system for each computer and using some common components, the authors preferred to build a single "kit" system. Not only were conception costs considerably reduced in this way, but so were maintenance costs, for one person can run the whole complex. Computer independence, which is one of the main characteristics of MUSS, comes from the fact it was simultaneously designed for several computers.

The major design choice, to build a portable system, had important consequences. The efficiency constraint, one of the most important, necessitated increased care, since portability and efficiency are often contradictory goals. System adaptability was of fundamental importance: The solution, as already mentioned, consisted in building a collection of processes to work on virtual machines. The system kernel, which was the most critical part, is very small. Computer independence was required for the interface between the kernel and virtual machines, as well as between the kernel and actual computers. In this way, efficiency constraints were locally satisfied in the kernel's implementation on a given machine.

The ideal machine.   The authors started from the principle that software would be portable if first its specification was itself portable. Although very important, the implementation technique is still a secondary consideration. The kernel being the most critical and difficult part of the system to write and validate, it had to be machine-independent if it were not to be rewritten many times. Note that this idea is the opposite of that upon which Unix was based.

The MUSS kernel is thus designed for an "ideal machine" (we would rather say an "abstract machine"), simulated by the only part of the software that is really machine-dependent. Determining the level of this ideal machine was obviously very difficult: If it were too low, it would be very difficult, perhaps impossible, to adapt it to an actual computer, if it were too high, the adaptation costs would be prohibitive. The authors made their choices based on the elegance of the kernel interface and the likelihood that their ideal machine would be close to many real machines.

The abstract-machine adaptation to a real machine is made in the easiest way. Communication between the kernel and a computer is done through specialized registers, accessible only by special routines. There are also some routines for the treatment of the actual machine interrupts, either making them or transmitting them to the kernel. The size of the machine-dependent part of the adaptation is about 500 instructions.

Device drivers.   Because of many possible variations between devices, device drivers are obviously the most machine-dependent part of the system. Thus the authors assumed the existence of ideal devices, adapted to the ideal machine. Pseudoregisters and fictitious manual buttons and displays can be specified and simulated, and still adapted to what exists in reality. For instance, the ideal card reader has various signals (at work, error), control switches (on, off, release), and control registers (address, count, state). The effects of all these different states or actions can be described by a very simple automaton.

Ideal devices are supposed to work by blocks. They use a standard character set that includes control characters. Device management is simplified—e.g., the most esoteric possibilities are not covered. Functions whose results depend on the device are treated in a more formal way: For example, a result banner is treated very differently on a printer, on a punch card, and on a paper tape.

It can be noted that the principle of an ideal device follows current hardware evolution. Peripherals are more and more powerful, and generally include a microprocessor. Operations are thus distributed between the computer and the devices, and the computer only knows a few high-level capabilities of the device. Of course, if this separation of work were not done, it would have to be simulated by software, depending on the computer and the particular device.

Memory management.   Though simulation of an ideal machine may be reasonable for device drivers, since the cost of input-output is much higher than the cost of instructions controlling a device, simulation is not feasible for memory management: Simulation of addressing would be too expensive because of the extra cost of each instruction.

The method adopted by MUSS is based on the definition of a family of ideal machines, including a representative for each general class of memory management. Minor variations are hidden by the model used. Thus there is a special version of the system for each category: Paged memory and multiple base registers are the only ones currently defined, since they are the only ones that are necessary. Anyway, only a few modules are concerned with differences in addressing.

The interface between the kernel and the virtual machine is defined by the data structures used for translating addresses. The virtual memory for a process is described by a local segment table. Processes share a table of common segments, and a global table permits access to physical segments. In the case of paged memory, this global table gives the address of a table of all pages associated with a segment. In the case of multiple base registers, it only gives the segment address.

Evaluation.   The portability of MUSS is easily measured: The system has actually been installed on six different computers (see the discussion earlier in this section), using either a paged memory or multiple base registers. Each new implementation requires about four to six person-months, since it is done by a member of the initial team. The expertise of the implementors is obviously very important. Performance was judged to be not only acceptable but good; the fears of the authors about ideal machine inefficiency proved unfounded. Moreover, the resident kernel is about 16K bytes, which makes it usable on small computers. Thus MUSS demonstrates that a real and efficient operating system can be portable. The authors estimate that this success comes from the concentration of most of their efforts on the system itself rather than on the tools of portability: Programming languages and their portable compilers are considered important, but secondary to system design. This does not contradict the importance of porta-ble-compiler implementation methods, since these methods are usable in many situations. Only the general ideas of the MUSS design are reusable, and only for operating systems.

7.3.4 MUSS languages

Languages for the compilers. Among the main components of a program-ming system, compilers are the most important. If the system is to be portable, the compilers must also be portable and, at the same time, efficient. The authors of MUSS kept to the rule that a method minimizing the work involved in a port would be adopted only if it was not detrimental to efficiency.

The principle chosen for the construction of compilers was not particularly original, since it involved a single intermediate language targeted to an abstract machine. However, two very different languages were used. The first one, CTL [CMR72], had been designed to be of the highest possible level in order to sim-plify compiler front ends, depending on source languages. Adapted to Algol 60, Algol 68, PL/I, and Fortran, it permitted the construction of reasonably efficient compilers, but with huge portability costs since the back end was in fact a real compiler (see the discussion below).

Because of this, the authors reconsidered their first choice, and recently they have used TML [BCP79]. The abstract-machine model is of a lower level, much closer to actual machines, and is therefore simpler, more portable, and more efficient. It is similar to Janus (see Secs. 5.2.3 and 7.4.4), but is designed for direct code generation, and the intermediate language is not human-readable. It has been used to implement Algol 60, Fortran, Pascal, Cobol, and Algol 68.

Compared with languages such as O-code or P-code (see Sec 5.2.2), the major difference is that CTL and TML are not related to a unique source language. Moreover, like in Janus, structures of any possible source language are found in the abstract machine model. Since these are not actual languages, but only com-munication protocols, they may be used to give information to the front end, as well as to describe a program to the back end.

The CTL language. At first, principles used for the design of CTL look quite natural: Since this language is used by multiple and varied compiler front ends as an interface to a machine-specific back end, it would be beneficial to have an intermediate language as close as possible to the source language. Thus front ends would be small, since they do not have much work to do, and the back end, which does a more complex job, would be shared between all compilers.

Most of the advantages expected from this approach were actually achieved. CTL was used to build operational Fortran and Algol 60 compilers and experimental PL/I and Algol 68 compilers. A high-level intermediate language makes modifications in the object code easier, and a technique to improve the object code is beneficial for all compilers. Likewise, modifying the object-code form is also a relatively easy operation. Finally, the closeness between CTL and source languages makes it relatively easy to build high-level debuggers, which are available for each compiler.

But this method had drawbacks that caused the authors to forsake it. Its main disadvantage was poor compile-time performance. The Fortran compiler, for instance, was twice as slow as expected, mainly because of work duplication between its front end and its back end: In some ways, CTL is a higher-level language than Fortran. On the other hand, dependencies between source languages and object languages are not well-delimited, CTL being too close to a source language, and no clear interface is defined. And, above all, the cost of transporting the back end (a translator from CTL to machine code) was much too high, since it is like porting an ordinary compiler not designed to be portable.

The TML language.   TML is a family of intermediate languages, designed for a basic abstract-machine model. This basic machine is adapted to Fortran, Basic, or MUPL (see discussion below), and it must be expanded to be adapted to a new source language. Thus there is a specific abstract machine for each source language, which avoids performance degradation in the case of simple languages. Components of TML are only chosen at port time (even more specifically, when the abstract machine must be adapted to a target machine).

The abstract machine has typed operands, and structured data are still in the intermediate language, like in Janus. Also like in Janus, data are either parameters; local, nonlocal, or global variables; or temporary variables, all of which avoids supposing a method of addressing. Arrays and records permit the representation of either homogeneously or heterogeneously structured data. Each data object has a descriptor through which its characteristics are accessed. Procedure calls are expressed independently of the source language.

Global optimizations are not made in the TML translator (the compiler back end), but knowledge of target-machine registers allows the usual techniques to generate good code. However, this part of the translator must be reprogrammed for each new target machine.

The MUPL language.   MUSS language processors are written in MUPL, a system-writing language inspired by Algol 60, but with machine-level possibilities. The MUPL compiler itself uses TML as its intermediate language. To implement these processors on a new target machine, one can proceed in a "classical" way: (1) modification of MUPL compiler back end (translator from TML into object language); (2) self-compilation using first the original machine and then the target machine; (3) recompilation of compiler front ends. Such an implementation includes Algol 60, Fortran, Basic, and MUPL. These four languages are all available on the MU5, but the other machines of the complex offer only some of them.

Without the existence of MUPL, it would have been necessary to use more complex and expensive methods—telescopic generation from a primary code or building an interpreter for TML, which was not designed for interpretation.

Performance of the MUSS language processors is good on stack and multiple-register machines, but it is doubtful that these performances could be maintained on more exotic architectures. Performance comparisons between implementations using CTL and those using TML reveal a gain in compilation time of from 15 to 50 percent, a reduction of memory use from 10 to 25 percent, and a stable execution time, which perfectly justify the change of intermediate language.

7.3.5 An assessment

The total cost, over 10 years, of constructing the MUSS system was 70 person-years. A group of from three to ten persons, half of them students, worked on this project. The cost of portability is difficult to evaluate, if only because it cannot be determined which characteristic or which component is specific to portability. Nevertheless, portability had a positive, if not a measurable, effect.

Complete development of the system was done in five steps:

- The definition of basic concepts and the first implementation on an ICL 1905E
- Redefinition and development on an MU5
- New redefinition to make the system a multitarget one
- A complete restudy of the system and its implementation
- Performance, evaluation, and tuning

Porting the MUSS system usually consists of porting the basic system, with Fortran, Algol 60, and MUPL compilers. As software is available in the form of text produced by Flocoder, and written in MUDL for the ideal machine, the port is accomplished by the following steps:

- Translation from MUDL to the target machine code: This can be done by writing a specific translator, but it is most often done by hand, a job of one person-month.
- Adaptation of the ideal machine to the actual computer (pseudosimulation): This step is the most difficult and critical and takes four to six weeks.
- Tests and verifications: since verification-specific tools are not portable, this step takes a long, if indeterminate, time.

In all, the port represents a work of about three person-months, although sometimes a module version is produced only at port time because it is useless before. Verifications and system start-up generally represent six to ten weeks of work, the extremes varying from a few days to a year, depending on the implementor's competence.

There is no automatic help for system maintenance. For all the MU5 complex it is a single person's job. The machine time used for maintenance (one hour dedicated every day) is rarely used. Modifications are made to nonprivileged modules during normal operation. Compilation of the complete system takes six minutes on the ICL 2960.

Performance, measured by a detailed evaluation [ThF79b], has proved to be better than expected, which is quite rare in the domain of operating systems and deserves to be mentioned. MUSS proves that an operating system having industrial qualities can also be portable.

7.4 The Mobile Programming System (MPS)

7.4.1 Introduction

Although the Mobile Programming System is not new, we decided to include it in this chapter to illustrate the method of telescopic generation mentioned in Sec. 4.1. The superposition of abstract machines allowed the construction of a programming environment that would be easily portable from one computer to another. The system starts with a basic abstract machine, called Flub, implemented with a macroprocessor, *SIMCMP* (standing for *simple compiler*). Then the macroprocessor Stage2, described in Sec. 3.1.6, is implemented using Flub; once it is installed on a new computer, it can in turn be used to implement new abstract machines of a higher level—Texed, for instance, or Janus. Texed is text-oriented and supports the text editor Mitem. Janus (see Sec. 5.2.3) is more ambitious, since it can theoretically be used for the implementation of any programming language. To our knowledge, it has been used so far with Pascal and Algol 68 compilers.

The whole system is based on the idea that data types and fundamental operations needed to solve a particular problem can be seen as a definition of a new and specific abstract machine, which then can be simulated on actual computers by implementing these data types and operations. Thus the specific abstract machines had to be carefully designed according to the problem to be solved—and according to the actual computers on which they would be implemented. In particular, limitations imposed by available tools had to be taken into account.

The authors of MPS were confronted with the problem of transferring already debugged and used software onto new computers, without any knowledge of the available tools. Thus they decided to build their own environment in such a way that they would be able to install it on any computer within a few days; as soon as their environment was installed, their usual programs would become instantly available. Using the method of telescopic generation, only the very basic abstract machine had to be implemented with the new computer's tools. Since there was the possibility that the target system had no tools, the new environment, MPS, had to be as simple as possible. Using the abstract machine, they could install a general-purpose macroprocessor, which could then be used to describe each new abstract machine of the system: With each operation corresponding to a macro definition, it was easy to adapt the abstract machine to the actual computer.

Note that in this particular case, the ability to get MPS running in a short time was more important than efficiency and that what is described in the rest of this section is the first implementation of the system. If this software were to be used on a permanent basis, many improvements could be made—first of all, by avoiding the use of Fortran and writing the macro definitions so as to generate an assembly language, and by rewriting the lower-level input-output operations. The quality of the generated code could also be improved afterwards by skipping one or more levels of abstract machines.

With that as a basis, we will describe the first abstract machine and how it is used in the implementation of other levels.

7.4.2 Flub

The abstract machine. The Flub machine was especially designed for the implementation of the powerful, general-purpose macroprocessor, Stage2. Hence it had to be particularly well adapted to the manipulation of structures such as trees, character strings, and integers; it did not need to support real numbers, arrays, and other features found in most languages. Figure 7.1 shows its organization.

Each of the 36 registers is composed of three fields: (1) a flag, indicating its state; (2) a value (an integer, character, or string); and (3) a pointer referencing the memory (string address). Some fields are preinitialized and represent the only constants of the machine; the others are used for instructions.

The instruction set includes about 30 instructions, all needed for the implementation of Stage2. These instructions, with the exception of control transfers, are all register-to-register operations. (Of course, these "registers" may not be actual registers on an actual computer, but they allow the representation of memory and registers to be differentiated.)

Flub's memory is organized in words, which, like the registers, consist of three fields. A string is represented by a word containing its length and a pointer to its first character, and by as many words as characters in it. Thus, the distinction between memory and register can be particularly useful, since memory can be packed and registers can still allow easy access to each field.

All Flub input-output goes through a general interface (which is present in all MPS). Information is transferred character by character between the buffer (a

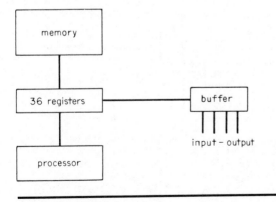

Figure 7.1 The Flub machine.

line) and general registers, and is transferred line by line from input-output channels to the buffer.

Implementation of Flub.   To implement Flub on an actual computer, a simple macroprocessor called SIMCMP, which was specifically designed for this purpose, is used. Flub operations are implemented by macro definitions. Macro bodies, input-output interfaces, and SIMCMP are machine-dependent. In fact, SIMCMP is a Fortran program of 90 lines (comments included), which can either be adapted to a new Fortran compiler (in case of incompatibility) or rewritten by hand in a new language. Input-output and macro bodies are also written in Fortran, but they should be carefully rewritten, because the input-output operations, at least, will be present in the whole system.

Implementation of Stage2.   The Flub machine supports the implementation of Stage2, which will be used to implement more elaborate abstract machines. Stage2 (see [Wai70b] and Sec. 3.1.6) is implemented from the [Stage2, Flub] macroprocessor (a processor for Stage2, written in the language of the Flub machine) and from the [Flub, SIMCMP, Fortran] translator. (The notation is defined in Sec. 5.3.) Since SIMCMP is itself a macrolanguage, the translator is, in fact, a set of macro definitions, transformed by the [SIMCMP, Fortran] macroprocessor. The [Stage2, Flub] macroprocessor is written in Flub, and we already have a translator for it—[Flub, SIMCMP, Fortran]. We suppose that a Fortran compiler is available on the machine on which Stage2 is to be implemented, and we already have [SIMCMP, Fortran].

Therefore all the processors necessary to translate [Stage2, Flub] are available and can be used without transformation. They lead to a first running version of Stage2, as shown by Fig. 7.2.

This first version is implemented with three writing-language operators, one object language operator, and one interpretation operator. (This last one is, in fact, a macro treatment that we assimilated to an interpretation; see Sec. 5.3.) In fact, some additional steps would be preferable to obtain a satisfactory implementation, as mentioned earlier.

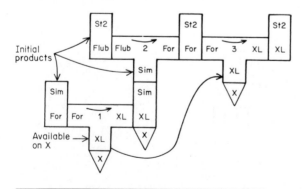

Figure 7.2   The first version of Stage2.

An assessment. This method was defined to provide a potential implementor of MPS with a first version of Stage2 in a minimal period of time. This explains why it was based on Fortran, and above all, why it used two levels of macroprocessing. Although the resulting product is inefficient, it can be used to implement another version with better performance.

The conventions used by Stage2 and SIMCMP are very much alike, and SIMCMP may be considered to be a subset of Stage2. This means that a new set of macros, [Flub, Stage2, Fortran], can then be written so that Stage2 facilities will produce a better code. Or, even better, the first version of Stage2 [Stage2, X] can be used to translate a new set of macros, [Flub, Stage2, X], avoiding the Fortran phase.

Thus a first version is obtained at low cost, with no help from the source machine, which was the important design point of this method. The consequences of this approach are examined by the authors in Newey et al. [NPW72].

7.4.3 Texed

Texed is an abstract machine that uses Stage2 and not Flub for its implementation. Its purpose is to support the implementation of an elaborate system of text manipulation called Mitem.

The general architecture of the Flub machine was kept more or less intact: memory, central processor, input-output channels, buffers, and registers. A number of instructions were added, and array types and a stack, which is used for temporary register management and parameter passing, were introduced. But the main difference is the complexity of input-output operations that Mitem requires. The operations include simultaneous access to several devices; new operations such as return to initial position, end-of-file, etc.; and the possibility of changing from one device to another without losing the current state (for example, putting the content of two files into a third file which must be modified). Therefore, the notion of device is included in the abstract machine. Devices are conceptualized by files connected to the machine by channels, each of which is associated with a buffer (see Fig. 7.3). Most input-output operations perform transfers between general and specialized buffers.

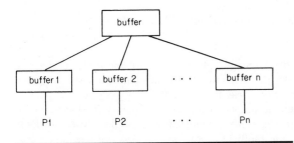

Figure 7.3 The Texed machine.

The main part of the implementation of Texed relies on input-output. This module is implemented as a collection of subprograms with integer parameters. As with SIMCMP, there is a Fortran version of the module, which can be used for a first implementation of Texed, or as a reference if the implementor decides to rewrite this module in assembly language.

The implementation of Texed resembles the implementation of Flub, with the difference that it relies on Stage2 instead of SIMCMP, which makes its adaptation to a new machine easier.

7.4.4   Janus

The abstract machine.   Janus is another abstract machine of the MPS family, designed to implement high-level programming languages. It thus must reflect the architecture of most computers, as well as the concepts found in most "classical" programming languages.

The abstract machine includes:

- A stack of dynamic variables of any type, existing only upon activation of a procedure.

- A processor, which contains the Janus program, what is needed for its execution, and three registers accessible by the programmer (who may be the implementor of a programming language): condition code, base register, and index register.

- A memory, characterized by a tree structure: Each child of the root represents a different category (static, constants, extern, etc.), and the objects are organized according to the category of their declaration.

What makes Janus a member of the MPS family is its implementation, which is based on Stage2. The language itself is very dependent on Stage2, and the instruction formats are defined so as to be processed by Stage2 as easily as possible—which leads to a heavy and almost unreadable syntax: fixed format, redundant information, etc.

Implementation of Janus.   The standard implementation of Janus is accomplished in several steps:

- Janus → J1, subset of Janus

- J1 → J2, another simplified abstract machine (J2 has a linear memory)

- J2 → assembly language

Some macro definitions, written in Stage2, allow a fast implementation of the first two steps. For the third step, the implementor must complete a set of macro skeletons with the target-machine assembly language.

Like the others, this version of Janus can only be a temporary version, since its implementation by these four steps (the last one is the assembler), three of which use Stage2, ensures a slow and inefficient program.

With the last set of macro definitions that he or she must complete, the implementor also has to write a run-time system. Janus has been used to implement a compiler for Algol 68 [Boo78] and a Pascal compiler, which has been ported from a CDC 6400 to a Sigma 3 and an Interdata [HaW78b]. The main advantage of this method is that it necessitates only a little work in order to yield the first usable version of the product. Moreover, it is economical to obtain a version with acceptable efficiency, because Janus can be used for various language compilers.

7.4.5 An assessment

MPS relies on the use of superposable abstract machines, as well as on the use of macroprocessors to adapt the abstract machines to actual computers. This method is relatively easy to start: According to the authors, Stage2 can be implemented in about a week, and each abstract machine requires from one to six weeks of work to implement a first version. However, this is usually insufficient to obtain software that is really usable and, in fact, much more work is needed.

The main difficulty is the design of abstract machines. The multiplication of these machines, which have very little in common, aside from the fact they all use Stage2 for their implementation, has led to multiple implementations. It would have been more useful if each implementation could have benefited from parts of the previous implementation, or if, for each abstract machine, the standard implementation could have consisted of macro definitions that generated a high-level language. But this was possible only for Flub, the most basic machine.

Note that this technique, especially the idea of a macroprocessor as the basis of the process, has been almost entirely abandoned.

7.5 Conclusion

7.5.1 Portable applications

A final category of portable programs—application programs, either alone or gathered in a "tool set"—has not really been described in the previous case studies. The Mobile Programming System described in Sec. 7.4 could be classified in this way, but it completely hides the programming environment on which it is installed rather than improving or completing it. On the contrary, some of the tools included in Unix, like VI [Joy79] and Bruwin [MeM81], depend completely on the Unix system.

Aside from commercial programs, which are the reason for the existence of many service companies but which are almost never described in the scientific literature (we thus can only guess about the methods that are used to make them available in different environments), portable programming tools are becoming more and more available. Since their specifications must be environment-independent, they do not use any nonsequential files, and they stay within the domain of text manipulation (in the more universal meaning of this term).

Let us mention, for example, the text editor Chef [MaP81, PeM81], which is a classical line editor, inspired by the Unix editor and by Kernighan and Plaugher's tools (see below). Its portability is due to the use of BCPL as the writing language, to a strong parameterization of programs, and to a very careful attempt to avoid host-system dependencies, which are too often considered unavoidable in this kind of program.

Tools for input-output management, designed by D. R. Hanson, are another example. The goal is to hide a rather hostile environment by simulating a friendlier environment close to the one provided by Unix or Multics. The input-output manager [Han83] is based on a directory manager [Han80b], but they are not necessarily used together, if the facilities provided by one of them are already available. The implementation method relies on Fortran or Ratfor, with the drawbacks we have already seen in the implementation of Icon (see Sec. 6.3.4).

Another example (which is better known because of the book on which it relies) is the case of Kernighan and Plaugher's software tools [KeP76], already mentioned in Sec. 4.4.2. These tools include a few very short programs as well as a complete Ratfor preprocessor [Ker75]. They were first designed to illustrate "good" programming, but the philosophy of the authors, which is based on the concept of providing only executable programs, led them to build a coherent environment relying on full input-output support.

Some of the basic ideas of these software tools are similar to the basic ideas of Unix and the philosophy of the tool set (see Sec 7.2), and this contributed to the popularity of the book and of the tools described in it, leading eventually to the establishment of a users' group. The users generally try to simulate a Unixlike environment on their own environment, using a "virtual operating system" [HSS80]. The implementation cost is much less than that of transporting Unix itself, but it still is nonnegligible, since it can consume six person-months [Han81]. Moreover, a transport of these tools, made by a semiautomated translation from Ratfor to BCPL [Sno78b], required less work (three person-months) than an installation without translation but with an implementation of efficient input-output.

In the long run, the use of Ratfor, and therefore of Fortran, was found to be an obstacle, and Kernighan and Plaugher rewrote their book and their tools using Pascal [KeP82]. Unfortunately, the results are not as good as might have been expected, since no effort was made to modify the external appearance of the tools or to improve the programming style that was inherited from Ratfor and C. The input-output operations, for example, were implemented so that the facilities of Fortran were simulated in Pascal, rather than basing the tools directly on the Pascal input-output operations. The cost of implementing the new version of the tools is about the same as the previous cost.

7.5.2 An assessment

Portability of operating and programming systems is currently less developed than portability of compilers. The portability of systems relies on the use of high-level programming languages and on the simulation of virtual machines; there are still no automated methods to construct portable operating systems. The construction of most of them even now involves a large number of programmers, which explains why they are still built mostly by big computer firms, as well as why the results are still far from good with respect to efficiency, reliability, and robustness, not to mention coherence.

Thus the recent appearance, and actual use, of portable operating systems is a positive development, even if they are mainly intended for micro- or minicomputers. Such systems are usually built by research laboratories or small software companies —therefore, there is no need for industrial distribution, no cumbersome management, and no long-planned deadlines—but they tend to replace the systems provided by the builders themselves.

The diffusion of systems such as CP/M, UCSD Pascal, and Unix has had a positive effect by encouraging exchanges between users, and makes the writing of portable programs adapted to these systems more valuable.

However, this situation has its negative aspects, as well. The broad diffusion of the systems mentioned above does not come from the fact that they are the best, but from the fact that they are available. Although each of them has desirable qualities, none is above criticism—far from it—a fact often concealed by the personal computer literature (which is mainly commercial) [Pec83]. The user is generally presented with an imperfect and unstable situation, where no system is really standard or reliable. (Rebooting an operating system that "hangs" from time to time, for an unknown reason, is often the usual way to work.) Also, the recent advances in user-interface design have made great ergonomic progress; there is a risk that traditional operating systems, which have changed little—as demonstrated by their command languages—will be left behind by these advances.

Perhaps more progress will be possible as portable operating systems become more of a reality. Users will finally find that they have a choice, and this will put pressure on computer companies to improve their products.

Chapter

8

Conclusion

We have tried throughout this book to explain, both in general and with specific examples, what is meant by "software portability," a term that covers many diverse concepts, ranging from the legal to the technical aspects of computer science. One of the challenges we faced when organizing the contents of this book was to try to cover all those different aspects as fully as possible. Hence Chap. 2 was devoted to a description of the major problems that may be encountered when transporting software, and Chaps. 3, 4, and 5 discussed solutions that have actually been used or that might be used. Among the problems that were discussed, the physical differences between machines is certainly the least likely to be solved in the near future, those differences being too wide to permit an acceptable uniformity. On the other hand, the legal aspects of portable software are rapidly evolving, as computers penetrate more and more into daily life and protections from theft and unauthorized access becomes more and more necessary.

High-level programming languages were featured in Chaps. 3 and 4, since, in effect, the portability of a program is often based on the language in which it is written. If the language is perfectly standardized, sufficiently powerful for the application, and widely available, the situation is perfect. Unfortunately, this is almost never the case, and such tools as filters and verifiers must be employed if the language is too permissive or if it has too many incompatible implementations. It may also be necessary, using extensible or augmented languages, to expand a language that is insufficient for the application. Research into this area has not given truly satisfactory results, and sometimes this has caused the definition of a new language for the sole purpose of writing a single application. As a consequence, it becomes necessary to define an implementation system for the language. The multiplicity of languages and the need for a standard implementation of each one explains the importance of compiler-generation systems. These systems are generally within the state of the art when handling the analysis, or "front-end," phases of the compilation process, but are more within the realm of research when applied to the machine-dependent parts of a compiler.

Chapters 5 and 6 were dedicated to a study of high-level-language implementation systems, first of all from a theoretical point of view, and later augmented by many examples chosen either because of their relative success (Pascal, for example) or because of their very original implementation methods (Icon).

Often programs have been written to be portable, starting with numerical applications and including compilers. In recent years, programs that were thought to be completely machine-dependent, such as operating systems and file-management systems and editors, have also been made portable. Chapter 7 showed several examples.

Since software portability, as we showed in the introduction, is becoming more and more necessary, the examples will surely multiply. A certain number of problems will be resolved when we discover how to base programs on a model that includes most computers, but this research is only in its early stages.

Bibliography

The following list of references is displayed in alphabetic order of the reference abbreviation. These abbreviations are composed using the first three letters of the author's last name, or the initials of the authors' last names when there are several. When several abbreviations have the same form, they are distinguished by an appended letter: [Gri77a], [Gri77b], and so on.

We used as little as possible those bibliographic references that are not easy to find—internal reports, theses, and papers published in obscure reviews. For the sources used most frequently, we employ the following abbreviations:

- *CACM: Communications of the ACM*
- *Computer J.: Computer Journal* (British Computer Society)
- *LNCS: Lecture Notes in Computer Science* (Springer-Verlag)
- *Sigplan: ACM Sigplan Notices*
- *SP&E: Software—Practice and Experience*

Should a reader be aware of any errors or glaring omissions in this bibliography we would be grateful to be notified of them.

[ABG77] Aird, T. J., E. L. Battiste, and W. C. Gregory: "Portability of Mathematical Software Coded in Fortran," *ACM Transactions on Mathematical Software 3,* no. 2, 1977, pp. 113–127.

[Abr73] Abramson, H.: *Theory and Application of a Bottom-Up Syntax-Directed Translator,* Academic Press, New York, 1973.

[Afn82] Association Française de Normalisation (AFNOR): *Norme Z70-001: Modèle de référence de base pour l'interconnexion des systèmes ouverts,* ISO/DIS 7498, Paris, 1982.

[AGG80] Albrecht, P. F., P. E. Garrison, S. L. Graham, R. H. Hyerle, P. Ip, and B. Krieg-Brückner: "Source-to-Source Translation: Ada to Pascal and Pascal to Ada," *Sigplan 15,* no. 11, 1980, pp. 183–193.

[AhJ76] Aho, A. V., and S. C. Johnson: "Optimal Code Generation for Expression Trees," *Journal of the ACM 23,* no. 3, 1976, pp. 488–501.

[Aho80] Aho, A. V.: "Translator Writing Systems: Where Do They Now Stand?" *IEEE Computer 13,* no. 8, 1980, pp. 9–15.

[AhS77] Aho, A. V., and R. Sethi: "How Hard Is Compiler Generation?" *LNCS 52,* 1977, pp. 1–15.

[AhU72] Aho, A. V., and J. D. Ullman: *The Theory of Parsing, Translation, and Compiling. Vol. 1: Parsing,* Prentice-Hall, Englewood Cliffs, New Jersey, 1972.

[AhU73] Aho, A. V., and J. D. Ullman: *The Theory of Parsing, Translation, and Compiling. Vol. 2: Compiling,* Prentice-Hall, Englewood Cliffs, New Jersey, 1973.

[AhU77] Aho, A. V., and J. D. Ullman: *Principles of Compiler Design,* Addison-Wesley, Reading, Massachusetts, 1977.

[Amm74] Ammann, U.: "The Method of Structured Programming Applied to the Development of a Compiler," *International Computing Symposium 73,* North-Holland, Amsterdam, 1974.

[Amm81] Ammann, U.: "The Zurich Implementation," in D. W. Barron (ed.), *Pascal—The Language and Its Implementation,* John Wiley, Chichester, England, 1981, pp. 63–82.

[AnN76] Anderson, M., and B. Niblett: "Software Protection: A Survey of the UK Industry," *Computer Bulletin 2,* no. 8, 1976, pp. 10–11.

[ARM83] *Ada Reference Manual,* ANSI/MIL-STD 1815A, 1983.

[Atk77] Atkinson, M. P.: "IDL—A Machine-Independent Data Language," *SP&E 7,* no. 6, 1977, pp. 671–684.

[Bac78] Backus, J.: "Can Programming Be Liberated from the Von Neumann style?" *CACM 21,* no. 8, 1978, pp. 613–641.

[Bac81] Backus, J.: "Is Computer Science Based on the Wrong Fundamental Concept of Program? An Extended Concept," in J. W. de Bakker and J. C. Van Vliet (eds.), *Algorithmic Languages,* North-Holland, Amsterdam, 1981, pp. 133–165.

[BaE74] Bauer, F. L., and J. Eickel (eds.): *Compiler Construction—An Advanced Course,* LNCS 21, Springer-Verlag, Berlin, 1974.

[BaM73] Battani, G., and H. Meloni: *Interpréteur du langage de programmation Prolog,* Groupe d'intelligence artificielle, U.E.R. de Luminy, Université d'Aix-Marseille II, 1973.

[BaT75] Basili, V. R., and A. J. Turner: "A Transportable Extendable Compiler," *SP&E 5,* no. 3, 1975, pp. 269–278.

[BCP79] Barringer, H., P. C. Capon, and R. Philipps: "The Portable Compiling Systems of MUSS," *SP&E 9,* no. 8, 1979, pp. 645–655.

[BdV76] Bron, C., and W. de Vries: "A Pascal Compiler for PDP-11 Minicomputers," *SP&E 6,* no. 1, 1976, pp. 109–116.

[Ben81a] Bensoussan, A.: "Introduction aux problèmes du droit en informatique," *Informatique et Gestion 123,* 1981, pp. 43–46.

[Ben81b] Bensoussan, A.: "Risques informatiques et assurances," *Informatique et Gestion 127,* 1981, pp. 39–42.

[Ben81c] Bensoussan, A.: "Dix années de jurisprudence," *01 Informatique 155,* 1981, pp. 81–94.

[Ben82a] Bensoussan, A.: *Le droit des logiciels,* Premier colloque de génie logiciel, AFCET-Informatique, Paris, June 1982.

[Ben82b] Bensoussan, A.: "Le droit des logiciels," *Technique et Science Informatiques 1,* no. 4, 1982, pp. 349–354.

[Ber78] Berry, R. E.: "Experience with the Pascal-P compiler," *SP&E 8,* no. 5, 1978, pp. 617–627.

[Ber81] Berry, R. E.: *Programming Language Translation,* John Wiley, New York, 1981.

[Ber82] Berera, E.: "Les réseaux et leur diversification," *Informatique et Gestion 136,* 1982, pp. 53–61.

[BGM79] Bonkowski, G. B., W. M. Gentleman, and M. A. Malcolm: "Porting the Zed Compiler," *Sigplan 14,* no. 8, 1979, pp. 92–97.

[BiF76] Birss, E. W., and J. P. Fry: "Generalized Software for Translating Data," *AFIPS NCC*, AFIPS Press, Montvale, New Jersey, 1976, pp. 889–897.

[BjJ78] Bjørner, D., and C. B. Jones (eds.): *The Vienna Development Method: The Meta-Language, LNCS 61*, Springer-Verlag, Berlin, 1978.

[BMM63] Brooker, R. A., I. R. MacCallum, D. Morris, and J. S. Rohl: "The Compiler Compiler," *Annual Review in Automatic Programming 3*, 1963, pp. 229–275.

[BMS80] Boyle, D., P. Mundy, and T. M. Spence: "Optimization and Code Generation in a Compiler for Several Machines," *IBM Journal of Research and Development 24*, no. 6, 1980, pp. 677–683.

[BoD74] Boyle, J. M., and K. W. Dritz: "An Automated Programming System to Facilitate the Development of Quality Mathematical Software," in J. R. Rosenfeld (ed.), *Information Processing 74*, North-Holland, Amsterdam, 1974, pp. 542–546.

[Boo78] Boom, H. J.: *Code Generation in Algol68H: An Overview*, Afdeling Informatica, IW 103/78, Mathematisch Centrum, Amsterdam, 1978.

[Bou79] Bouchet, P.: *Procédures de reprise*, Monographies d'Informatique de l'AFCET, Editions Hommes et Techniques, Paris, 1979.

[BoW78] Bochmann, G. V., and P. Ward: "Compiler Writing System for Attribute Grammars," *Computer J. 21*, no. 6, 1978, pp. 144–148.

[Bow78] Bowles, K. L.: "A (Nearly) Machine Independent Software System for Micro and Mini Computers," *Byte 20*, May 1978.

[Boy77] Boyle, J. M.: "Mathematical Software Transportability Systems—Have the Variations a Theme?" *LNCS 57*, 1977, pp. 223–245.

[Bra61] Bratman, H.: "An Alternate Form of the Uncol Diagram," *CACM 4*, no. 3, 1961, p. 142.

[BrA80] Brainerd, W., and J. Adams: "Fortran for the 1980's," in S. H. Lavington (ed.), *Information Processing 80*, North-Holland, Amsterdam, 1980, pp. 361–366.

[Bra80] Braubach, R. P.: "Protection internationale des programmes d'ordinateurs," *PIBD 249*, II, 1980, pp. 5–6.

[BrF80] Brown, W. S., and S. Feldman: "Environment Parameters and Basic Functions for Floating Point Computations," *ACM Transactions on Mathematical Software 6*, 1980, pp. 510–523.

[BrH76] Brinch-Hansen, P.: "The Solo Operating System," *SP&E 6*, no. 2, 1976, pp. 141–200.

[Bro67] Brown, P. J.: "The ML/1 Macroprocessor," *CACM 10*, no. 10, 1967, pp. 618–623.

[Bro69] Brown, P. J.: "Using a Macro-Processor to Aid Software Implementation," *Computer J. 12*, no. 4, 1969, pp. 327–331.

[Bro72] Brown, P. J.: "Levels of Language for Portable Software," *CACM 15*, no. 12, 1972, pp. 1059–1062.

[Bro74] Brown, P. J.: *Macro-Processors and Techniques for Portable Software*, John Wiley, New York, 1974.

[Bro77a] Brown, P. J. (ed.): *Software Portability—An Advanced Course*, Cambridge University Press, Cambridge, England, 1977.

[Bro77b] Brown, P. J.: "Basic Implementation Concepts," in P. J. Brown (ed.), *Software Portability—An Advanced Course*, Cambridge University Press, Cambridge, England, 1977, pp. 20–30.

[Bro77c] Brown, P. J.: "Macro-Processors," in P. J. Brown (ed.), *Software Portability—An Advanced Course*, Cambridge University Press, Cambridge, England, 1977, pp. 89–98.

[Bro78] Brown, W. S.: "A Realistic Model of Floating-Point Computation," in Rice (ed.), *Numerical Software,* vol. 3, Academic Press, New York, 1978.

[Bro79] Brown, P. J.: "Macros without Tears," *SP&E 9,* no. 6, 1979, pp. 433–437.

[Bro80a] Brown, P. J.: "Supermac: A Macro Facility That Can Be Added to Existing Compilers," *SP&E 10,* no. 6, 1980, pp. 431–434.

[Bro80b] Brosgol, B. M.: "TCOL Ada and the Middle End of the PQCC Ada Compiler," *Sigplan 15,* no. 11, 1980, pp. 101–102.

[Bro81] Brown, W. S.: *A Simple but Realistic Model of Floating Point Computation,* computing science terminal report, Bell Laboratories, Murray Hill, New Jersey, 1981.

[BrO83] Brown, P. J., and J. A. Ogden: "The Supermac Macro Processor in Pascal," *SP&E 13,* no. 4, 1983, pp. 295–304.

[Bru76] Bruynoogh, M.: *An Interpreter for Predicate Logic Programs,* Report CW10, Applied Mathematics and Programming Division, Université Catholique de Louvain, Belgium, 1976.

[CaC73] Calderbank, M., and V. J. Calderbank: "A Portable Language for System Development," *SP&E 3,* no. 3, 1973, pp. 309–321.

[Cam78] Campbell, W. R.: "A Compiler Definition Facility Based on the Syntactic Macro," *Computer J. 21,* no. 1, 1978, pp. 35–41.

[Cat80] Cattell, R. G. G.: "Automatic Derivation of Code Generators from Machine Descriptions," *ACM Transactions on Programming Languages and Systems 2,* no. 2, 1980, pp. 173–190.

[CFJ68] Cheatham, T. E. Jr., A. Fischer, and P. Jorrand: "On Basis for ELF; Extensible Language Facility," *AFIPS FJCC 33 (2),* AFIPS Press, Montvale, New Jersey, 1968, pp. 937–948.

[CGV80] Cunin, P. Y., M. Griffiths, and J. Voiron: *Comprendre la compilation,* Springer-Verlag, Berlin, 1980.

[Che82] Cheriton, D. R.: *The Thoth System: Multi-Process Structuring and Portability,* North-Holland, New York, 1982.

[ChS69] Christensen, C., and C. J. Shaw (eds.): "Proceedings of Sigplan Extensible Language Symposium," *Sigplan 4,* no. 8, 1969.

[ClM81] Clocksin, W. F., and C. S. Mellish: *Programming in Prolog,* Springer-Verlag, Berlin, 1981.

[CMM79] Cheriton, D. R., M. A. Malcolm, L. S. Melen, and G. R. Sager: "Thoth, a Portable Real-Time Operating System," *CACM 22,* no. 2, 1979, pp. 105–115.

[CMR72] Capon, P. C., D. Morris, J. S. Rohl, and I. R. Wilson: "The MU5 Compiler Target Language and Autocode," *Computer J. 15,* no. 2, 1972, pp. 109–112.

[CNL79] Cattell, R. G. G., V. M. Newcomer, and B. W. Leverett: "Code Generation in a Machine-Independent Compiler," *Sigplan 14,* no. 8, 1979, pp. 65–75.

[Cod82] Cody, W. J.: "Floating Point Parameters, Models and Standards," in J. K. Reid (ed.), *Relationship Between Numerical Computations and Programming Languages,* North-Holland, Amsterdam, 1982, pp. 51–69.

[CoF79] Cohen, H. A., and R. S. Francis: "Macro-Assemblers and Macro-Based Languages in Micro-Processor Software Development," *IEEE Computer 2,* no. 2, 1979, pp. 53–64.

[CoK78] Comer, D., and B. W. Kernighan: "Mouse4: An Improved Implementation of the Ratfor Preprocessor," *SP&E 8,* no. 1, 1978, pp. 35–40.

[Col76] Cole, A. J.: *Macro-Processors,* Cambridge University Press, Cambridge, England, 1976.

[Col81] Cole, A. J.: *Macro-Processors,* 2d ed., Cambridge University Press, Cambridge, England, 1981.

[Com79] Comer, D.: "Map: A Pascal Macro-Preprocessor for Large Program Development," *SP&E 9,* no. 3, 1979, pp. 203–209.

[Coo76] Cook, A. J.: "Experience with Extensible, Portable Fortran Extensions," *Sigplan 11,* no. 9, 1976, pp. 10–17.

[Cow77] Cowell, W. (ed.): *Portability of Numerical Software,* Springer-Verlag, Berlin, 1977.

[CPW74] Coleman, S. S., P. C. Poole, and W. M. Waite: "The Mobile Programming System: Janus," *SP&E 4,* no. 1, 1974, pp. 5–23.

[CSI82] *Club SOL Info,* #0, Agence de l'Informatique, Paris, September 1982.

[DaF80] Davidson, J. W., and C. W. Fraser: "The Design and Application of a Retargetable Peephole Optimizer," *ACM Transactions on Programming Languages and Systems 2,* no. 2, 1980, pp. 191–202.

[DaF84] Davidson, J. W., and C. W. Fraser: "Automatic Generation of Peephole Optimizations," *Sigplan 19,* no. 6, 1984, pp. 111–116.

[Dah84] Dahlstrand, I.: *Software Portability and Standards,* Ellis Horwood, Chichester, England, 1984.

[DaM81] Davie, A. J. T., and R. Morrison: *Recursive Descent Compiling,* John Wiley, New York, 1981.

[DeB77] Dewar, R. B. K., and K. E. Belcher: "The Implementation of Spitbol. Part I: Spitbol/360," in J. André and J. P. Banâtre (eds.), *Implementation and Design of Algorithmic Languages,* IRIA, Rocquencourt, France, 1977, pp. 421–425.

[DeB80] Delamarre, G., and A. Bestougeff: "Secret et confidentialité des informations," *Informatique et Gestion 114,* April 1980.

[Dew71] Dewar, R. B. K.: "Spitbol Version 2.0," S4D23, Illinois Institute of Technology, Chicago, Illinois, 1971.

[Dew75] Dewar, R. B. K.: "Indirect Threaded Code," *CACM 18,* no. 6, 1975, pp. 330–331.

[DiC82] Diakite, L., and P. Chemla: "Bilan de l'action de transport du système Unix sur CII-HB Mini-6," Rapport INRIA Sys. 1556. INRIA, Rocquencourt, France, June 1982.

[DMC77] Dewar, R. B. K., and A. P. McCann: "Macro-Spitbol: A Snobol4 Compiler," *SP&E 7,* no. 1, 1977, pp. 95–113.

[DMV79] Demuynck, M., P. Moulin, and S. Vinson: "Bases de données et portabilité des programmes," *01 Informatique 126,* 1979, pp. 93–99.

[DuC82] Du Croz, J. J.: "Programming Languages for Numerical Subroutine Libraries" in J. K. Reid (ed.), *Relationship Between Numerical Computations and Programming Languages,* North-Holland, Amsterdam, 1982, pp. 17–32.

[EaS70] Earley, J., and H. Sturgis: "A Formalism for Translator Interactions," *CACM 13,* no. 10, 1970, pp. 607–617.

[ELG80] Ebert, R., J. Lugger, and R. Goecke (eds.): *Practice in Software Adaptation and Maintenance,* North-Holland, Amsterdam, 1980.

[Ell78] Ellis, R. A.: "On the Interactive Use of a Macro-Processor to Generate Operating System Batch Streams," *IEEE Transactions on Software Engineering 4,* no. 2, 1978, pp. 146–148.

[ELR78] Evans, R. V., G. S. Lockington, and T. N. Reid: "A Compiler-Compiler and Methodology for Problem-Oriented Language Compiler Implementors," *Computer J. 21,* no. 2, 1978, pp. 117–121.

[Els79] Elsworth, E. F.: "Compilation via an Intermediate Language," *Computer J.* 22, no. 3, 1979, pp. 226–233.

[ErK77] Ershov, A., and C. H. A. Koster (eds.): *Methods of Algorithmic Language Implementation, LNCS 47,* Springer-Verlag, Berlin, 1977.

[Eva64] Evans, A., Jr.: "An Algol 60 Compiler," *Annual Review in Automatic Programming 4,* 1964. Published again in B. W. Pollack (ed.), *Compiler Techniques,* Auerbach, Princeton, New Jersey, 1972, pp. 381–407.

[Far84] Farrow, R.: "Generating a Production Compiler from an Attribute Grammar," *IEEE Software 1,* no. 4, 1984, pp. 77–93.

[FBC79] Ford, B., J. Bentley, J. J. Du Croz, and S. H. Hague: "The NAG Library Machine," *SP&E 9,* no. 1, 1979, pp. 65–72.

[FeG68] Feldman, J., and D. Gries: "Translator Writing Systems," *CACM 11,* no. 2, 1968, pp. 77–113.

[FeG82] Feuer, A. R., and N. H. Gehani: "A Comparison of the Programming Languages C and Pascal," *Computing Surveys 14,* no. 2, 1982, pp. 73–92.

[FeG84] Feuer, A. R., and N. H. Gehani (eds.): *Comparing and Assessing Programming Languages—Ada, C, and Pascal,* Prentice-Hall, Englewood Cliffs, New Jersey, 1984.

[Fel79] Feldman, S. I.: "Implementation of a Portable Fortran 77 Compiler Using Modern Tools," *Sigplan 14,* no. 8, 1979, pp. 98–106.

[Fel82] Feldman, S.: "Language Support for Floating Point," in J. K. Reid (ed.), *Relationship Between Numerical Computation and Programming Languages,* North-Holland, Amsterdam, 1982, pp. 263–274.

[FHS78] Fox, P. A., A. D. Hall, and N. L. Schryer: "The PORT Mathematical Subroutine Library," *ACM Transactions on Mathematical Software 4,* 1978, pp. 104–126.

[FiG84] Fisher, D. L., and P. E. Gibson: "Cobol 74 Is Portable," *Computers and Standards 3,* 1984, pp. 143–148.

[Fis79] Fischer, W. P.: "Micro-Processor Assembly Language Draft Standard," *IEEE Computer 12,* no. 12, 1979, pp. 96–109.

[FMN80] Filipski, G. L., D. R. Moore, and J. E. Newton: "Ada as a Software Transition Tool," *Sigplan 15,* no. 11, 1980, pp. 176–182.

[For78] Ford, B.: "Parameterization of the Environment for Transportable Numerical Software," *ACM Transactions on Mathematical Software 4,* 1978, pp. 100–103.

[FoS76] Ford, B., and D. K. Sayers: "Development of a Single Numerical Algorithm Library for Different Machine Ranges," *ACM Transactions on Mathematical Software 2,* 1976, pp. 115–131.

[FoS80] Ford, B., and D. K. Sayers: "Evaluation of Numerical Software Intended for Many Machines," in M. A. Hennel and L. M. Delves (eds.), *Production and Assessment of Numerical Software,* Academic Press, London, 1980, pp. 211–222.

[Fox77] Fox, P. A.: "PORT–A Portable Mathematical Subroutine Library," *LNCS 57,* 1977, pp. 165–177.

[Fre79] Freak, R. A.: "The Translation of High-Level Computer Languages to Other High-Level Languages," Master's thesis, University of Tasmania, Hobart, Tasmania, 1979.

[Fre81] Freak, R. A.: "A Fortran to Pascal Translator," *SP&E 11,* no. 7, 1981, pp. 717–732.

[FrH82] Fraser, C. W., and D. R. Hanson: "A Machine-Independent Linker," *SP&E 12*, no. 4, 1982, pp. 351–366.

[Fri82] Fritsch, F. N. (discussion ed.): "The Fortran of the Future," in J. K. Reid (ed.), *Relationship Between Numerical Computations and Programming Languages*, North-Holland, Amsterdam, 1982, pp. 317–328.

[FrT79a] Frank, G. R., and C. J. Theaker: "The Design of the MUSS Operating System," *SP&E 9*, no. 8, 1979, pp. 599–620.

[FrT79b] Frank, G. R., and C. J. Theaker: "MUSS—The User Interface," *SP&E 9*, no. 8, 1979, pp. 612–631.

[Gam76] Gammin, R. C.: "GPMX—A Portable General-Purpose Macro-Processor Adapted for Preprocessing Fortran," *AFIPS NCC 76*, AFIPS Press, Montvale, New Jersey, 1976, pp. 927–934.

[Gan79] Ganzinger, H.: "On Storage Optimatization for Automatically Generated Compilers," *LNCS 67*, 1979, pp. 132–141.

[Gas70] Gaskins, R., Jr.: *CAL Snobol Reference Manual*, computer center, University of California, Berkeley, California, 1970.

[Gau81] Gaudel, M. C.: "Compiler Generation from Formal Definition of Programming Languages: A Survey," *LNCS 107*, 1981, pp. 97–114.

[GeH80] Genz, A. C., and T. R. Hopkins: "Portable Numerical Software for Microcomputers," in M. A. Hennell and L. M. Delves (eds.), *Production and Assessment of Numerical Software*, Academic Press, London, 1980, pp. 179–189.

[Gem83] Geminiani, M. C.: "Legal Protection of Software: A Survey," *Advances in Computers 22*, 1983, pp. 1–44.

[GeT68] Gentleman, W. M., and J. F. Traub: "The Bell Laboratories Numerical Mathematics Program Library Project," *Proceedings of ACM National Conference 23*, 1968, pp. 485–490.

[GFH82] Ganapathi, M., C. N. Fischer, and J. L. Hennessy: "Retargetable Compiler Code Generation," *Computing Surveys 14*, no. 4, 1982, pp. 573–592.

[GGM82] Ganzinger, H., R. Giegerich, U. Möncke, and R. Wilhelm: "A Truly Generative Semantics-Directed Compiler Generator," *Sigplan 17*, no. 6, 1982.

[GHJ79] Graham, S. L., C. B. Haley, and W. N. Joy: "Practical LR Error Recovery," *Sigplan 14*, no. 8, 1979, pp. 168–175.

[GHK79] Griswold, R. E., D. R. Hanson, and J. T. Korb: "The Icon Programming Language—Overview," *Sigplan 14*, no. 4, 1979, pp. 18–31.

[Gie79] Giegerich, R.: *Introduction to the Compiler Generating System MUG2*, technical report TUM-INFO-7913, Technischen Universität München, 1979.

[Gie81] Gien, M.: *Spécification du noyau du système SOL*, Project pilote SOL, INRIA, Rocquencourt, France, September 1981.

[Gie82] Giegerich, R.: "Automatic Generation of Machine-Specific Code Optimizers," *Sigplan 17*, no. 9, 1982, pp. 75–81.

[Gim74a] Gimpel, J. F.: *Sitbol User's Manual, UM-3*, University Computing Center, University of Arizona, Tucson, Arizona, April 1974.

[Gim74b] Gimpel, J. F.: "Some Highlights of the Sitbol Language Extensions for Snobol4," *Sigplan 9*, no. 10, 1974, pp. 11–20.

[GLN76] Grosse-Lindemann, C. O., and H. H. Nagel: "Postlude to a Pascal Compiler Bootstrap on a DECSystem-10," *SP&E 6*, no. 1, 1976, pp. 29–42.

[Gor79] Gordon, M. J. C.: *The Denotational Description of Programming Languages,* Springer-Verlag, Berlin, 1979.

[Got77] Gotzen, F.: "Le droit d'auteur face à l'ordinateur," *Le droit d'auteur,* Genève, 1977, pp. 15–21.

[Got81] Gotzen, F.: "Les programmes d'ordinateurs comme objets de droits intellectuels," *L'Ingénieur-Conseil 7.9,* 1981, pp. 241–247.

[GPP68] Griswold, R. E., J. F Poage, and I. P. Polonsky: *The Snobol4 Programming Language,* Prentice-Hall, Englewood Cliffs, New Jersey, 1968.

[GPP71] Griswold, R. E., J. F. Poage, and I. P. Polonsky: *The Snobol4 Programming Language,* 2d ed., Prentice-Hall, Englewood Cliffs, New Jersey, 1971.

[Gra80] Graham, S. L.: "Table-Driven Code Generators," *IEEE Computer 13,* no. 8, 1980, pp. 25–34.

[Gra84] Graham, R. L.: "The Legal Protection of Computer Software," *CACM 27,* no. 5, 1984, pp. 422–427.

[GrG83] Griswold, R. E., and M. T. Griswold: *The Icon Programming Language,* Prentice-Hall, Englewood Cliffs, New Jersey, 1983.

[GrH77] Griswold, R. E., and D. R. Hanson: "An Overview of SL5," *Sigplan 12,* no. 4, 1977, pp. 40–50.

[GrH79] Griswold, R. E., and D. R. Hanson: *Icon System Implementation Kit,* Department of Computer Science, University of Arizona, Tucson, Arizona, January 1979.

[GrH81] Griss, M. L., and A. C. Hearn: "A Portable Lisp Compiler," *SP&E 11, no. 6,* 1981, pp. 541–605.

[Gri71] Gries, D.: *Compiler Construction for Digital Computers,* John Wiley, New York, 1971.

[Gri72] Griswold, R. E.: *The Macro-Implementation of Snobol4,* W.H. Freeman, San Francisco, California, 1972.

[Gri77a] Griffiths, M.: "Verifiers and Filters," in P. J. Brown (ed.), *Software Portability—An Advanced Course,* Cambridge University Press, Cambridge, England, 1977, pp. 33–52.

[Gri77b] Griffiths, M.: "Translation Between High Level Languages," in P. J. Brown (ed.), *Software Portability—An Advanced Course,* Cambridge University Press, Cambridge, England, 1977, pp. 106–113.

[Gri77c] Griswold, R. E.: "Engineering for Portability," in P. J. Brown (ed.), *Software Portability—An Advanced Course,* Cambridge University Press, Cambridge, England, 1977, pp. 117–126.

[Gri77d] Griswold, R. E.: "The Macro-Implementation of Snobol4," in P. J. Brown (ed.), *Software Portability—An Advanced Course,* Cambridge University Press, Cambridge, England, 1977, pp. 180–191.

[Gri77e] Griswold, R. E.: "An Alternative to SIL," in P. J. Brown (ed.), *Software Portability—An Advanced Course,* Cambridge University Press, Cambridge, England, 1977, pp. 291–298.

[Gri82] Griswold, R. E.: "A Tool to Aid in the Installation of Complex Software Systems," *SP&E 12,* no. 2, 1982, pp. 251–267.

[GRW77] Ganzinger, H., K. Ripken, and R. Wilhelm: "Automatic Generation of Optimizing Multipass Compilers," in B. Gilchrist (ed.), *Information Processing 77,* North-Holland, Amsterdam, 1977, pp. 535–540.

[Gui80] Guilbert, J. F.: "La sécurité dans un grand réseau de transport d'information: Transpac," *Informatique et Gestion 119,* November 1980.

[HaF76] Hague, S. J., and B. Ford: "Portability: Prediction and Correction," *SP&E 6*, no. 1, 1976, pp. 61–69.

[HaH80] Hamle, R. G., and R. M. Haralick: "Transportable Package Software," *SP&E 10*, no. 9, 1980, pp. 743–749.

[Hal65] Halpern, M. I.: "Machine Independence: Its Technology and Economics," *CACM 8*, no. 12, 1965, pp. 782–785.

[Hal80] Halstead, K.: "Portable Software and Machine Specific Efficiency," in M. A. Hennell and L. M. Delves (eds.), *Production and Assessment of Numerical Software*, Academic Press, London, 1980, pp. 191–197.

[Han77] Hanson, D. R.: "Ratsno—An Experiment in Software Adaptability," *SP&E 7*, no. 5, 1977, pp. 625–630.

[Han80a] Hanson, D. R.: "A Portable Storage Management System for the Icon Programming Language," *SP&E 10*, no. 6, 1980, pp. 489–500.

[Han80b] Hanson, D. R.: "A Portable File Directory System," *SP&E 10*, no. 8, 1980, pp. 623–634.

[Han81] Hanson, D. R.: *Installing Version 3 of the Software Tools*, technical report TR 81-23, Department of Computer Science, University of Arizona, Tucson, Arizona, 1981.

[Han83] Hanson, D. R.: "A Portable Input/Output System," *SP&E 13*, no. 1, 1983, pp. 95–100.

[HaW78a] Haddon, B. K., and W. M. Waite: *The Universal Intermediate Language Janus* (draft definition), software engineering group, University of Colorado, Boulder, Colorado, 1978.

[HaW78b] Haddon, B. K., and W. M. Waite: "Experience with the Universal Intermediate Language Janus," *SP&E 8*, no. 5, 1978, pp. 601–616.

[HeD80] Hennell, M. A., and L. M. Delves (eds.): *Production and Assessment of Numerical Software*, Academic Press, London, 1980.

[Hem77] Hembert, P. W.: "Criteria for Transportable Algol Libraries," *LNCS 57*, 1977, pp. 145–157.

[Hew69] Hewitt, C.: "Planner: A Language for Manipulating Models and Proving Theorems in a Robot," *Proceedings IJCAI*, Washington, D.C., 1969.

[HiM80] Hill, I. D., and B. L. Meek (eds.): *Programming Language Standardization*, John Wiley, New York, 1980.

[Hoa69] Hoare, C. A. R.: "An Axiomatic Basis for Computer Programming," *CACM 12*, no. 10, 1969, pp. 576–583.

[Hoa81] Hoare, C. A. R.: "The Emperor's Old Clothes," *CACM 24*, no. 2, 1981, pp. 75–83.

[HoH79] Howkins, J. J., and M. T. Harandi: "Towards More Portable Cobol," *Computer J*, 22, no. 4, 1979, pp. 290–295.

[Hol82] Holt, R. C.: "Tunis, a Unix Look-Alike Written in Concurrent Euclid," abstract, *ACM Operating Systems Review*, January 1982.

[HoM80] Horspool, R. N., and N. Marovac: "An Approach to the Problem of Detranslation of Computer Programs," *Computer J*. 23, no. 3, 1980, pp. 223–229.

[Hop80] Hopkins, T. R.: "PBasic—A Verifier for Basic," *SP&E 10*, no. 3, 1980, pp. 175–181.

[HoU69] Hopcroft, J. E., and J. D. Ullman: *Formal Languages and Their Relation to Automata*, Addison-Wesley, Reading, Massachusetts, 1969.

[HoW73] Hoare, C. A. R., and N. Wirth: "An Axiomatic Definition of the Programming Language Pascal," *Acta Informatica 2*, no. 4, 1973, pp. 335–355.

[HSC79] Hansen, G. J., G. A. Shoults, and J. D. Cointment: Construction of a Transportable, Multi-Pass Compiler for Extended Pascal, *Sigplan 14,* no. 8, 1979, pp. 117–126.

[HSS80] Hall, D. E., D. K. Scherrer, and J. S. Svewtek: "A Virtual Operating System," *CACM 23,* no. 9, 1980, pp. 495–502.

[InK77] Inglis, J., and P. J. H. King: "Data Portability," in P. J. Brown (ed.), *Software Portability—An Advanced Course,* Cambridge University Press, Cambridge, England, 1977, pp. 213–223.

[Iro70] Irons, E. T.: "Experience with an Extensible Language," *CACM 13,* no. 1, 1970, pp. 31–40.

[Iso80] *Data Processing—Open Systems Interconnection—Basic Reference Model,* ISO/TC 97/SC 16/N 537, December 1980.

[Iso81] Van Griethuysen, J. J. (ed.): *Concepts and Terminology for the Conceptual Schema,* ISO/TC 97/SC 5/WG 3, February 1981.

[JeW75] Jensen, K., and N. Wirth: *Pascal—User Manual and Report,* Springer-Verlag, Berlin, 1975. Third edition revised by A. B. Mickel and J. F. Miner, Springer-Verlag, New York, 1985.

[Joh78] Johnson, S. C.: "A Portable Compiler: Theory and Practice," *Sigplan 13,* no. 1, 1978, pp. 97–104.

[Joh79] Johnson, S. C.: *A Tour through the Portable C Compiler,* 7th ed., Unix programmer's manual, Bell Laboratories, January 1979.

[Joh80] Johnson, S. C.: "Language Development Tools on the Unix System," *IEEE Computer 13,* no. 8, 1980, pp. 16–21.

[JoH81] Joy, W., and M. Horton: *Termcap and Termlib,* Unix programmer's manual, 7th ed., Berkeley release 4.1. University of California, Berkeley, June 1981.

[JoL78] Johnson, S. C., and M. E. Lesk: "Language Development Tools," *Bell System Technical Journal 57,* no. 6. 1978, pp. 2155–2175.

[Jon80] Jones, N. D. (ed.): *Semantics-Directed Compiler Generation, LNCS 94,* Springer-Verlag, Berlin, 1980.

[JoR78] Johnson, S. C., and D. M. Ritchie: "Unix Time-Sharing System: Portability of C Programs and the Unix System," *Bell System Technical Journal 57,* no. 6, 1978, pp. 2021–2048.

[JoS80] Jones, N. D., and D. A. Schmidt: "Compiler Generation from Denotational Semantics," *LNCS 94,* 1980, pp. 70–93.

[Joy79] Joy, W.: *An Introduction to Display Editing with VI,* Unix programmer's manual, 7th ed., Berkeley release, University of California, Berkeley, 1979.

[JPA68] Johnson, W. L., J. H. Porter, S. I. Ackley, and D. T. Ross: "Automatic Generation of Efficient Lexical Analysers Using Finite State Techniques," *CACM 11,* no. 12, 1968, pp. 805–813.

[KeP76] Kernighan, B. W., and P. L. Plauger: *Software Tools,* Addison-Wesley, Reading, Massachusetts, 1976.

[KeP82] Kernighan, B. W., and P. L. Plauger: *Software Tools in Pascal,* Addison-Wesley, Reading, Massachusetts, 1976.

[Ker75] Kernighan, B. W.: "Ratfor—A Preprocessor for a Rational Fortran," *SP&I 5,* no. 4, 1975, pp. 395–406.

[KeR78] Kernighan, B. W., and D. M. Ritchie: *The C Programming Language,* Prentice-Hall, Englewood Cliffs, New Jersey, 1978.

[Kil81] Kildall, G.: "CP/M: A Family of 8 and 16 Bit Operating Systems," *Byte 23*, June 1981, pp. 216–232.

[KKM80] Kornerup, P., B. B. Kristensen, and O. L. Madsen: "Interpretation and Code Generation Based on Intermediate Languages," *SP&E 10*, no. 8, 1980, pp. 635–658.

[KMR68] Kulburn, T., D. Morris, J. S. Rohl, and F. H. Sumner: "A System Design Proposal," *Information Processing 1968*, North-Holland, Amsterdam, 1968, pp. 806–811.

[Knu68] Knuth, D. E.: "Semantics of Context-Free Languages," *Mathematical Systems Theory 2*, 1968, pp. 127–145.

[Knu71] Knuth, D. E.: "An Empirical Study of Fortran Programs," *SP&E 1*, no. 1, 1971, pp. 105–133.

[Kos71a] Koster, C. H. A.: "Affix Grammars," in J. E. L. Peck (ed.), *Algol 68 Implementation*, North-Holland, Amsterdam, 1971, pp. 95–109.

[Kos71b] Koster, C. H. A.: *A Compiler Compiler*, Report MR-127. Mathematisch Centrum, Amsterdam, 1971.

[Kos74a] Koster, C. H. A.: "Portable Compilers and the Uncol Problem," in W. L. Van der Poel and L. A. Maarssen (eds.), *Machine-Oriented Higher Level Languages*, North-Holland, Amsterdam, 1974, pp. 253–261.

[Kos74b] Koster, C. H. A.: "Using the CDL Compiler-Compiler," *LNCS 21*, 1974, pp. 366–426.

[Kos77] Koster, C. H. A.: "CDL—A Compiler Implementation Language," *LNCS 47*, 1977, pp. 341–351.

[KVC80] Kanoui, H., and M. Van Caneghem: "Implementing a High-Level Language on a Very Low Cost Computer," in S. H. Lavington (ed.), *Information Processing 80*, North-Holland, Amsterdam, 1980, pp. 349–354.

[Lak80] Lakos, C. A.: "Implementing BCPL on the Burroughs B6700," *SP&E 10*, no. 8, 1980, pp. 673–684.

[Lar73] Larmouth, J.: "Serious Fortran," *SP&E 3*, no. 1, 1973, pp. 87–107, no. 2, 1973, pp. 197–225.

[Lar81] Larmouth, J.: "Fortran 77 Portability," *SP&E 11*, 1981, no. 10, pp. 1071–1117.

[LCH80] Leverett, B. W., R. G. G. Cattell, S. O. Hobbs, J. M. Newcomer, A. H. Reiner, B. R. Schatz, and W. A. Wulf: "An Overview of the Production-Quality Compiler-Compiler Project," *IEEE Computer 13*, no. 8, 1980, pp. 38–49.

[LeB74] Lecarme, O., and G. V. Bochmann: "A (Truly) Usable and Portable Compiler Writing System," in J. L. Rosenfeld (ed.), *Information Processing 74*, North-Holland, Amsterdam, 1974, pp. 218–221.

[Lec77a] Lecarme, O.: "Development of a Pascal Compiler for the CII Iris 50—A Partial History," *Pascal News 8*, 1977.

[Lec77b] Lecarme, O.: "Usability and Portability of a Compiler Writing System," *LNCS 47*, 1977, pp. 41–62.

[Lec81a] Lecarme, O.: "Pascal and Portability," in D. W. Barron (ed.), *Pascal—The Language and Its Implementation*, John Wiley, Chichester, England, 1981, pp. 21–35.

[Lec81b] Lecarme, O.: "Une famille de langages de programmation: Snobol, SL5 et Icon," *RAIRO Informatique 15*, no. 2, 1981, pp. 111–154.

[Lec83] Lecarme, O.: "A Point of View about Software Tools in Pascal," *Technology and Science of Informatics 2*, no. 3, 1983, pp. 213–219.

[LeG73] Leach, G., and H. Golde: "Bootstrapping XPL to an XDS Sigma 5 Computer," *SP&E 3*, no. 3, 1973, pp. 235–244.

[LeP84] Lecarme, O., and M. Pellissier: *La transportabilité du logiciel,* Masson, Paris, 1984.

[Les75] Lesk, M. E.: *LEX—A Lexical Analyzer Generator,* computer science technical report #39, Bell Laboratories, 1975.

[LeS80] Le Stanc, C.: "La protection des programmes d'ordinateurs par le droit d'auteur dans les pays d'Europe centrale," *PIBD 257,* II, 1980, pp. 102–104.

[LeS82] Ledgard, H. T., and A. Singer: "Scaling Down Ada (or Towards a Standard Ada Subset)," *CACM 25,* no. 2, 1982, pp. 121–125.

[LPT78] Lecarme, O., and M. C. Peyrolle-Thomas: "Self-Compiling Compilers: An Appraisal of Their Implementation and Portability," *SP&E 8,* no. 2, 1978, pp. 149–170.

[LPT82a] Lecarme, O., M. Pellissier, and M. C. Thomas: "Computer-Aided Implementation of Language Implementation Systems: A Review and Classification," *SP&E 12,* no. 9, 1982, pp. 785–824.

[LPT82b] Lecarme, O., M. Pellissier, and M. C. Thomas: "La transportabilité du logiciel (version préliminaire)," IMAN-NC-8, Laboratoire d'Informatique, Université de Nice, 1982.

[LRS76] Lewis, P. M., D. J. Rosenkrantz, and R. E. Stearns: *Compiler Design Theory,* Addison-Wesley, Reading, Massachusetts, 1976.

[Luc81] Lucas, A.: "La protection du logiciel," *Informatique et Gestion 125,* 1981, pp. 32–34.

[Mac80] Mackenzie, C. E.: *Coded Character Sets, History and Development,* Addison-Wesley, Reading, Massachusetts, 1980.

[Mad80] Madsen, O. L.: "On Defining Semantics by Means of Extended Attribute Grammars," *LNCS 94,* 1980, pp. 259–299.

[MaP81] Maclean, M. A., and J. E. L. Peck: "Chef—A Versatile Portable Text Editor," *SP&E 11,* no. 5, 1981, pp. 467–477.

[MCA62] McCarthy, J., P. W. Abrahams, D. J. Edwards, T. P. Hart, and M. I. Levin: *Lisp 1.5 Programmer's Manual,* MIT Press, Cambridge, Massachusetts, 1962.

[MCD77] McCann, A. P., and R. B. K. Dewar: "The Implementation of Spitbol—Part II: Macro-Spitbol," in J. André and J. P. Banâtre (eds.), *Implementation and Design of Algorithmic Languages,* IRIA, Rocquencourt, France, 1977, pp. 426–435.

[MDF72] Morris, D., G. D. Detlefsen, G. R. Frank, and T. J. Sweeney: "The Structure of the MU5 Operating System," *Computer J. 15,* no. 2, 1972, pp. 113–116.

[MeM81] Meyrowitz, N., and M. Maser: "Bruwin: An Adaptable Design Strategy for Window Manager/Virtual Terminal Systems," proceedings of the eighth symposium on operating system principles, *ACM Operating Systems Review,* December 1981.

[MeP79] Meesson, R., and A. Pyster: "Overhead in Fortran Preprocessors," *SP&E 9,* no. 12, 1979, pp. 987–999.

[Met79] Metzner, J. R.: "A Graded Bibliography on Macro Systems and Extensible Languages," *Sigplan 14,* no. 1, 1979, pp. 57–68.

[Mil84] Miles, D. E.: "Copyrighting Computer Software after Apple V. Franklin," *IEEE Software 1,* no. 2, 1984, pp. 84–88.

[Mir80] Miranda, S. M.: *Aspects of Data Security in General Purpose Management Systems,* IEEE proceedings of the 1980 symposium on security and privacy, April 1980.

[MKH70] McKeemann, W. M., J. J. Horning, and D. B. Wortman: *A Compiler Generator,* Prentice-Hall, Englewood Cliffs, New Jersey, 1970.

[MKL71] Morris, D., T. G. Kennedy, and L. Last: "Flocoder," *Computer J. 14,* 1971, pp. 221–223.

[MKR79] Milton, D. R., L. N. Kirchhoff, and B. R. Rowland: "An All(1) Compiler Generator," *Sigplan 14*, no. 8, 1979, pp. 152–157.

[MLB76] Marcotty, M., H. F. Ledgard, and G. V. Bochmann: "A Sampler of Formal Definitions," *Computing Surveys 8*, 1976, pp. 191–276.

[MoD65] Mooers, C. N., and L. P. Deutsch: "Trac, a Text Handling Language," *Proceedings of ACM National Conference 20*, 1965, pp. 229–246.

[MoI79] Morris, D., and R. N. Ibbett: *The MU5 Computer System*, Macmillan, London, 1979.

[Moo75] Mooers, C. N.: "Computer Software and Copyright," *Computing Surveys 7*, no. 1, 1975, pp. 45–72.

[Mos75] Mosses, P. D.: "Mathematical Semantics and Compiler Generation," doctoral thesis, Oxford University, Oxford, England, 1975.

[MuS80] Munn, R. J., and J. M. Stewart: "Ratmac: A Preprocessor for Writing Portable Scientific Software," *SP&E 10*, no. 9, 1980, pp. 743–749.

[MWC70] Morris, D., I. R. Wilson, and P. C. Capon: "A System Program Generator," *Computer J. 13*, no. 3, 1970, pp. 248–254.

[NaF80] Napper, R. B. E., and R. N. Fischer: "RCC: A User-Extensible System Implementation Language," *Computer J. 23*, no. 3, 1980, pp. 212–223.

[Nag80] Nagata, H.: "Formal: A Language with a Macro-Oriented Extension Facility," *Computer Languages 5*, no. 2, 1980, pp. 65–76.

[NAJ75] Nori, K. V., U. Ammann, K. Jensen, and H. Nägeli: *The Pascal (P) Compiler Implementation Notes*, Institut für Informatik, Eidgenössische Technische Hochschule, Zürich, 1975. Reprinted in D. W. Barron (ed.), *Pascal—The Language and Its Implementation*, John Wiley, Chichester, England, 1981, pp. 125–170.

[Nel79] Nelson, P. A.: "A Comparison of Pascal Intermediate Languages," *Sigplan 14*, no. 3, 1979, pp. 208–213.

[NeW78] Neal, D., and V. Wallentine: "Experiences with the Portability of Concurrent Pascal," *SP&E 8*, no. 3, 1978, pp. 341–353.

[Nib77a] Niblett, B.: "Commercial Considerations in Software Portability," in P. J. Brown (ed.), *Software Portability*, Cambridge University Press, Cambridge, England, 1977, pp. 159–163.

[Nib77b] Niblett, B.: "Legal Protection of Portable Software," in P. J. Brown (ed.), *Software Portability*, Cambridge University Press, Cambridge, England, 1977, pp. 164–168.

[NiW84] Nissen, J., and P. J. L. Wallis (eds.): *Portability and Style in Ada*, Cambridge University Press, Cambridge, England, 1984.

[NPW72] Newey, M. C., P. C. Poole, and W. M. Waite: "Abstract Machine Modelling to Produce Portable Software: A Review and Evaluation," *SP&E 2*, no. 2, 1972, pp. 107–136.

[Nud77] Nudds, D.: "The Design of the Max Macro Processor," *Computer J. 20*, no. 1, 1977, pp. 30–36.

[NWW82] Nissen, J. C. D., P. Wallis, B. A. Wichmann, et al.: "Ada-Europe Guidelines for Portability of Ada Programs," *Ada Letters 1*, no. 3, 1982.

[OlW83] Oliveria, R. J., and I. R. Wilson: "An Analysis of Microcomputer Implementation of Pascal," *SP&E 13*, no. 4, 1983, pp. 373–384.

[OrW69] Orgass, R. J., and W. M. Waite: "A Base for a Mobile Programming System," *CACM 12*, no. 8, 1969, pp. 507–510.

[OsF76a] Osterweil, L. J., and L. D. Fosdick: "Dave—A Validation Error Detection and Documentation System for Fortran Programmers," *SP&E 6*, no. 4, 1976, pp. 473–486.

[OsF76b] Osterweil, L. J., and L. D. Fosdick: "Some Experience with Dave—A Fortran Program Analyzer," *AFIPS NCC*, AFIPS Press, Montvale, New Jersey, 1976, pp. 909–915.

[Pag80] Pagan, F. G.: "On the Generation of Compilers from Language Definitions," *Information Processing Letters 10*, no. 2, 1980, pp. 104–107.

[Pap79] Papakonstantinou, G.: "A Poor Man's Realization of Attribute Grammars," *SP&E 9*, no. 9, 1979, pp. 719–728.

[Par76] Parker, D. B.: *Crime by Computer*, Scribner, New York, 1976.

[Pau82] Paulson, L.: "A Semantics-Directed Compiler Generator," *Sigplan 17*, no. 1, 1982, pp. 224–233.

[Pec83] Pechura, M. A.: "Comparing Two Microcomputer Operating Systems: CP/M and HDOS," *CACM 26*, no. 3, 1983, pp. 188–195.

[PeD82] Pemberton, S., and M. C. Daniels: *Pascal Implementation—The P4 Compiler*, Ellis Horwood, Chichester, England, 1982.

[Pel80] Pellissier, M.: "Langages intermédiaires et méthodes d'implémentation de compilateurs transportables," thèse de troisième cycle, Université de Nice, 1980.

[PeM81] Peck, J. E. L., and M. A. Maclean: "The Construction of a Portable Editor," *SP&E 11*, no. 5, 1981, pp. 479–489.

[Pia82] Piard, Y. S.: "Réseaux locaux: l'embarras du choix," *Informatique et Gestion 136*, 1982, pp. 38–43.

[Poo74] Poole, P. C.: "Portable and Adaptable Compilers," *LNCS 21*, 1974, pp. 427–497.

[PoW73] Poole, P. C., and W. M. Waite: "Portability and Adaptability," in F. L. Bauer (ed.), *Advanced Course in Software Engineering*, Springer-Verlag, Berlin, 1973, pp. 183–277.

[Pow79] Powell, M. S.: "Experience of Transporting and Using the Solo Operating System," *SP&E 9*, no. 7, 1979, pp. 561–569.

[Pow84] Powell, M. L.: "A Portable Optimizing Compiler for Modula-2," *Sigplan 19*, no. 6, 1984, pp. 310–316.

[PrH77] Prudom, A., and M. A. Hennel: "Some Problems Concerning the Automatic Translation of Fortran to Algol 68," *Sigplan 12*, no. 6, 1977, pp. 138–143.

[PyD78] Pyster, A., and A. Dutta: "Error-Checking Compilers and Portability," *SP&E 8*, no. 1, 1978, pp. 99–108.

[RAB79] Richards, M., A. R. Aylward, P. Bond, R. D. Evans, and B. J. Knight: "Tripos—A Portable Operating System for Mini-Computers," *SP&E 9*, no. 6, 1979, pp. 513–526.

[Rai80a] Raihä, K. J.: "Bibliography on Attribute Grammars," *Sigplan 15*, no. 3, 1980, pp. 35–44.

[Rai80b] Raihä, K. J.: "Experiences with the Compiler Writing System HLP," *LNCS 94*, 1980, pp. 350–362.

[Rem82] Remer, D.: *Legal Care for Your Software*, Addison-Wesley, Reading, Massachusetts, 1982.

[Ric71] Richards, M.: "The Portability of the BCPL Compiler," *SP&E 1*, no. 2, 1971, pp. 135–146.

[Ric73] Richards, M.: *The BCPL Programming Manual*, computer laboratory, Cambridge University, Cambridge, England, 1973.

[Ric74] Richards, M.: "Bootstrapping the BCPL Compiler Using Intcode," in W. L. Van der Poel and L. A. Maarssen (eds.), *Machine Oriented Higher Level Languages*, North-Holland, Amsterdam, 1974.

[Ric77a] Richards, M.: "Portable Compilers," in P. J. Brown (ed.), *Software Portability—An Advanced Course,* Cambridge University Press, Cambridge, England, 1977, pp. 99–105.

[Ric77b] Richards, M.: "The Implementation of BCPL," in P. J. Brown (ed.), *Software Portability—An Advanced Course,* Cambridge University Press, Cambridge, England, 1977, pp. 192–202.

[RiH77] Richardson, M. G., and S. J. Hague: "The Design and Implementation of the NAG Master Library File System," *SP&E 7,* no. 1, 1977, pp. 127–137.

[Rip75] Ripken, K.: "Generating an Intermediate Code Generator in a Compiler-Writing System," *LNCS 75,* 1975, pp. 121–127.

[Rit80] Ritchie, D. M.: "The Evolution of the Unix Time-Sharing System," in J. M. Tobias (ed.), *Language Design and Programming Methodology,* Springer-Verlag, Berlin, 1980, pp. 25–35.

[RJL78] Ritchie, D. M., S. C. Johnson, M. E. Lesk, and B. W. Kernighan: "Unix Time-Sharing System: The C Programming Language," *Bell System Technical Journal 57,* no. 6(2), 1978, pp. 1991–2019.

[Ros77] Rosin, R. F.: "A Graphical Notation for Describing System Implementation," *SP&E 7,* no. 2, 1977, pp. 239–250.

[RTM82] Roubine, O., J. Teller, and O. Maurel: *Lolita: A Low-Level Intermediate Language for Ada,* ACM Adatec proceedings, October 1982.

[Rud79] Rudnik, A.: "Portable Compiler Code Generation Strategies," *CIPS 79,* Canadian Information Processing Society, 1979, pp. 241–247.

[RuS76] Russell, D. L., and J. Y. Sue: "Implementation of a Pascal Compiler for the IBM 360," *SP&E 6,* no. 3, 1976, pp. 371–376.

[RWS80] Richards, M., and C. Whitby-Strevens: *BCPL: the Language and Its Compiler,* Cambridge University Press, Cambridge, England, 1980.

[Ryd74] Ryder, B. G.: "The PFORT Verifier," *SP&E 4,* no. 5, 1974, pp. 359–377.

[Sab76] Sabin, M. A.: "Portability—Some Experiences with Fortran," *SP&E 6,* no. 3, 1976, pp. 393–396.

[Sam69] Sammet, J. E.: *Programming Languages—History and Fundamentals,* Prentice-Hall, Englewood Cliffs, New Jersey, 1969.

[Sam81a] Sammet, J. E.: "An Overview of High-Level Languages," *Advances in Computers 20,* 1981, pp. 199–259.

[Sam81b] Samet, H.: "Experience with Software Conversion," *SP&E 11,* no. 10, 1981, pp. 1053–1069.

[SaM70] Santos, P. J., Jr., and D. W. Maurer: "Compilation of a Subset of Snobol4," *Sigplan 5,* no. 12, 1970, pp. 60–68.

[San71] Santos, P. J.: *Fasbol, a Snobol4 Compiler,* ERL-M134, electronics research laboratory, University of California, Berkeley, California, December 1971.

[Sch71] Schuman, S. A. (ed.): "Proceedings of International Symposium on Extensible Programming Languages," *Sigplan 6,* no. 12, 1971.

[ScV84] Schmidt, U., and R. Voller: "A Multi-Language Compiler System with Automatically Generated Code Generators," *Sigplan 19,* no. 6, 1984, pp. 202–211.

[SeU70] Sethi, R., and J. D. Ullman: "The Generation of Optimal Code for Arithmetic Expressions," *Journal of the ACM 17,* no. 4, 1970, pp. 715–728.

[SFR68] Sklansky, J., M. Finkestein, and E. C. Russel: "A Formalism for Program Translation," *Journal of the ACM 15,* no. 2, 1968, pp. 165–175.

[Ske82] Skelly, P. G.: "The ACM Position on Standardization of the Ada Language," *CACM 25*, no. 2, 1982, pp. 118–120.

[SMO58] Strong, J. (ed.), O. Mock, T. Olsztyn, T. Steel, A. Tritter, and J. Weigstein: "The Problem of Programming Communication with Changing Machines: A Proposed Solution," *CACM 1*, no. 8 (12–18); no. 9 (9–15), 1958.

[Sno78a] Snow, C. R.: "An Exercise in the Transportation of an Operating System," *SP&E 8*, no. 1, 1978, pp. 41–50.

[Sno78b] Snow, C. R.: "The Software Tools Project," *SP&E 8*, 1978, pp. 585–599.

[SoY74] Solntseff, N., and A. Yezerski: "A Survey of Extensible Programming Languages," *Annual Review in Automatic Programming 7*, 1974, pp. 267–307.

[Sta75] Standish, T. A.: "Extensibility in Programming Language Design," *AFIPS NCC 44*, AFIPS Press, Montvale, New Jersey, 1975, pp. 287–290.

[Str65] Strachey, C.: "A General-Purpose Macro-Generator," *Computer J. 8*, no. 3, 1965, pp. 225–241.

[Str69] Strubble, G.: *Assembler Language Programming: The IBM System/360*, Addison-Wesley, Reading, Massachusetts, 1969.

[StS72] Stoy, J. E., and C. Strachey: "OS6—An Experimental Operating System for a Small Computer," *Computer J. 15*, 1972, pp. 117–124, 195–203.

[Tab82] Tabourier, Y.: "Problèmes de normalisation et de décomposition dans les modèles conceptuels de données," *Informatique et Gestion 133*, May 1982.

[Tan76] Tanenbaum, A. S.: "A General-Purpose Macro-Processor as a Poor Man's Compiler-Compiler," *IEEE Transactions on Software Engineering 2*, no. 2, 1976, pp. 121–125.

[Ter77] Terashima, N.: "The Hierarchical Language System," *Sigplan 12*, no. 9, 1977, pp. 103–113.

[Tes77] Teskey, N.: Date; A Macro-Processor for Extending Command Languages, *Computer J. 20*, no. 2, 1977, pp. 187–189.

[ThF79a] Theaker, C. J., and G. R. Frank: "MUSS—A Portable Operating System," *SP&E 9*, no. 8, 1979, pp. 633–643.

[ThF79b] Theaker, C. J., and G. R. Frank: "An Assessment of the MUSS Operating System," *SP&E 9*, no. 8, 1979, pp. 657–670.

[ThP77] Thomas-Peyrolle, M. C.: "La transportabilité des compilateurs," thèse de doctorat de spécialité, Université de Nice, 1977.

[TKB78] Tanenbaum, A. S., P. Klint, and W. Bohm: "Guidelines for Software Portability," *SP&E 8*, no. 6, 1978, pp. 681–698.

[TLD69] Thompson, F. B., P. C. Lovckemann, B. Dostert, and R. S. Deverill: "Rel, a Rapidly Extensible Language System," *ACM National Conference 24*, 1969, pp. 399–417.

[Tri78a] Triance, J. M.: "A Study of Cobol Portability," *Computer J. 21*, no. 3, 1978, pp. 278–281.

[Tri78b] Triance, J. M.: "A Macro Facility for Cobol," *LNCS 65*, 1978, pp. 420–431.

[TrY80] Triance, J. M., and F. S. Yow: "MCobol: A Prototype Macro Facility for Cobol," *CACM 23*, no. 8, 1980, pp. 432–439.

[TSK81] Tanenbaum, A. S., H. Van Staveren, E. G. Keizer, and J. W. Stevenson: *A Practical Toolkit for Making Portable Compilers*, IR-74, Vrije Universiteit Amsterdam, October 1981.

[TSS82] Tanenbaum, A. S., H. Van Staveren, and J. W. Stevenson: "Using Peephole Optimization on Intermediate Code," *ACM Transactions on Programming Languages and Systems 4,* no. 1, 1982, pp. 21–36.

[Tur80] Turchin, V. F.: "Semantics Definition in Refal and Automatic Production of Compilers," *LNCS 94,* 1980, pp. 441–474.

[Val84] Valdorf, G.: "Dedicated, Distributed and Portable Operating Systems: A Structuring Concept," *SP&E 14,* no. 11, 1984, pp. 1079–1096.

[Van79] Vanderperre, P.: "La protection juridique du logiciel," *PIBD 228 II,* 1979, pp. 30–31.

[WaC81] Waite, W. M., and L. R. Carter: "An Analysis/Synthesis Interface for Pascal Compilers," *SP&E 11,* no. 8, 1981, pp. 769–787.

[WaG84] Waite, W. M., and G. Goos: *Compiler Construction,* Springer-Verlag, Berlin, 1984.

[WaH82] Walker, M. G., and R. G. Harrison: "Program Portability," *Datamation 28,* no. 1, 1982, pp. 140–149.

[Wai67] Waite, W. M.: "A Language Independent Macro-Processor," *CACM 10,* no. 7, 1967, pp. 433–440.

[Wai70a] Waite, W. M.: "Building a Mobile Programming System," *Computer J. 13,* 1970, pp. 28–31.

[Wai70b] Waite, W. M.: "The Mobile Programming System: Stage2," *CACM 13,* no. 7, 1970, pp. 415–421.

[Wai73] Waite, W. M.: *Implementing Software for Non-Numeric Applications,* Prentice-Hall, Englewood Cliffs, New Jersey, 1973.

[Wai75] Waite, W. M.: "Hints on Distributing Portable Software," *SP&E 5,* no. 4, 1975, pp. 295–308.

[Wai77a] Waite, W. M.: "System Interface," in P. J. Brown (ed.), *Software Portability—An Advanced Course,* Cambridge University Press, Cambridge, England, 1977, pp. 127–135.

[Wai77b] Waite, W. M.: "Janus," in P. J. Brown (ed.), *Software Portability—An Advanced Course,* Cambridge University Press, Cambridge, England, 1977, pp. 277–290.

[Wal78] Wallis, P. J. L.: "The Design of a Portable Programming Language," *Acta Informatica 10,* 1978, pp. 157–167.

[Wal80] Wallis, P. J. L.: "Numerical Software Portability and the PPL Project," in M. A. Hennel and L. M. Delves (eds.), *Production and Assessment of Numerical Software,* Academic Press, London, 1980, pp. 199–210.

[Wal82] Wallis, P. J. L.: *Portable Programming,* Macmillan, London, 1982.

[Wel81] Welsh, J.: "Two 1900 Compilers," in D. W. Barron (ed.), *Pascal—The Language and Its Implementation,* John Wiley, Chichester, 1981, pp. 171–179.

[WeQ72] Welsh, J., and C. Quinn: "A Pascal Compiler for ICL 1900 Series Computers," *SP&E 2,* no. 1, 1972, pp. 73–77.

[WhP73] White, J. R., and Presser, L.: "A Structured Language for Translator Construction," *Computer J. 18,* no. 1, 1973, pp. 34–42.

[Wir68] Wirth, N.: "PL/360, a Programming Language for the 360 Computers," *Journal of the ACM 15,* no. 1, 1968, pp. 37–74.

[Wir71a] Wirth, N.: "The Programming Language Pascal," *Acta Informatica 1,* 1971, pp. 35–63.

[Wir71b] Wirth, N.: "The Design of a Pascal Compiler," *SP&E 1,* no. 3, 1971, pp. 309–333.

[Wir73] Wirth, N.: *The Programming Language Pascal*, revised report, Berichte der Fach-gruppe Computer-Wissenschaften Nr. 5, Eidgenössische Technische Hochschule, Zu-rich, 1973.

[Wir75] Wirth, N.: "Pascal-S: A Subset and Its Implementation," Institut für Informatik, Eidgenössische Technische Hochschule, Zurich, 1975. Reprinted in D. W. Barron (ed.), *Pascal—The Language and Its Implementation*, John Wiley, Chichester, England 1981, pp. 199–259.

Index

ABOUT THE AUTHORS

OLIVIER LECARME, currently a professor of informatics at the Université de Nice, has extensive teaching and research experience in the design and implementation of programming languages, software portability, and programming methodology. He holds a Doctorat de Spécialité and a Doctorat d'Etat in computer science, and he is the author or coauthor of several books and numerous articles in the field.

MIREILLE PELLISSIER GART is employed with Intermetrics, of Cambridge, Massachusetts, where she is a senior programmer for an Ada compiler project. She held a similar position at the CII-Honeywell Bull Research Center in Louveciennes, France. Ms. Pellissier Gart earned a Doctorat de Troisième Cycle in computer science from the Université de Nice and spent one year at the University of Montreal on a postdoctorate fellowship.